ORSHIP
by the Book

D1057320

WORSHIP
by the Book

D. A. CARSON
EDITOR

Mark Ashton

R. Kent Hughes

Timothy J. Keller

ZONDERVAN™

GRAND RAPIDS, MICHIGAN 49530 USA

5/13

We want to hear from you. Please send your comments about this book to us in care of the address below. Thank you.

GRAND RAPIDS, MICHIGAN 49530 USA

WWW.ZONDERVAN.COM

ZONDERVAN™

Worship by the Book
Copyright © 2002 by D. A. Carson, Timothy Keller, Mark Ashton, and Kent Hughes

Requests for information should be addressed to:
Zondervan, *Grand Rapids, Michigan 49530*

Library of Congress Cataloging-in-Publication Data

Worship by the book/D. A. Carson, editor; with Mark Ashton, R. Kent Huges,
   and Timothy J. Keller.
     p. cm.
   Includes bibliographical references and index.
   ISBN 0-310-21625-7
   1. Public worship. 2. Worship programs.   I. Carson, D. A.
  BV15.W66 2002
  264—dc21   2002000789

Acknowledgments and permission statements for copyrighted materials used in this book
are provided on page 9, which hereby becomes part of this copyright page.

Interior design by Beth Shagene

Printed in the United States of America

---

09 10 11 12 13 /❖ DC/ 20 19 18 17 16 15 14 13 12 11

CONTENTS

PREFACE

$\mathcal{T}$here are so many books on the subject of worship these days that I had better make clear right away what we are trying to accomplish in this volume.

This is not a comprehensive theology of worship. Still less is it a sociological analysis of current trends or a minister's manual chock full of "how to" instructions. We have not attempted detailed historical analyses of our respective traditions, nor have we devoted much space to interaction with other discussions. Rather, after a preliminary chapter on the biblical theology of worship, the remaining three chapters move from theological reflection to practical implementation of patterns of corporate worship in the local churches we represent. Complete service outlines are included, for many ministers will find the arguments more helpful and fruitful if they are fleshed out in detailed outlines.

Three of us are currently pastors—an Anglican, a Baptist, and a Presbyterian. The fourth teaches at a seminary but has served as pastor in earlier years. What unites us is our strong commitment to the ministry of the Word; our respect for historical rootedness; and our deep commitment, nevertheless, to contemporaneity and solid engagement with unconverted, unchurched people. We are as suspicious of mere traditionalism as we are of cutesy relevance. What we provide is the theological reasoning that shapes our judgments in matters of corporate worship, along with examples that have emerged from our ministries. In each case we have tried to interact with our respective traditions without being padlocked to them.

For reasons of brevity and clarity, we have included relatively few footnotes and interacted with a minimum of the voluminous secondary literature. It will not take long for readers to discover where we disagree with one another. Sometimes the disagreement is over something tied to our respective denominational distinctives; sometimes disagreements reflect the different subcultures in which we serve; sometimes they are mere judgment calls. Nevertheless, the degree of agreement is impressive—partly, I think, because each of us takes biblical theology seriously.

We would be the first to acknowledge that on countless points brothers and sisters in Christ in other cultures may want to "tweak" what we say to better fit their own worlds. For example, Korean patterns of public prayer are rather different from most of what is found in the West, and musical styles in the rising indigenous churches of sub-Saharan black Africa would generate a somewhat different discussion of some points. But we are addressing the worlds we know best from the Word we love best. Our prayer is that this record of our own struggles, reflections, and practices may stimulate others to careful, biblically informed reformation of corporate worship.

I want to record my thanks to Dr. Don Hedges, who efficiently tracked down the copyright holders of the pieces cited on the service sheets, and to my graduate assistant, Sigurd Grindheim, who ably compiled the indexes.

Soli Deo gloria.

D. A. CARSON

ACKNOWLEDGMENTS

*T*hree of the four chapters of this book include detailed service sheets used in specific churches. These service sheets include numerous hymns and choruses, sometimes only the words, and sometimes both words and music. Every effort has been taken to track down copyright holders and secure permission. We have inserted a credit line at each place in the text where permission has been granted, but it seems appropriate to group those acknowledgments here as well. In the relatively few instances of songs where no credit line is provided, the material, as far as we have been able to determine, lies in the public domain.

We gratefully acknowledge permission to use the following:

J. S. Bach, "Alleluia! O Praise the Lord Most Holy," © 1971 Concordia Publishing House.

Michael Baughen, "Sing to God New Songs of Worship," © Jubilate Hymns Ltd. (admin. by Hope Publishing Company).

Michael Christ, "It's Your Blood," © 1985 Mercy / Vineyard Publishing (ASCAP).

Samuel Crossman, "My Song Is Love Unknown" (in this version) © Jubilate Hymns Ltd. (admin. by Hope Publishing Company).

Anita Davidson, "It's Not the Bright Light," permission secured from the author.

William Dix, "As with Gladness Men of Old" (in this version) © Jubilate Hymns Ltd. (admin. by Hope Publishing Company).

Les Garrett, "This Is the Day," © 1967 Scripture in Song (a division of Integrity Music, Inc.)/ASCAP.

Jack Hayford, "Worship Christ the Risen King," © 1986 Rocksmith Music / Annamarie Music (ASCAP) (all rights admin. by Brentwood-Benson Music Publishing, Inc.).

Chapter 1

WORSHIP UNDER THE WORD

D. A. CARSON

The Challenge

To construct a theology of worship turns out to be a difficult task. In addition to the ordinary difficulties associated with constructing an informed, balanced, and reasonably comprehensive theology of almost any biblical theme, the preparation of a theology of worship offers special challenges.

1. At the empirical level, the sad fact of contemporary church life is that there are few subjects calculated to kindle more heated debate than the subject of worship. Some of these debates have less to do with an intelligible theology of worship than with mere preferences for certain styles of music (older hymns versus contemporary praise choruses) and kinds of instruments (organs and pianos versus guitars and drums). Other flash points concern the place of "special music" (the North American expression for performance music), congregational singing, liturgical responses, clapping, drama. All sides claim to be God-centered. The moderns think the traditionalists defend comfortable

11

and rationalistic truths they no longer feel, while the stalwarts from the past fret that their younger contemporaries are so enamoured of hyped experience they care not a whit for truth, let alone beauty. Sometimes one senses that for many there are only two alternatives: dull (or should we say "stately"?) traditionalism, or faddish (or should we say "lively"?) contemporaneity. We are asked to choose between "as it was in the beginning, is now, and ever more shall be, world without end," and "old is cold, new is true." The one side thinks of worship as something we experience, often set over against the sermon (first we have worship, and then we have the sermon, as if the two are disjunctive categories); while the other side thinks of worship as ordered stateliness, often set over against all the rest of life.

In fact, the issues are more complicated than this simplistic polarization suggests. One must reckon with the propensity of not a few contemporary churches to reshape the corporate meetings of the church to make them more acceptable to every sociologically distinguishable cultural subgroup that comes along—boomers, busters, Gen Xers, white singles from Cleveland, or whatever. Although one wants to applaud the drive that is willing, for the sake of the gospel, to remove all offenses except the offense of the cross, sooner or later one is troubled by the sheer lack of stability, of a sense of heritage and substance passed on to another generation, of patterns of corporate worship shared with Christians who have gone before, or of any shared vision of what corporate worship should look like. This in turn generates a swarm of traditionalists who like things that are old regardless of whether or not they are well founded. They cringe at both inclusive litanies and guitars and start looking for an "alternative to alternative worship."[1]

Moreover, to gain perspective on the possible options, one must reflect on some of the historical studies that examine the worship practices of some bygone era, sometimes explicitly with the intention of enabling contemporaries to recover their roots or rediscover past

---

1. The quip is from Martin Marty in his foreword to Marva J. Dawn, *Reaching Out Without Dumbing Down: A Theology of Worship for the Turn-of-the-Century Culture* (Grand Rapids: Eerdmans, 1995).

practices.[2] Intriguingly, many of the new nontraditional services have already become, in some churches, entrenched traditions—and, on a historical scale, arguably inferior ones.

What cannot be contested is that the subject of worship is currently "hot." The widespread confusion is punctuated by strongly held and sometimes mutually exclusive theological stances that make attempts to construct a biblical theology of worship a pastorally sensitive enterprise.

2. The sheer diversity of the current options[3] not only contributes to the sense of unrest and divisiveness in many local churches but leads to confident assertions that all the biblical evidence supports those views and those alone. Contemporary attempts at constructing a theology of worship are naturally enmeshed in what "worship" means *to us,* in our vocabularies and in the vocabularies of the Christian communities to which we belong. Ideally, of course, our ideas about worship should be corrected by Scripture, and doubtless that occurs among many individuals with time. But the opposite easily happens as well: we unwittingly read our ideas and experiences of worship back into Scripture, so that we end up "finding" there what, with exquisite confidence, we know jolly well *ought* to be there. This is especially easy

---

2. To mention a few quite diverse examples: Paul F. Bradshaw, *The Search for the Origins of Christian Worship: Sources and Methods for the Study of Early Liturgy* (Oxford: University Press, 1993); James McKinnon, ed., *Music in Early Christian Literature* (Cambridge: Cambridge University Press, 1986); Melva Wilson Costen, *African American Christian Worship* (Nashville: Abingdon, 1993); Horton Davies, *The Worship of the American Puritans, 1629–1730* (New York: Peter Lang, 1990); idem, *Worship and Theology in England*, vol. 1, *From Cranmer to Baxter and Fox (1534–1690)*; vol. 2, *From Watts and Wesley to Martineau (1690–1900)*; vol. 3, *The Ecumenical Century (1900 to Present)* (Grand Rapids: Eerdmans, 1996). Cf. James F. White, *A Brief History of Christian Worship* (Nashville: Abingdon, 1993); J. G. Davies, ed., *A New Dictionary of Liturgy and Worship* (Philadelphia: Westminster Press, 1987); Gordon S. Wakefield, *An Outline of Christian Worship* (Edinburgh: T & T Clark, 1998); Andrew Wilson-Dickson, *The Story of Christian Music* (Minneapolis: Fortress, 1996); Hughes Oliphant Old, *The Reading and Preaching of the Scriptures in the Worship of the Christian Church*, vol. 1, *The Biblical Period;* vol. 2, *The Patristic Age;* vol. 3, *The Medieval Church* (Grand Rapids: Eerdmans, 1998–99).

3. See, for instance, the useful analysis of Mark Earey, "Worship—What do we think we are doing?" *Evangel* 16/1 (Spring 1998): 7–13.

to do when, as we shall see, the semantic range of our word *worship*, in *any* contemporary theory of worship, does not entirely match up with any one word or group of words in the Bible. What it means to be corrected by Scripture in this case is inevitably rather complex.

The result is quite predictable. A person who loves liturgical forms of corporate worship often begins with Old Testament choirs and antiphonal psalms, moves on to liturgical patterns in the ancient synagogue, and extols the theological maturity of the liturgy in question. A charismatic typically starts with 1 Corinthians 12 and 14. A New Testament scholar may begin with the ostensible "hymns" of the New Testament and then examine the brief texts that actually describe some element of worship, such as the Lord's Supper. And so it goes. It is not easy to find an agreed-upon method or common approach to discovering precisely how the Bible should re-form our views on worship.

That brings us to some of the slightly more technical challenges.

3. Unlike *Trinity*, the word *worship* is found in our English Bibles. So one might have thought that the construction of a doctrine of worship is easier than the construction of a doctrine of the Trinity. In the case of the Trinity, however, at least we agree on, more or less, what we are talking about. Inevitably, anything to do with our blessed triune God involves some hidden things that belong only to God himself (cf. Deut 29:29); nevertheless, in terms of the sphere of discussion, when we talk about the doctrine of the Trinity we have some idea to what we are referring, and we know the kinds of biblical and historical data that must feed into the discussion. By contrast, a cursory scan of the literature on worship soon discloses that people mean very different things when they talk about worship. To construct a theology of worship when there is little agreement on what worship is or refers to is rather daunting. The task cries out for some agreed-upon definitions.

But although the word *worship* occurs in our English Bibles, one cannot thereby get at the theme of worship as easily as one can get at, say, the theology of grace by studying all the occurrences of the word *grace*, or get at the theology of calling by examining all the passages that use the word *call*. Of course, even in these cases much more is involved than mere word study. One wants to examine the context of every passage with *grace* in it, become familiar with the synonyms, probe the concepts and people to which *grace* is tied (e.g., faith, the Lord Jesus, peace, and so forth). We rapidly recognize that different biblical authors may use words in slightly different ways. As is well known, *call* in Paul's writings is effective: those who are "called" are truly saved. By contrast, in the Synoptic Gospels the "call" of God means something like "invitation": many are *called* but few are chosen. Still, it is possible to provide a more or less comprehensive summary of the various things the Bible means by *call* simply by looking at all the examples and analyzing and cataloguing them. But the same thing cannot be done with *worship*, not least because for almost any definition of worship there are many passages that have a bearing on this subject that do not use the Hebrew or Greek word that could be rendered by the word *worship* itself. Moreover, the Hebrew and Greek words that are sometimes rendered by the English word *worship* sometimes mean something rather different from what *we* mean by worship. So we cannot get at this subject by simplistic word studies. We shall need to arrive at definitions that we can agree upon.

4. Constructing a theology of worship is challenging because of the different kinds of answers that are provided, in this case, by biblical theology and systematic theology. This observation is so important and lies so much at the heart of this chapter that a fuller explanation is warranted.

I begin with two definitions. For our purposes, *systematic theology* is theological synthesis organized along topical and atemporal lines. For example, if we were trying to construct a systematic theology of God, we would ask what the Bible as a whole says about God: What is he like? What are his attributes? What does he do? The answers to these and many similar questions would be forged out of the entirety of what the Bible says in interaction with what Christians in other generations have understood. We would not primarily be asking narrower questions, such as: What does the book of Isaiah say about God? How is God progressively revealed across the sweep of redemptive history? What distinctive contributions to the doctrine of God are made by the different genres found in the Bible (e.g., apocalyptic literature, parables, poetry, and so forth)?

By contrast, *biblical theology* is theological synthesis organized according to biblical book and corpus and along the line of the history of redemption. This means that biblical theology does not ask, in the first instance, what the Bible as a whole says about, say, God. Rather, it asks what the Synoptic Gospels say about God, or what the gospel of Mark or the book of Genesis says. It asks what new things are said about God as we progress through time.[4] Biblical theology is certainly interested in knowing how the biblical texts have been understood across the history of the church, but above all it is interested in inductive study of the texts themselves (including such matters as their literary genre: for instance, it does not fall into the mistake of treating proverbs as if they were case law in some insensitive, proof-texting approach), as those texts are serially placed against the backdrop of the Bible's developing plotline.

How, then, do these considerations bear on how we go about constructing a theology of worship? If we ask what worship is, *intending our question to be answered out of the matrix of systematic theology,* then we are looking for "whole Bible" answers—that is, what the Bible says as a whole. That will have one or more effects. On the positive side, we will be trying to listen to the *whole* Bible and not to one favorite passage on the subject—say, 1 Corinthians 14. At its best, such attentiveness fosters more comprehensive answers and fewer idiosyncratic answers. On the other hand, if we try to read the whole Bible without reflecting on the distinctions the Bible itself introduces regarding worship, we may end up looking for the lowest common denominators. In other words, we may look for things to do with worship that are true in every phase of redemptive history and thus lose the distinctive features. For example, we might say that worship is bound up with confessing the sheer centrality and worthiness of God. That is wonderfully true, yet it says nothing about the place of the sacrificial systems in Old Testament worship or the role of the choirs David founded, and so forth.

Alternatively, if we use the whole Bible indiscriminately to construct our theology of worship, we may use it idiosyncratically. For

---

4. That the *order* in which something is revealed may be extremely important if we are to understand the Bible aright is made very clear in chapters like Romans 4 and Galatians 3, where the apostle's argument several times turns on which events happened first.

instance, we note that the temple service developed choirs, so we conclude that our corporate worship must have choirs. Perhaps it should—but somewhere along the line we have not integrated into our reflection how the Bible fits together. We do not have a "temple" in the Old Testament sense. On what grounds do we transfer Old Testament choirs to the New Testament and not an Old Testament temple or priests? Of course, some of the church fathers during the early centuries did begin to think of ministers of the gospel as equivalent to Old Testament priests. The New Testament writers prefer to think of Jesus as the sole high priest (see Hebrews) or, alternatively, of all Christians as priests (e.g., 1 Pet 2:5; Rev 1:6). But even if we continue to think of contemporary clergy as priests, sooner or later we will have to ask similar questions about many other elements of Old Testament worship that were bound up with the temple—for example, the sacrifices of the Day of Atonement and of Passover. All Christians understand these sacrifices to be transmuted under the new covenant, such that they are now fulfilled in the sacrifice of Christ.

But the point is simply that the "pick-and-choose" method of constructing a theology of worship from the whole Bible lacks methodological rigor and therefore stability. Thus, constructing a theology of worship out of the matrix of systematic theology may actually *define* what we mean by "worship." The methods and approaches characteristic of the discipline (more precisely, they are characteristic of the discipline of the kind of systematic theology that is insufficiently informed by biblical theology) will to some extent determine the outcome.

If we ask what worship is, *intending our question to be answered out of the matrix of biblical theology,* then we are looking for what distinct books and sections of the Bible say on this subject and how they relate to one another. Inevitably we will be a little more alert to the differences; in particular, we will be forced to reflect at length on the differences one finds when one moves from the Mosaic covenant to the new covenant (on which more below). The dangers here are almost the inverse of the dangers of a systematic approach. Now we may so focus in a merely descriptive way on this or that corpus that we fail to construct an adequate theology of worship. For a theology of worship erected out of the matrix of biblical theology must still be a "whole

Bible" theology in the sense that the diverse pieces must fit together. Loss of nerve at this point will produce description with antiquarian interest but no normative power.

To summarize: The construction of a responsible theology of worship is made difficult by strongly held and divergent views on the subject, by a variety of linguistic pressures, and by the sharp tendencies to produce quite different works, depending in part on whether the theologian is working out of the matrix of systematic theology or of biblical theology.

Toward a Definition

Before pressing on to a definition, it may be worth taking two preliminary steps. First, it is worth thinking about our English word *worship*. Both the noun and the verb form have changed in meaning significantly over the centuries. Although from the tenth century on the word *worship* often had God as its object, nevertheless from the 1200s on it was often connected with the condition of deserving honor or a good reputation or with the source or ground of that honor. Chaucer, for instance, can say that it is a great worship to a man to keep himself from noise and strife. Knights win worship by their feats of arms. In the fifteenth century a "place of worship" may be a good house, and a "town of worship" is an important town. By easy transfer, worship came to refer to the honor itself that is shown a person or thing. That usage goes back a thousand years, and it is by no means restricted to God as the object. For example, in the marriage service of the old English Prayer Book the groom tells his bride, "With my body I thee worship"—which certainly does not make her a deity.

In all such usages one is concerned with the "worthiness" or the "worthship" (Old English *weorthscipe*) of the person or thing that is reverenced. From a Christian perspective, of course, only God himself is truly worthy of all possible honor, so it is not surprising that in most of our English Bibles, "worship" is bound up either with the worship of God or with the prohibition of worship of other beings, whether supernatural (e.g., Satan in Matt 4:9) or only ostensibly so (e.g., the sun).

What makes this even more difficult is that there are several underlying words in both Greek and Hebrew that are sometimes rendered "worship" and sometimes not. In other words, there is no one-to-one relationship between any Hebrew or Greek word and our word *worship*. For example, the Greek verb *proskyneō* is rendered "to worship" in Matthew 2:2 ("We saw his star in the east and have come *to worship* him"). Herod too promises to "go and *worship* him" (2:8), though certainly he is not thinking of worship of a supernatural being. What he is (falsely) promising is to go and pay homage to this child born to be a king. However, in the parable of the unmerciful servant in Matthew 18:26, when the servant turns out to be bankrupt and his family is threatened with slavery, he *"fell on his knees [pesōn . . . prosekynei]* before [his master]"*: certainly there is no question here of "worship" in the contemporary sense. Thus, our word *worship* is more restrictive in its object than this Greek verb but may be broader in the phenomena to which it refers (regardless of the object). In any case, the construction of a theology of worship will not be possible unless we come to reasonable agreement about what we mean by *worship*.

The second preliminary step that may prove helpful is to reflect on a few books and articles that exhibit one or more of the challenges involved in writing a theology of worship. Each of these pieces is competent and thoughtful. If I raise questions about them, it is not because I am not indebted to them but because this interaction will help to establish the complexities of the subject and prepare the way for what follows.

Andrew Hill has written an informative book whose subtitle, *Old Testament Worship for the New Testament Church*, discloses the content.[5] Most of its chapters are devoted to one element or another of worship in the Old Testament: the vocabulary of worship in the Hebrew canon; the nature of the "fear of the Lord" (which Hill ties to personal piety); historical developments; the sacred forms, sacred places, and sacred times of worship; sacred actions such as the lifting up of the hands; the roles of priest and king in worship; the place of the

---

5. Andrew E. Hill, *Enter His Courts with Praise! Old Testament Worship for the New Testament Church* (Grand Rapids: Baker, 1993).

tabernacle and temple; and the significance of the Psalms and of artistic decoration for worship. Hill concludes his book by trying to establish the legitimate connections between these Old Testament patterns and New Testament worship. Six appendices include treatments of the Hebrew religious calendar, sacrifice and music in the Old Testament, and the use of psalms for today's church. The book is full of useful information, thoughtfully presented.

One may quibble about this or that point, but for our purposes the greatest questions arise out of Hill's last chapter. He argues that Jewish patterns of worship were stamped on the nascent church primarily by two means. First, the synagogue structure and liturgy were largely duplicated by the early church. For example, Hill says, a typical synagogue liturgy, both ancient and modern, runs as follows: call to worship (often a "psalmic blessing"); a cycle of prayers (focusing especially on God as Creator and on God's covenant love for Israel); recitation of the Shema (Deut 6:4–9) and other texts (Deut 11:13–21; Num 15:37–41), which served as both a confession of faith and as a benediction; a second cycle of prayers, usually led by someone other than the ruler of the synagogue and including both praise and petition along with the congregational recitation of the Eighteen Benedictions; Scripture reading (including translation if necessary and even brief exposition) from at least one passage in the Torah, one in the Prophets, and perhaps one from the Writings; a benediction (often from the Psalms); the sermon; and the congregational Blessing and Amen. Following W. E. Oesterley,[6] Hill then ticks off the various ways in which the early church allegedly mirrored synagogue practices in its own worship: call to worship, credal affirmation, prayer, reading and exposition of Scripture, and so forth. Hill adds a few additional links: a covenant community gathering for worship, baptism, the concept of corporate personality within the community, alms collection/monetary offerings, liturgical benedictions, and lay participation.[7]

Second, Hill appeals to typology. The New Testament writers read the Old Testament as an incomplete and still-imperfect revelation that

---

6. W. E. Oesterley, *The Jewish Background of Christian Liturgy* (New York: Oxford University Press, 1965), 111–54.

7. Hill, *Enter His Courts*, 232–33.

is fulfilled in the new covenant and reread the sacred text from a christological perspective. Hill briefly notes some of the obvious typological connections: the sanctuary of the Mosaic covenant becomes the sanctuary not made with hands (Heb 9:1–23), the "sacrificial worship" of the Mosaic covenant by the single sacrifice of Christ (Heb 9:23–10:18), and so forth. From this Hill infers that the book of Hebrews in particular "provides a window into the spiritual principles implicit in Old Testament worship."[8] For example, "the Old Testament prophetic charge to do justice and love mercy instead of offering animal sacrifice takes on new meaning in light of Paul's command to the believer in Christ to be a living sacrifice (Hos 6:6; Amos 5:21–24; cf., Rom 12:1–2)."[9]

A plethora of questions arises. On the first point, the relationship between the church and the synagogue: (1) To what extent does the synagogue liturgy reflect Old Testament theology? Our actual sources for synagogue liturgy postdate the New Testament, emerging from a period of systematic reflection *after* the fall of the temple and the rise of Christianity. At this point the synagogue no longer exercised the relatively restricted role it occupied while the temple was still the center of the Jewish world; the synagogue now necessarily replaced it. Inevitably there arose important and influential theological strands that had to compensate for the loss of the temple and with it the loss of the entire sacrificial system. Oesterley's work is now very dated, and much scholarship since then has warned against anachronism. Jewish lectionaries, for example, come from a period later than the latest New Testament writing.[10] (2) By the same token, we have no detailed *first-century* evidence of an entire Christian service. Doubtless there are things to learn from the patristic sources, but they should not be read back into the canonical sources. Certainly the New

---

8. Ibid., 237.

9. Ibid.

10. If all we are saying is that early church corporate worship mirrored the synagogue in (1) reading the Scripture; (2) singing; (3) praying; and (4) a homily, that is doubtless true. It is the attempt to ground entire liturgical structures in the New Testament or in first-century Jewish synagogues that proves so elusive and finally so anachronistic.

Testament documents do not themselves provide a "model service" of the sort advocated by Hill (however admirable that model may be), nor do they command that the church adhere to a synagogal liturgy (of whatever date). (3) At least some of the parallels Hill finds between the synagogue and the early church—a covenant community gathering for worship, monetary offerings, lay participation—are either so generic as to be meaningless (What religion does not collect money? How many religions foster some form of lay participation?) or at least raise some fundamental questions about the implicit definition of worship. Under the new covenant, for instance, is it true to say that the community gathers for worship? I shall return to that question in a moment.

On the second point, the nature of typology, although I heartily agree that a properly defined typology lies at the heart of a great deal of the New Testament's use of the Old, slight adjustments in one's understanding of typology or in the exegesis of particular texts will result in a rather different theology of worship from the one Hill is advocating. For instance, while some interpreters think of typology as an interpretive method that provides us with nothing more than "spiritual principles" (which presupposes an atemporal relationship), others—myself included—think that several forms of typology embrace a teleological element, a predictive element. In that case, one must ask what those Old Testament patterns of worship are *pointing toward*. This shift in interpretive priority tilts toward biblical theology.

Turning from Hill's important work, we may more briefly reflect on several other discussions of worship of very different complexion. Many studies have focused on the theme of worship in a particular biblical corpus—on some element of the Psalms,[11] on a critical Old Testament chapter,[12] or on Matthew,[13] Hebrews,[14] or

---

11. E.g., Terence E. Fretheim, "Nature's Praise of God in the Psalms," *Ex Auditu* 3 (1987): 16–30.

12. E.g., John W. Hilber, "Theology of Worship in Exodus 24," *Journal of the Evangelical Theological Society* 39 (1996): 177–89.

13. E.g., Mark Allan Powell, "A Typology of Worship in the Gospel of Matthew," *Journal for the Study of the New Testament* 57 (1995): 3–17.

14. E.g., John Dunnill, *Covenant and Sacrifice in the Letter to the Hebrews*, Society of New Testament Studies Monograph Series, vol. 75 (Cambridge: Cambridge University Press, 1992).

Revelation.[15] Inevitably, such essays vary considerably. Some are contributions to the theology of the particular book; others are attempts to get behind the book to the worship patterns and priorities of the ostensible community served by the book. Until such studies are integrated into a larger sweep, they have the important but limited function of opening our eyes to aspects of worship we might overlook, even though they cannot themselves impose a unified vision. Thus, we may value one of the observations of Marianne Meye Thompson regarding the book of Revelation:

> Worship serves the indispensable function of uniting us with "all the saints," living and dead. In fact one of the most important things that worship accomplishes is to remind us that we worship not merely as a congregation or a church, but as part of the church, the people of God. John reminds his readers that their worship is a participation in the unceasing celestial praise of God. So too, the worship of God's people today finds its place "in the middle" of a throng representing every people and nation, tribe and tongue.[16]

Perhaps the volume that most urgently calls for thoughtful evaluation is the biblical-theological study written by David Peterson.[17] His important book not only traces out the development of worship in the Old Testament but also highlights the vivid contrast introduced by the New Testament. From Moses on, the heart of Old Testament worship, Peterson insists, is connected with the tabernacle and then with the temple. But what is striking about the New Testament is not only that Jesus is explicitly worshiped and that the theological impulses of the New Testament documents draw many Old Testament strands into Jesus himself (thus he is the temple, the priest, the Passover lamb, the

15. E.g., Donald Guthrie, "Aspects of Worship in the Book of Revelation," in *Worship, Theology and Ministry in the Early Church,* Journal for the Study of New Testament Supplement Series, vol. 87 (Sheffield: Academic Press, 1992), 70–83; Marianne Meye Thompson, "Worship in the Book of Revelation," *Ex Auditu* 8 (1992): 45–54.

16. Thompson, "Worship," 53.

17. David Peterson, *Engaging with God* (Leicester: Apollos, 1992). See also the early essays in *Worship: Adoration and Action,* ed. D. A. Carson (Grand Rapids: Baker, 1993).

bread of life) and thereby necessarily transmute Old Testament patterns of worship, but that worship *language* moves the locus away from a place or a time to all of life. Worship is no longer something connected with set feasts, such as Passover; or a set place, such as the temple; or set priests, such as the Levitical system prescribed. It is for all the people of God at all times and places, and it is bound up with how they live (e.g., Rom 12:1–2).

We shall briefly survey some of the evidence below; it is very impressive. But one of the entailments is that we cannot imagine that the church gathers for worship on Sunday morning if by this we mean that we then engage in something that we have not been engaging in the rest of the week. New covenant worship terminology prescribes *constant* "worship." Peterson therefore examines afresh just why the New Testament church gathers, and he concludes that the focus is on mutual edification, not on worship. Under the terms of the new covenant, worship goes on all the time, including when the people of God gather together. But mutual edification does not go on all the time; it is what takes place when Christians gather together. Edification is the best summary of what occurs in corporate singing, confession, public prayer, the ministry of the Word, and so forth. Then, at the end of his book, Peterson examines his own denominational heritage (Anglican) and enters a quiet plea for continued and proper use of the *Book of Common Prayer*.

It will soon become obvious that I am very sympathetic to much of Peterson's exegesis. Especially in his examination of praise vocabulary and the "cultic" vocabulary in the New Testament—words for priestly service, sacrifice, offering, and so on—Peterson is very convincing. I am not sure he always captures the affective element in the corporate worship of both Testaments; moreover, I shall suggest a slight modification to his way of thinking of the meetings of the church.

With respect to his attachment to the *Book of Common Prayer,* he is of course following the great Anglican Richard Hooker, who argued that where the Bible neither commands nor forbids, the church is free to order its liturgical life as it pleases for the sake of good order. If Hooker's principle is followed, Peterson says in effect, let the ordering be done well with rich theological principles in mind. Yet one must wrestle with the competing claims of Hooker's principle and the Presbyterian Regulative Principle (on which more below). Furthermore, it is difficult to avoid the feeling that there is something of a "disconnect" between Peterson's conclusions on the Prayer Book and the rest of his work. By this I do not mean that his judgments on Anglican worship are inappropriate or theologically unjustified. Rather, the bulk of his book is supported by close exegesis of Scripture and is testable by the canons of exegesis, while the material on the Prayer Book is necessarily disconnected from such exegesis and therefore has more of the flavor of fervently held personal opinion (regardless of how theologically informed that opinion is). Moreover, after so vigorously defining new covenant worship in the most comprehensive categories embracing all of life, Peterson finds he wants to talk about what we shall call corporate worship in the regular "services" of the church after all.

Peterson, of course, allows that when the people of God gather together corporately, they are still worshiping. What he insists is that the *distinctive* element of their corporate meetings is not worship but edification. Inevitably, there are some who go farther. Observing not only how "cultic" language is used in the New Testament to refer to all of Christian life, and noting the lack of any mention of worship when the New Testament writers provide purpose clauses as to why the people of God meet together, these scholars conclude that we should *stop* thinking of "worship services" and meeting together "to worship" and the like.[18] They make some good points, but a good part of their argument turns on a definition of worship that is tightly tied to cultus.

So I must come to a definition. After the definition, much of the rest of this chapter will be an exposition of that definition, followed by some practical suggestions.

---

18. See, with various emphases, I. Howard Marshall, "How far did the early Christians *worship* God?" *Churchman* 99 (1985): 216–29; A. Boyd Luter Jr., "'Worship' as Service: The New Testament Usage of *latreuo*," *Criswell Theological Review* 2 (1988): 335–44; and the discussion between John P. Richardson, "Is Worship Biblical?" *Churchman* 109 (1995): 197–218; *idem,* "Neither 'Worship' nor 'Biblical': A Response to Alastair Campbell," *Churchman* 111 (1997): 6–18, and Alastair Campbell, "Once More: Is Worship 'Biblical'?" *Churchman* 110 (1996): 131–39.

Definition and Exposition

Robert Shaper asserts that worship, like love, is characterized by intuitive simplicity (everybody "knows" what worship is, just as everyone "knows" what love is) and philosophical complexity (the harder you press to unpack love or worship, the more difficult the task).[19] Worship embraces relationship, attitude, act, life. We may attempt the following definition:

> *Worship* is the proper response of all moral, sentient beings to God, ascribing all honor and worth to their Creator-God precisely because he is worthy, delightfully so. This side of the Fall, *human worship* of God properly responds to the redemptive provisions that God has graciously made. While all true worship is God-centered, *Christian worship* is no less Christ-centered. Empowered by the Spirit and in line with the stipulations of the new covenant, it manifests itself in all our living, finding its impulse in the gospel, which restores our relationship with our Redeemer-God and therefore also with our fellow image-bearers, our co-worshipers. Such worship therefore manifests itself both in adoration and in action, both in the individual believer and in *corporate worship*, which is worship offered up in the context of the body of believers, who strive to align all the forms of their devout ascription of all worth to God with the panoply of new covenant mandates and examples that bring to fulfillment the glories of antecedent revelation and anticipate the consummation.

Doubtless this definition is too long and too complex. But it may provide a useful set of pegs on which to hang a brief exposition of the essentials of worship. This exposition is organized under an apostolic number of points of unequal weight that arise from the definition.

1. The first (and rather cumbersome) sentence of the definition asserts that worship is "the proper response of all moral, sentient beings to God." There are two purposes to this phrase. First, the inclusive "all" reminds us that worship is not restricted to human beings alone. The angels worship; they are commanded to do so, and in a passage such as Revelation 4, they orchestrate the praise offered in heaven. Among other things, this means that worship cannot properly

---

19. Robert Shaper, *In His Presence* (Nashville: Thomas Nelson, 1984), 13.

be defined as *necessarily* arising out of the gospel, for one of the great mysteries of redemption is that in his wisdom God has provided a Redeemer for fallen human beings but not for fallen angels. The angels who orchestrate the praise of heaven do not offer their worship as a response borne of their experience of redemption. For our part, when we offer our worship to God, we must see that this does not make us unique. The object of our worship, God himself, is unique in that he alone is to be worshiped; we, the worshipers, are not.

Second, by speaking of worship as the proper response "of moral, sentient beings," this definition excludes from worship rocks and hawks, minnows and sparrows, cabbages and toads, a mote of dust dancing on a sunbeam. Of course, by understandable extension of the language, all creatures, sentient and otherwise, are exhorted to praise the Lord (e.g., Ps 148). But they do not do so in conscious obedience; they do so because they are God's creatures and are constituted to reflect his glory and thus bring him glory. In this extended sense all of the created order "owns" its Lord. As all of it now participates in death and "groans" in anticipation of the consummation (Rom 8:22–23), so also on the last day it participates in the glorious transformation of the resurrection: our hope is a new heaven and a new earth. In this extended sense, all creation is God-oriented and "ascribes" God's worth to God alone. But it is an *extended* sense. For our purposes, we will think of worship as something offered to God by "all moral, sentient beings."

2. Worship is a "proper response" to God for at least four reasons. First of all, in both Testaments worship is repeatedly enjoined on the covenant people of God: they worship because worship is variously commanded and encouraged. God's people are to "ascribe to the LORD the glory due his name. Bring an offering and come before him; worship the LORD in the splendor of his holiness" (1 Chr 16:29). "Come, let us bow down in worship, let us kneel before the LORD our Maker; for he is our God and we are the people of his pasture, the flock under his care" (Ps 95:6–7). "Worship the LORD with gladness; come before him with joyful songs" (Ps 100:2). When he was tempted to worship the devil, Jesus insisted, "Worship the Lord your God, and serve him only" (Matt 4:10). It follows that the worship of any other god is simply

idolatry (Ps 81:9; Isa 46:6; Dan 3:15, 28). It is a mark of terrible judgment when God gives a people over to the worship of false gods (Acts 7:42–43). In the courts of heaven, God has no rival. No homage is to be done to any other, even a glorious interpreter of truth: "Worship God" and him alone (Rev 19:10).

Second, worship is a "proper response" because it is grounded in the very character and attributes of God. If worship is repeatedly enjoined, often the link to the sheer greatness or majesty or splendor of God is made explicit. In other words, the "worth" of God is frequently made explicit in the particular "worth-ship" that is being considered. Sometimes this is comprehensive: "Ascribe to the LORD *the glory due his name*" (1 Chr 16:29; cf. Ps 29:2)—that is, the glory that is his due, since in biblical thought God's name is the reflection of all that God is. That text goes on to exhort the reader to "worship the Lord *in the splendor of his holiness*." That is tantamount to saying that we are to worship the Lord in the splendor of all that makes God God. Like white light that shines through a prism and is broken into its colorful components, so this truth can be broken down into its many parts. Many elements contribute to the sheer "Godness" that constitutes holiness in its purest form. Thus, people will speak of "the glorious splendor of [his] majesty" (Ps 145:3–5). If 2 Kings 17:39 commands the covenant community to "worship the LORD your God," it gives a reason: "it is he who will deliver you from the hand of all your enemies." But all of the focus is on God.

Third, one of the most striking elements of God's "worth-ship," and therefore one of the most striking reasons for worshiping him, is the fact that he alone is the Creator. Sometimes this is linked with the fact that he reigns over us. "Come, let us bow down in worship," the psalmist exhorts, "let us kneel *before the LORD our Maker*" (the first element); "*for he is our God and we are the people of his pasture*" (the second element) (Ps 95:6–7). If we are to worship the Lord with gladness (Ps 100:2), it is for this reason: "It is he who made us, and we are his; we are his people, the sheep of his pasture" (v. 3). Nowhere, perhaps, is this more powerfully expressed than in Revelation 4. Day and night the four living creatures never stop ascribing praise to God: "Holy, holy, holy is the Lord God Almighty, who was, and is, and is to come" (4:8). Whenever they do so (and we have just been told that they never stop), the twenty-four elders "fall down before him who sits on the throne, and worship him who lives for ever and ever" (4:10). Moreover, "they lay their crowns before the throne" (4:10), an act that symbolizes their unqualified recognition that they are dependent beings. Their worship is nothing other than recognizing that God alone is worthy "to receive glory and honor and power, *for you created all things and by your will they were created and have their being*" (4:11, italics added). Worship is the proper response of the creature to the Creator. Worship does not create something new; rather, it is a transparent response to what is, a recognition of our creaturely status before the Creator himself.[20]

Fourth, to speak of a "proper response" to God calls us to reflect on what God himself has disclosed of his own expectations. How does God want his people to respond to him? Although God always demands faith and obedience, the precise outworking of faith and obedience may change across the years of redemptive history. Suppose that at some point in history God insisted that believers be required to build great monuments in his honor. For them, the building of such monuments would be part of their "proper response" precisely because it would have been mandated by God. Once the Mosaic covenant was in place, the people of Israel were mandated to go up to the central tabernacle/temple three times a year: this was part of their proper response. What this means for members of the new covenant is that our response to God in worship should begin by carefully and reflectively examining what God requires of us under the terms of this covenant. We should not begin by asking whether or not we *enjoy* "worship," but by asking, "What is it that God expects of us?" That will frame our proper response. To ask this question is also to take the first step in reformation. It demands self-examination, for we soon discover where we do *not* live up to what God expects. This side of the Fall,

---

20. This is the sort of theme that is often movingly treated by Marva J. Dawn, *A Royal "Waste" of Time: The Splendor of Worshiping God and Being Church for the World* (Grand Rapids: Eerdmans, 1999). But because she does not set her discussion within the context of biblical theology (see below), she rather consistently reduces worship to what we have called "corporate worship."

every age has characteristic sins. To find out what they are by listening attentively to what the Bible actually says about what God demands will have the effect of reforming every area of our lives, including our worship. Cornelius Plantinga makes the point almost as an aside:

> If we know the characteristic sins of the age, we can guess its foolish and fashionable assumptions—that morality is simply a matter of personal taste, that all silences need to be filled up with human chatter or background music, that 760 percent of the American people are victims,[21] that it is better to feel than to think, that rights are more important than responsibilities, that even for children the right to choose supersedes all other rights, that real liberty can be enjoyed without virtue, that self-reproach is for fogies, that God is a chum or even a gofer whose job is to make us rich or happy or religiously excited, that it is more satisfying to be envied than respected, that it is better for politicians and preachers to be cheerful than truthful, *that Christian worship fails unless it is fun.*[22]

3. We worship our Creator-God "precisely because he is worthy, *delightfully so.*" What ought to make worship delightful to us is not, in the first instance, its novelty or its aesthetic beauty, but its object: God himself is delightfully wonderful, and we learn to delight in him.

In an age increasingly suspicious of (linear) thought, there is much more respect for the "feeling" of things—whether a film or a church service. It is disturbingly easy to plot surveys of people, especially young people, drifting from a church of excellent preaching and teaching to one with excellent music because, it is alleged, there is "better worship" there. But we need to think carefully about this matter. Let us restrict ourselves for the moment to corporate worship. Although there are things that can be done to enhance corporate worship, there

---

21. At this point Plantinga refers to an essay by John Leo, who has observed that "a lot of Americans qualify for victim status in multiple ways: they are victims of AIDS, the press, rock music or pornography, warped upbringing, anti-nerd bias, public hostility toward smokers, addiction, patriarchy, being black, being white, belonging to male bonding groups that beat drums in the woods, and so on" ("A 'Victim' Census for Our Time," *U.S. News and World Report,* 23 November 1992, 22).

22. Cornelius Plantinga Jr., *Not the Way It's Supposed to Be: A Breviary of Sin* (Grand Rapids: Eerdmans, 1995), 126–27 (emphasis mine).

is a profound sense in which excellent worship cannot be attained merely by pursuing excellent worship. In the same way that, according to Jesus, you cannot find yourself until you lose yourself, so also you cannot find excellent corporate worship until you stop trying to find excellent corporate worship and pursue God himself. Despite the protestations, one sometimes wonders if we are beginning to worship *worship* rather than worship *God*. As a brother put it to me, it's a bit like those who begin by admiring the sunset and soon begin to admire themselves admiring the sunset.

This point is acknowledged in a praise chorus like "Let's forget about ourselves, and magnify the Lord, and worship him." The trouble is that after you have sung this repetitious chorus three or four times, you are no farther ahead. The *way* you forget about yourself is by focusing on God—not by singing about doing it, but by doing it. There are far too few choruses and services and sermons that expand our vision of God—his attributes, his works, his character, his words. Some think that corporate worship is good because it is lively where it had been dull. But it may also be shallow where it is lively, leaving people dissatisfied and restless in a few months' time. Sheep lie down when they are well fed (cf. Ps 23:2); they are more likely to be restless when they are hungry. "Feed my sheep," Jesus commanded Peter (John 21); and many sheep are unfed. If you wish to deepen the worship of the people of God, above all deepen their grasp of his ineffable majesty in his person and in all his works.

This is not an abstruse theological point divorced from our conduct and ethics. Nor is it an independent point, as if there were two independent mandates: first of all, worship God (because he deserves it), and then live rightly (because he says so). For worship, properly understood, shapes who we are. We become like whatever is our god. Peter Leithart's comments may not be nuanced, but they express something important:

> It is a fundamental truth of Scripture that we become like whatever or whomever we worship. When Israel worshipped the gods of the nations, she became like the nations—bloodthirsty, oppressive, full of deceit and violence (cf. Jeremiah 7). Romans 1 confirms this principle by showing how idolaters are delivered over to sexual deviations and

eventually to social and moral chaos. The same dynamic is at work today. Muslims worship Allah, a power rather than a person, and their politics reflects this commitment. Western humanists worship man, with the result that every degrading whim of the human heart is honoured and exalted and disseminated through the organs of mass media. Along these lines, Psalm 115:4–8 throws brilliant light on Old Covenant history and the significance of Jesus' ministry. After describing idols as figures that have every organ of sense but no sense, the Psalmist writes, "Those who make them will become like them, everyone who trusts in them." By worshipping idols, human beings become speechless, blind, deaf, unfeeling, and crippled—but then these are precisely the afflictions that Jesus, in the Gospels, came to heal![23]

Pray, then, and work for a massive display of the glory and character and attributes of God. We do not expect the garage mechanic to expatiate on the wonders of his tools; we expect him to fix the car. He must know how to use his tools, but he must not lose sight of the goal. So we dare not focus on the mechanics of corporate worship and lose sight of the goal. We focus on God himself, and thus we become more godly and learn to worship—and collaterally we learn to edify one another, forbear with one another, challenge one another.

Of course, the glories of God may be set forth in sermon, song, prayer, or testimony. It is in this sense that the title of one of Mark Noll's essays is exactly right: "We Are What We Sing."[24] What is clear is that if you try to enhance "worship" simply by livening the tempo or updating the beat, you may not be enhancing worship at all. On the other hand, dry-as-dust sermons loaded with clichés and devoid of the presence of the living God mediated by the Word do little to enhance worship either.

What we must strive for is growing knowledge of God and delight in him—not delight in worship per se, but delight in God. A place to begin might be to memorize Psalm 66. There is so much more to know about God than the light diet on offer in many churches; and genuine believers, when they are fed wholesome spiritual meals, soon delight all the more in God himself. This also accounts for the importance of

---

23. Peter Leithart, "Transforming Worship," *Foundations* 38 (Spring 1997): 27.
24. *Christianity Today*, 12 July 1999, 37–41.

"re-telling" in the Bible (e.g., Pss 75–76). Retelling the Bible's story line brings to mind again and again something of God's character, past actions, and words. It calls to mind God's great redemptive acts across the panorama of redemptive history. This perspective is frequently lost in contemporary worship, where there are very few elements calculated to make us remember the great turning points in the Bible. I am thinking not only of those bland "services" in which even at Easter and Christmas we are deluged with the same sentimental choruses at the expense of hymns and anthems that *tell the Easter or Christmas story*, but also of the loss of hymns and songs that *told individual Bible stories* (e.g., "Hushed Was the Evening Hymn"). Similarly, whatever else the Lord's Table is, it is a means appointed by the Lord Jesus to remember his death and its significance.[25] The Psalms frequently retell parts of Israel's history, especially the events surrounding the exodus, serving both as review and as incentive to praise. Paul recognizes that writing "the same things" may be a "safeguard" for his readers (Phil 3:1). Written reminders may stimulate readers to "wholesome thinking" (2 Pet 3:1), for Peter wants them "to recall the words spoken in the past by the holy prophets and the command given by our Lord and Savior" through the apostles (3:2). In this he mirrors Old Testament exhortations, for there we are told that we must remember not only all that God has done for us, but every word that proceeds from the mouth of God, carefully passing them on to our children (Deut 6, 8). All of this presupposes that retelling ought to prove formative, nurturing, stabilizing, delightful.[26] Equally, it presupposes that even under the terms of the old covenant, everything that might be embraced by the term *worship* was more comprehensive than what was bound up with the ritual of tabernacle and temple.

Perhaps it is in this light that we ought to wrestle with the importance of repetition as a reinforcing pedagogical device. If mere traditionalism for the sake of aesthetics is suspect, surely the same is true of mere innovation for the sake of excitement. But there must be some

---

25. Cf. Tim Ralston, "'Remember' and Worship: The Mandate and the Means," *Reformation and Revival* 9/3 (2000): 77–89.

26. Cf. Eugene H. Merrill, "Remembering: A Central Theme in Biblical Worship," *JETS* 43 (2000): 27–36.

ways of driving home the fundamentals of the faith. In godly repetition and retelling, we must plant deeply within our souls the glorious truths about God and about what he has done that we will otherwise soon forget.

4. "This side of the Fall, *human worship* of God properly responds to the redemptive provisions that God has graciously made." The brief glimpse afforded of human existence before the Fall (Gen 2) captures a time when God's image-bearers delighted in the perfection of his creation and the pleasure of his presence precisely because they were perfectly oriented toward him. No redemptive provisions had yet been disclosed, for none were needed. There was no need to exhort human beings to worship; their entire existence revolved around the God who had made them.

At the heart of the Fall is the self-love that destroys our God-centeredness. Implicitly, of course, all failure to worship God is neither more nor less than idolatry. Because we are finite, we will inevitably worship something or someone. In *The Brothers Karamazov*, Dostoyevsky was not wrong to write, "So long as man remains free he strives for nothing so incessantly and so painfully as to find someone to worship." Yet because we are fallen, we gravitate to false gods: a god that is domesticated and manageable, perhaps a material god, perhaps an abstract god like power or pleasure, or a philosophical god like Marxism or democracy or postmodernism. But worship we will. Most of these gods are small and pathetic, prompting William James to denounce the "moral flabbiness born of the exclusive worship of the bitch-goddess *success*."

Worse yet, we stand guilty before God, for our Maker is also our Judge. That might have been the end of the story, but God progressively discloses his redemptive purposes. As he does so, he makes demands about what approach is acceptable to him, what constitutes acceptable praise and prayer, what constitutes an acceptable *corporate* approach before him. Thus, worship becomes enmeshed, by God's prescription, in ritual, sacrifice, detailed law, a sanctuary, a priestly system, and so forth. Three important points must be made here.

First, the changing and developing patterns of God's prescriptions for his people when they draw near to him constitute a complex and subtle history.[27] The first human sin calls forth the first death, the death of an animal to hide the nakedness of the first image-bearers. Sacrifice soon becomes a deeply rooted component of worship. By the time of the Mosaic covenant, the peace offering (Lev 17:11ff.) was the divinely prescribed means of maintaining a harmonious relationship between God and his covenant people. The sin offering (Lev 4) dealt with sin as a barrier between the worshipers and God. This sin offering was a slaughtered bull, lamb, or goat with which the worshiper had identified himself by laying his hands on its head. When the blood of the victim, signifying its life (Lev 17:11), was daubed on the horns of the altar, symbolizing the presence of God, God and the worshipers were united in a renewed relationship. Under the terms of the prescribed covenantal relationship, there could no longer be acceptable worship apart from conformity to the demands of the sacrificial system. By this system, God had prescribed the means by which his rebellious image-bearers could approach him. "Worship was thus Israel's response to the covenant relationship and the means of ensuring its continuance."[28]

There were many variations both before and after Sinai. In the patriarchal period, clans and individuals offered sacrifice in almost any location and without a priestly class. The Mosaic covenant prescribed that offerings be restricted to the tabernacle, a mobile sanctuary, and that they become an exclusive prerogative of the Levites; but both restrictions, especially the former, were often observed in the breach. With the construction of Solomon's temple, covenantal worship became more centralized, at least until the division of the kingdom. The high feasts brought pilgrims onto the roads by the thousands, going "up" to Jerusalem, the city of the great king. Choirs were in attendance, and musical instruments contributed to these festal occasions. Worship was powerfully tied to cultus.

The division of the kingdom and the spiraling degeneration of both Israel and Judah soon broke up even this degree of uniformity. The

---

27. See the relevant sections of Peterson, *Engaging with God;* Y. Hattori, "Theology of Worship in the Old Testament," in *Worship: Adoration and Action,* 21–50.

28. J. G. Davies, "Worship," *A Dictionary of Biblical Tradition in English Literature,* ed. David Lyle Jeffrey (Grand Rapids: Eerdmans, 1992), 851.

exile dispersed the northern tribes to sites that made access to the temple impossible; in due course, exile reached the kingdom of Judah and witnessed the utter destruction of the temple. The revolution in thinking that accompanied this obliteration of the central reality of the cultus is shown in many Old Testament texts, not least in the vision of Ezekiel 8–11, where it is the exilic community—not the Jews remaining in Jerusalem who are about to be destroyed along with the temple—who constitute the true remnant, the people for whom God himself will be a sanctuary (11:16). Such realities relativize the temple and with it the covenantal structure inextricably linked with it. The same effect is achieved by promises of a new covenant (Jer 31:31ff.; Ezek 36:25–27). As the author of Hebrews would later reason, the promise of a new covenant made the old covenant obsolete in principle (Heb 8:13). The restoration of a diminished temple after the exile did not really jeopardize these new anticipations, for neither the high-priestly line of Zadok nor the Davidic kingdom was ever restored.

Thus, the first point to observe is that however enmeshed in cultus, sacrifice, priestly service, covenantal prescription, and major festivals the worship of Israel had become, that worship kept changing its face across the two millennia from Abraham to Jesus.

Second, there is no reason to restrict all worship in ancient Israel to the cultus. The Psalms testify to a large scope for individual praise and adoration, even if some of them are addressed to a wide readership and even if some were intended for corporate use in temple services. The Old Testament provides ample evidence of individuals pouring out their prayers before God, quite apart from the religion of the cultus (e.g., Hannah, Daniel, and Job).

Third, and most important, a remarkable shift takes place with the coming of the Lord Jesus and the dawning of the new covenant he introduces. Under the terms of the new covenant, the Levitical priesthood has been replaced: either we are all priests (i.e., intermediaries, 1 Peter), or else Jesus alone is the high priest (Hebrews), but there is no priestly caste or tribe. Jesus' body becomes the temple (John 2:13–22); or, adapting the figure, the church is the temple (1 Cor 3:16–17); or the individual Christian is the temple (1 Cor 6:19). No church building is ever designated the "temple" (e.g., "Temple Baptist Church").

The pattern of type/antitype is so thorough that inevitably the way we think of worship must also change. The language of worship, so bound up with the temple and priestly system under the old covenant, has been radically transformed by what Christ has done.

We see the change in a well-known passage like Romans 12:1–2. To offer our bodies as "living sacrifices, holy and pleasing to God" is our "spiritual act of worship." In other words, Paul uses the worship language of the cultus, except that his use of the terminology transports us away from the cultus: what we offer is no longer a lamb or a bull but our bodies. We see the change again in another well-known passage. Jesus tells us we "must worship in spirit and in truth" (John 4:24). This does not mean that we must worship "spiritually" (as opposed to "carnally"?) and "truthfully" (as opposed to "falsely"?). The context focuses our Lord's argument. Samaritans held that the appropriate location for worship was at the twin mountains, Gerizim and Ebal; Jews held that it was Jerusalem. By contrast, Jesus says that a time is now dawning "when the true worshipers will worship the Father in spirit and truth. . . . God is spirit, and his worshipers must worship in spirit and in truth" (4:23–24). In the first instance, then, this utterance abolishes both Samaria's mountains and Jerusalem as the proper location for the corporate worship of the people of God. God is spirit, and he cannot be domesticated by mere location or mere temples, even if in the past he chose to disclose himself in one such temple as a teaching device that anticipated what was coming. Moreover, in this book—in which Jesus appears as the *true* vine, the *true* manna, the *true* Shepherd, the *true* temple, the *true* Son—to worship God "in spirit *and in truth*" is first and foremost a way of saying that we must worship God *by means of Christ*. In him the reality has dawned and the shadows are being swept away (cf. Heb 8:13). Christian worship is new covenant worship; it is gospel-inspired worship; it is Christ-centered worship; it is cross-focused worship.[29]

Elsewhere in the New Testament, we discover that Paul could think of evangelism as his *priestly* service (Rom 15). Jesus is our Passover lamb (1 Cor 5:7). We offer a sacrifice of praise (Heb 13:15),

---

29. On all these points, Peterson, *Engaging with God*, is very good.

not a sacrifice of sheep. Our worship is no longer focused on a particular form or festival. It must be bound up with all we are and do as the blood-bought people of God's Messiah. We offer up *ourselves* as living sacrifices. Augustine was not far off the mark when he wrote, "God is to be worshiped by faith, hope, and love." This is something we do all the time: under the terms of the new covenant, worship is no longer primarily focused in a cultus shaped by a liturgical calendar, but it is something in which we are continuously engaged.

To sum up: "This side of the Fall, *human worship* of God properly responds to the redemptive provision that God has graciously made." But because of the location of new covenant believers in the stream of redemptive history, the heart of what constitutes true worship changes its form rather radically. At a time when sacrificial and priestly structures anticipated the ultimate sacrifice and high priest, faithful participation in the corporate worship of the covenant community meant the temple with all its symbolism: sacrificial animals, high feasts, and so forth. This side of the supreme sacrifice, we no longer participate in the forms that pointed toward it; and the focus of worship language, priestly language, sacrificial language has been transmuted into a far more comprehensive arena, one that is far less oriented toward any notion of cultus.

5. Nevertheless, so that we do not err by exaggerating the differences between the forms of worship under the Mosaic covenant and under the new covenant, it is essential to recognize that "*all* true worship is God-centered." It is *never* simply a matter of conforming to formal requirements. The Old Testament prophets offer many passages that excoriate all worship that is formally "correct" while the worshiper's heart is set on idolatry (e.g., Ezek 8). Isaiah thunders the word of the Lord: "'The multitude of your sacrifices—what are they to me?' says the LORD. 'I have more than enough of burnt offerings, of rams and the fat of fattened animals; I have no pleasure in the blood of bulls and lambs and goats. . . . Stop bringing meaningless offerings! Your incense is detestable to me. New Moons, Sabbaths and convocations— I cannot bear your evil assemblies. . . . When you spread out your hands in prayer, I will hide my eyes from you. . . . Take your evil deeds out of my sight! Stop doing wrong, learn to do right!'" (Isa 1:11–17). "Will

you steal and murder, commit adultery and perjury, burn incense to Baal and follow other gods you have not known, and then come and stand before me in this house, which bears my Name, and say, 'We are safe'—safe to do all these detestable things?" (Jer 7:9–10). "Without purity of heart their pretense of worship was indeed an abomination," says Robert Rayburn. "Even the divinely authorized ordinances themselves had become offensive to the God who had given them because of the way they had been abused."[30]

This may clarify a point from Peterson that can easily be turned toward a doubtful conclusion. Peterson rightly points out, as we have seen, that the move from the old covenant to the new brings with it a transmutation of the language of the cultus. Under the new covenant the terminology of sacrifice, priest, temple, offering, and the like is transformed. No longer is there a supreme site to which pilgrimages of the faithful must be made: we worship "in spirit and in truth." This transformation of language is inescapable and is tied to the shift from type to antitype, from promise to reality, from shadow to substance. But we must not therefore conclude that, apart from instances of individual worship, in the Old Testament the formal requirements of the cultus exhausted what was meant by public worship.

In any legal structure there has always been a hierarchy of priorities. Jesus himself was quite prepared to deliver his judgment as to which was the greatest commandment in "the Law": "Love the Lord your God with all your heart and with all your soul and with all your mind" (Matt 22:37; cf. Deut 6:5). It follows that the greatest sin, the most fundamental sin, is to *not* love the Lord our God with all of our heart and soul and mind. The connection with worship, as we have defined it, is transparent. We cannot ascribe to the Lord all the glory due his name if we are consumed by self-love or intoxicated by pitiful visions of our own greatness or independence. Still less are we properly worshiping the Lord if we formally adhere to the stipulations of covenantal sacrifice when our hearts are far from him. To put the matter positively, worship is not merely a *formal* ascription of praise to God: it emerges from my

---

30. Robert G. Rayburn, *O Come, Let Us Worship* (Grand Rapids: Baker Book House, 1980), 19.

whole being to this whole God, and therefore it reflects not only my understanding of God but my love for him. "Praise the LORD, O my soul; all my inmost being, praise his holy name" (Ps 103:1).

Thus, the transition from worship under the old covenant to worship under the new is not characterized by a move from the formal to the spiritual, or from the cultus to the spiritual, or from the cultus to all of life. For it has *always* been necessary to love God wholly; it has *always* been necessary to recognize the sheer holiness and transcendent power and glory and goodness of God and to adore him for what he is. So we insist that "*all* true worship is God-centered." The transition from worship under the old covenant to worship under the new is characterized by the covenantal stipulations and provisions of the two respective covenants. The way wholly loving God works out under the old covenant is in heartfelt obedience to the terms of that covenant—and that includes the primary place given to the cultus, with all its import and purpose in the stream of redemptive history; and the implications of this outworking include distinctions between the holy and the common, between holy space and common space, between holy time and common time, between holy food and common food. The way wholly loving God works out under the new covenant is in heartfelt obedience to the terms of that covenant—and here the language of the cultus has been transmuted to all of life, with the implication, not so much of a desacralization of space and time and food, as with a sacralization of all space and all time and all food: what God has declared holy let no one declare unholy.

There is a further implication here that can only be mentioned, not explored. In theological analysis of work, it is a commonplace to say that work is a "creation ordinance" (the terminology varies with the theological tradition). However corrosive and difficult work has become this side of the Fall (Gen 3:17–19), work itself belongs to the initial paradise (Gen 2:15), and it continues to be something we do as creatures in God's good creation. That is true, of course, but under the new covenant it is also inadequate. If everything, including our work, has been sacralized in the sense just specified, then work itself is part of our worship. Christians work not only as God's creatures in God's creation, but as redeemed men and women offering their time, their energy, their work, their whole lives, to God—loving him with heart and mind and strength, understanding that whatever we do, we are to do to the glory of God.

This does not mean there is no place for corporate gathering under the new covenant, no corporate acknowledgement of God, no corporate worship—as we shall see. But in the light of the completed crosswork of the Lord Jesus Christ, the language of the cultus has necessarily changed, and with it our priorities in worship. What remains constant is the sheer God-centeredness of it all.

6. *Christian* worship is no less Christ-centered than God-centered. The set purpose of the Father is that all should honor the Son even as they honor the Father (John 5:23). Since the eternal Word became flesh (John 1:14), since the fullness of the Deity lives in Christ in bodily form (Col 2:9), since in the light of Jesus' astonishing obedience (even unto death!) God has exalted him and given him "the name that is above every name, that at the name of Jesus every knee should bow, in heaven and on earth and under the earth" (Phil 2:9–10), and since the resurrected Jesus quietly accepted Thomas's reverent and worshiping words, "My Lord and my God!" (John 20:28), contemporary Christians follow the example of the first generation of believers and worship Jesus without hesitation.

Nowhere is the mandate to worship the Lord Jesus clearer than in the book of Revelation, from chapter 5 on. In Revelation 4, in apocalyptic metaphor, God is presented as the awesome, transcendent God of glory before whom even the highest orders of angels cover their faces. This sets the stage for the drama in chapter 5. There an angel issues a challenge to the entire universe: Who is able to approach the throne of such a terrifying God, take the book in his right hand, and slit the seven seals that bind it? In the symbolism of the time and of this genre of literature, this is a challenge to bring to pass all God's purposes for the universe, his purposes of both blessing and judgment. No one is found who is worthy to accomplish this task, and John the seer is driven to despair (5:4). Then someone is found: the Lion of the tribe of Judah, who is also the Lamb—simultaneously a kingly warrior and a slaughtered Lamb—emerges to take the scroll from the right hand of the Almighty and slit the seals. But instead of approaching the throne of this transcendent and frankly terrifying God, he stands in the very center of the throne, one with Deity himself (5:6). This sets off a mighty chorus of worship addressed to the Lamb, praising him because he is *worthy* to take the scroll and open its seals (5:9). What makes him uniquely qualified to bring to pass God's purposes for judgment and redemption is not simply the fact that he emerges from the very throne of God, but that he was slain, and by his blood he purchased men for God from every tribe and language and people and nation (5:9). In short, not only his person but his atoning work make him uniquely qualified to bring to pass God's perfect purposes.

Thereafter in the book of Revelation, worship is addressed to "him who sits on the throne and to the Lamb," or some similar formulation. For in our era, Christian worship is no less Christ-centered than God-centered.

7. Christian worship is Trinitarian. This point deserves extensive reflection. One might usefully consider, for instance, a Trinitarian biblical theology of prayer.[31] But for our purposes it will suffice to repeat some of the insights of James Torrance. He writes:

> The [Trinitarian] view of worship is that it is the gift of participating through the Spirit in the incarnate Son's communion with the Father. That means participating in union with Christ, in what he has done for us once and for all, in his self-offering to the Father, in his life and death on the cross. It also means participating in what he is continuing to do for us in the presence of the Father and in his mission from the Father to the world. There is only one true Priest through whom and with whom we draw near to God our Father. There is only one Mediator between God and humanity. There is only one offering which is truly acceptable to God, and it is not ours. It is the offering by which he has sanctified for all time those who come to God by him (Heb. 2:11; 10:10, 14).... It takes seriously the New Testament teaching about the sole priesthood and headship of Christ, his self-offering for us to the Father and our life in union with Christ through the Spirit, with a vision of the Church which is his body.... So we are baptized in the name of the

---

31. See, for instance, the important essay by Edmund P. Clowney, "A Biblical Theology of Prayer," in *Teach Us To Pray: Prayer in the Bible and the World*, ed. D. A. Carson (Carlisle: Paternoster Press, 1990), 136–73.

Father, Son and Holy Spirit into the community, the one body of Christ, which confesses faith in the one God, Father, Son and Holy Spirit, and which worships the Father through the Son in the Spirit.[32]

This is very helpful, especially if it is not taken to refer to what must pertain only at 11:00 A.M. on Sunday morning. The justifying, regenerating, redeeming work of our triune God transforms his people: that is the very essence of the new covenant. New covenant worship therefore finds its first impulse in this transforming gospel, "which restores our relationship with our Redeemer-God and therefore with our fellow image-bearers, our co-worshipers."

8. Christian worship embraces both adoration and action.[33] By referring to both, I do not mean to reintroduce a distinction between the sacred and the common (see section 4 above). It is not that we withdraw into "adoration" and then advance into "action," with the former somehow gaining extra kudos for being the more spiritual or the more worshipful. We are to do everything to the glory of God. In offering our bodies as living sacrifices, which is our spiritual worship, we do with our bodies what he desires. Indeed, there may be something even more aggressive about this "action." As Miroslav Volf puts it, "There is something profoundly hypocritical about praising God for God's mighty deeds of salvation and cooperating at the same time with the demons of destruction, whether by neglecting to do good or by actively doing evil. Only those who help the Jews may sing the Gregorian chant, Dietrich Bonhoeffer rightly said, in the context of Nazi Germany. . . . Without action in the world, the adoration of God is empty and hypocritical, and degenerates into irresponsible and godless quietism."[34] Conversely, Christian action in this world produces incentive to adore God (i.e., 1 Pet 2:11–12).

---

32. James B. Torrance, *Worship, Community and the Triune God of Grace* (Downers Grove: InterVarsity Press, 1996), 20–22. This book often proves very insightful, even though in my view Torrance sometimes attacks a Zwinglian view of the Lord's Supper that is little more than a straw man.

33. See especially the essay by Miroslav Volf, "Reflections on a Christian Way of Being-in-the-World," in *Worship: Adoration and Action,* 203–11, to which I am indebted for some elements of this section.

34. Ibid., 211.

On the other hand, *mere* activism is not a particularly godly alternative either; for like active evil, it may be impelled by mere lust for power, or mere commitment to a tradition (no matter how good the tradition), or mere altruism or reformist sentiment. To resort to periods of adoration, whether personal and individual or corporate, is not, however, to retreat to the classic sacred/profane division, but it is to grasp the New Testament recognition of the rhythms of life in this created order. Jesus himself presupposes that there is a time and place for the individual to resort to a "secret" place for prayer (Matt 6:6). The church itself, as we shall see, is to gather regularly.

In short, precisely because Christian worship is impelled by the gospel "which restores our relationship with our Redeemer-God and therefore also with our fellow image-bearers, our co-worshipers," precisely because the ultimate triumph of God is a reconciled universe (Col 1:15–20), our worship must therefore manifest itself in both adoration and action.

9. Similarly, if the New Testament documents constitute our guide, our worship must manifest itself both in the individual believer and in "corporate worship, which is offered up in the context of the body of believers."

This corporate identity extends not only to other believers here and now with whom we happen to be identified but also to believers from all times and places. For the fundamental "gathering" of the people of God is the gathering *to God*, "to Mount Zion, to the heavenly Jerusalem, the city of the living God. You have come to thousands upon thousands of angels in joyful assembly, to the church of the firstborn, whose names are written in heaven. You have come *to God*, the judge of all men, to the spirits of righteous men made perfect, to Jesus the mediator of a new covenant, and to the sprinkled blood, that speaks a better word than the blood of Abel" (Heb 12:22–24; emphasis added). The local church is not so much a part of this church as the manifestation of it, the outcropping of it. Every church is simply the church.

Thus, whatever it is we do when we gather together—something still to be discussed—we do in the profound recognition that we believers constitute something much bigger than any one of us or even any empirical group of us. We are the church, the temple of God

(1 Cor 3:16–17).[35] One of the entailments of such a perspective is that, however much we seek to be contemporary for the sake of evangelistic outreach, there must also be a drive in us to align ourselves with the *whole* church in some deeply rooted and tangible ways. What it means to be the church was not invented in the last twenty years. The demands of corporate rootedness must be melded with the demands of living faithfully and bearing witness in a particular culture and age.

The New Testament speaks of the gathering or the coming together of the people of God in many contexts (e.g., Acts 4:31; 11:26; 14:27; 15:6, 30; 20:7–8; 1 Cor 5:4; 11:17, 33–34; 14:26).[36] "The church in assembly not only provides encouragement to its members but also approaches God (Heb 10:19–25)," writes Everett Ferguson.[37] But this could equally be put the opposite way: the church in assembly not only approaches God, but it provides encouragement to its members. Even in Ephesians 5:19 we speak "to one another" when we sing; and in Colossians 3:16, the singing of "psalms, hymns and spiritual songs" is in the context of teaching and admonishing one another—part of letting "the word of Christ dwell in you richly." This means that the purist model of addressing *only* God in our corporate worship is too restrictive. On the other hand, while one of the purposes of our singing should be mutual edification, that is rather different from making ourselves and our experience of worship the *topic* of our singing.

10. This body of believers strives "to align all the forms of their devout ascription of all worth to God with the panoply of new covenant mandates and examples." This will be true in the arena of conduct, to which the Apostle Paul devotes so much space. Again and again he exhorts his younger colleagues to help believers learn *how* to live and speak and conduct themselves.

But my focus here will be on the church in its gathered meetings. What does the New Testament mandate for such meetings, whether by

---

35. The context shows that in this passage the temple of God is *the church*, unlike 1 Corinthians 6:19–20, where in quite a different figurative usage the temple of God is the body of the individual Christian.

36. See the important work of Everett Ferguson, *The Church of Christ* (Grand Rapids: Eerdmans, 1996), esp. 231ff.

37. Ibid., 233.

prescription or description? Is it the case, under the terms of the new covenant, that it is *wrong* to say that our purpose in coming together (for instance, on Sunday morning) is for worship? Some, as we have seen, reply, "Yes, it is clearly wrong." Nor is this some newfangled iconoclasm. William Law, in his justly famous *A Serious Call to a Devout and Holy Life,* written more than two centuries ago, insists, "There is not one command in all the Gospel for public worship.... The frequent attendance at it is never so much as mentioned in all the New Testament." In the light of the New Testament's penchant for deploying all the old worship terminology in fresh ways, no longer bound up with temple and feast days but with all of Christian living, to say that we come together "to worship" implies that we are *not* worshiping God the rest of the time. And that is so out of touch with New Testament emphases that we ought to abandon such a notion absolutely. We do not come together for worship, these people say; rather, we come together for instruction, or we come together for mutual edification.

Yet one wonders if this conclusion is justified. Of course, if we spend the week *without* worshiping God and think of Sunday morning as the time when we come together to offer God the worship we have been withholding all week (to set right the balance, as it were), then these critics are entirely correct. But would it not be better to say that the New Testament emphasis is that the people of God should worship him in their individual lives and in their family lives and then, when they come together, worship him corporately?

In other words, worship becomes the category under which we order *everything* in our lives. Whatever we do, even if we are simply eating or drinking, whatever we say, in business or in the home or in church assemblies, we are to do all to the glory of God. That is worship. And when we come together, we engage in worship in a corporate fashion.

Some are uncomfortable with this analysis. They say that if worship is something that Christians should be doing all the time, then although it is formally true that Christians should be engaged in worship when they gather together, it is merely true in the same sense in which Christians should be engaged in breathing when they gather together. It is something they do all the time. But the analogy this makes between worship and breathing is misleading. We are not commanded to breathe; breathing is merely an autonomic function. But we are *commanded* to worship (e.g., Rev 19:10). And although it is true that the technical language of worship in the Old Testament is transmuted in the New from the cultus to all of life, there are odd passages where the language also refers to the Christian assembly (e.g., *proskyneô* in 1 Cor 14:25).

Moreover, just as in the light of the New Testament we dare not think we gather for worship because we have *not* been worshiping all week, so also it is folly to think that only part of the "service" is worship—everything but the sermon, perhaps, or only the singing, or only singing and responses. The notion of a "worship leader" who leads the "worship" part of the service before the sermon (which, then, is no part of worship!) is so bizarre, from a New Testament perspective, as to be embarrassing.[38] Doesn't even experience teach us that sometimes our deepest desires and heart prayers to ascribe all worth to God well up during the powerful preaching of the Word of God? I know that "worship leader" is merely a matter of semantics, a currently popular tag, but it is a popular tag that unwittingly skews people's expectations as to what worship is. At very least, it is misleadingly restrictive.[39]

---

38. Scarcely less bizarre is the contention of some that we should distinguish between services for worship and services for teaching (e.g., Robert E. Webber, in a generally helpful book, *Worship Old and New* [Grand Rapids: Zondervan, 1982], 125, 194).

39. Perhaps this is the place to reflect on the fact that many contemporary "worship leaders" have training in music but none in Bible, theology, history, or the like. When pressed as to the criteria by which they choose their music, many of these leaders finally admit that their criteria oscillate between personal preference and keeping the congregation reasonably happy—scarcely the most profound criteria in the world. They give little or no thought to covering the great themes of Scripture, or the great events of Scripture, or the range of personal response to God found in the Psalms (as opposed to covering the narrow themes of being upbeat and in the midst of "worship"), or the nature of biblical locutions (in one chorus the congregation manages to sing "holy" thirty-six times, while three are enough for Isaiah and John of the Apocalypse), or the central historical traditions of the church, or anything else of weight. If such leaders operate on their own with little guidance or training or input from senior pastors, the situation commonly degenerates from the painful to the pitiful. On this and many other practical and theological points, see the wise and informed counsel of David Montgomery, *Sing a New Song: Choosing and Leading Praise in Today's Church* (Edinburgh: Rutherford House and Handsel Press, 2000).

So what should we do, then, in corporate worship so understood? Although some might object to one or two of his locutions, Edmund Clowney provides one of the most succinct summaries of such evidence as the New Testament provides:

> The New Testament indicates, by precept and example, what the elements of [corporate] worship are. As in the synagogue, corporate prayer is offered (Acts 2:42; 1 Tim. 2:1; 1 Cor. 14:16); Scripture is read (1 Tim. 4:13; 1 Th. 5:27; 2 Th. 3:14; Col. 4:15, 16; 2 Pet. 3:15, 16) and expounded in preaching (1 Tim. 4:13; cf. Lk. 4:20; 2 Tim. 3:15–17; 4:2). There is a direct shift from the synagogue to the gathering of the church (Acts 18:7, 11; cf. 19:8–10). The teaching of the word is also linked with table fellowship (Acts 2:42; 20:7, cf. vv. 20, 25, 28). The songs of the new covenant people both praise God and encourage one another (Eph. 5:19; Col. 3:15; 1 Cor. 14:15, 26; cf. 1 Tim. 3:16; Rev. 5:9–13; 11:17f; 15:3, 4). Giving to the poor is recognized as a spiritual service to God and a Christian form of "sacrifice" (2 Cor. 9:11–15; Phil. 4:18; Heb. 13:16). The reception and distribution of gifts is related to the office of the deacon (Acts 6:1–6; Rom. 12:8, 13; cf. Rom. 16:1, 2; 2 Cor. 8:19–21; Acts 20:4; 1 Cor. 16:1–4) and to the gathering of believers (Acts 2:42; 5:2; 1 Cor. 16:2). The faith is also publicly confessed (1 Tim. 6:12; 1 Pet. 3:21; Heb. 13:15; cf. 1 Cor. 15:1–3). The people receive God's blessing (2 Cor. 13:14; Lk. 24:50; cf. Num. 6:22–27). The holy kiss of salutation is also commanded (Rom. 16:16; 1 Cor. 16:20; 2 Cor. 13:12; 1 Th. 5:26; 1 Pet. 5:14). The people respond to praise and prayer with the saying of "Amen" (1 Cor. 14:16; Rev. 5:14; cf. Rom. 1:25; 9:5; Eph. 3:21 etc.). The sacraments of baptism and the Lord's Supper are explicitly provided for. Confession is linked with baptism (1 Pet. 3:21); and a prayer of thanksgiving with the breaking of bread (1 Cor. 11:24).[40]

One might quibble over a few points. Some might say that explicit *permission* must be opened up for tongues as restricted by 1 Corin-

---

40. Edmund P. Clowney, "Presbyterian Worship," *Worship: Adoration and Action*, ed. D. A. Carson, 117. Cf. also Hughes Oliphant Old, *Themes and Variations for a Christian Doxology: Some Thoughts on the Theology of Worship* (Grand Rapids: Eerdmans, 1992); Michael B. Thompson, "Romans 12:1–2 and Paul's Vision for Worship," in *A Vision for the Church: Studies in Early Christian Ecclesiology*, ed. Markus N. A. Bockmuehl and Michael B. Thompson (Edinburgh: T & T Clark, 1998), esp. 129–30.

thians 14, for example. Still, Clowney's list is surely broadly right. But observe:

a. To compile such a list is already to recognize that there are some distinctive elements to what I have called "corporate worship." I am not sure that we would be wise to apply the expression "corporate worship" to any and all activities in which groups of Christians faithfully engage— going to a football match, say, or shopping for groceries. Such activities doubtless fall under the "do all to the glory of God" rubric and therefore properly belong to the ways in which we honor God; therefore, they do belong to worship in a broad sense. Yet the activities the New Testament describes when Christians gather together in assembly, nicely listed by Clowney, are more restrictive and more focused. Doubtless there can be some mutual edification going on when a group of Christians take a sewing class together, but in the light of what the New Testament pictures Christians doing when they assemble together, there is nevertheless something slightly skewed about calling a sewing class an activity of corporate worship. So there is a narrower sense of worship, it appears; and this narrower sense is bound up with corporate worship, with what the assembled church does in the pages of the New Testament. Yet it is precisely at this point that one must instantly insist that this narrower list of activities does *not* include all that the New Testament includes within the theological notion of worship in the broader sense. If one restricts the term *worship* to the list of church-assembly activities listed by Clowney, one loses essential elements of the dramatic transformation that occurs in the move from the old covenant to the new;[41] conversely, if one uses the term *worship* only in its broadest and theologically richest sense, then sooner or later one finds oneself looking for a term that embraces the particular activities of the gathered people of God described in the New Testament. For lack of a better alternative, I have chosen the term *corporate worship*— but I recognize the ambiguities inherent in it.

---

41. This, of course, is the use of the word *worship* found in most older studies or in recent studies that do not take into account the redemptive-historical developments within the canon. See, for example, D. E. Aune ("Worship, Early Christian," in *Anchor Bible Dictionary* 6.973–89), who ties worship to such activities and responses as these: acclamation, awe, blessing, commemoration, confession, doxology, fear, hymn, invocation, offering, praise, prayer, prophecy, prostration, sacrifice, supplication, and thanksgiving.

b. It is worth reflecting on how many of the items listed by Clowney are related, in one way or another, to the Word. Joshua is told that the Word will be with him wherever he goes if he but meditates on the law day and night, careful to do everything written in it (Josh 1:5–9). The book of Psalms opens by declaring that the just person is the one who delights in the law of the Lord and meditates on it day and night (Ps 1:2). Jesus asserts, in prayer, that what will sanctify his disciples is the Word (John 17:17). Doyle puts his finger on this integrating factor:

> The characteristic response we are to make to God as he comes to us clothed in his promises, clothed with the gospel, is faith. In the context of the New Testament's vision of what church is to be, this faith most appropriately takes the form of confession. To each other we confess and testify to the greatness of God. We do this by the very activity of making God's Word the centre of our activities—by reading it, preaching it, making it the basis of exhortation, and even setting it to music in hymns and praise. The Spirit uses all this, we are assured, to build us up in Christ. Praise is integral to our activities in church, because it is another form of our response of faith. It is part of our whole life of worship, but only one part of it.[42]

What this also suggests, yet again, is that an approach to corporate worship that thinks of only *some* of the activities of assembled Christians, such as singing and praying, as worship, but not the ministry of the Word itself, is badly off base. Worse yet are formulations that are in danger of making "worship" a substitute for the gospel. It is not uncommon to be told that "worship leads us into the presence of God" or that "worship takes us from the outer court into the inner court" or the like. There is a way of reading those statements sympathetically (as I shall note in a moment), but taken at face value they are simply untrue. Objectively, what brings us into the presence of God is the death and resurrection of the Lord Jesus. If we ascribe to worship (meaning, in this context, our corporate praise and adoration) something of this power, it will not be long before we think of such worship as being meritorious, or efficacious, or the like. The small corner of truth that such expressions hide (though this truth is poorly worded)

---

42. Robert Doyle, "The One True Worshipper," *The Briefing*, (29 April 1999), 8.

is that when we come together and engage in the activities of corporate worship (including not only prayer and praise but the Lord's Supper and attentive listening to the Word, and the other items included in Clowney's list), we encourage one another, we edify one another, and so we often *feel* encouraged and edified. As a result, we are renewed in our awareness of God's love and God's truth, and we are encouraged to respond with adoration and action. In this subjective sense, *all* of the activities of corporate worship may function to make us more aware of God's majesty, God's presence, God's love. But I doubt that it is helpful to speak of such matters in terms of worship "leading us into the presence of God": not only is the term *worship* bearing a meaning too narrow to be useful, but the statement is in danger of conveying some profoundly untrue notions.

c. Although the *elements* Clowney lists are obviously the elements of corporate worship mentioned in the New Testament, there is no explicit mandate or model of a particular order or arrangement of these elements. Of course, this is not to deny that there may be better and worse arrangements. One might try to establish liturgical order that reflects the theology of conversion, or at least of general approach to God: confession of sin before assurance of grace, for instance. Nevertheless, the tendency in some traditions to nail everything down in great detail and claim that such stipulations are biblically sanctioned is to "go beyond what is written" (to use the Pauline phrase, 1 Cor 4:6).

It is at this point that perhaps I should comment on some Reformed parodies of popular evangelical corporate worship services. One that is circulating nicely on the Web at the moment is several pages long: there is space here to include only some excerpts:

> Fellowshippers shall enter the sanctuary garrulously, centering their attention on each other, and gaily exchanging their news of the past week.
>
> If there be an overhead projector, the acolytes shall light it.
>
> The Minister shall begin Morning Fellowship by chanting the greeting, "Good Morning." Then shall not more than 50% and not less [*sic*] than 10% of the fellowshippers respond, chanting in this wise, "Good Morning." . . .

The Glad-handing of the Peace: Then may the Minister say: "Why don't we all shake hands with the person on our left and on our right and say 'Good morning.'" . . .

The Reading: Then shall be read an arbitrary Scripture passage of the Minister's choosing, so long as it does not relate to the time of the Church year. . . .

And much more of the same, becoming progressively more amusing. But before we laugh too hard, we should perhaps analyze why this is funny. It is amusing because there is an obvious clash between the categories of traditional, liturgical worship (with copious references to acolytes "lighting" something, chanting, slightly dented allusions to traditional segments of the service, etc.) and the sheer informalism of much evangelical corporate worship. But the plain fact of the matter is that the liturgical template on which the evangelical informalism has been grafted in order to construct this amusing piece *has no particular warrant in the New Testament.*[43]

This is not to deny that experience may teach us better and worse ways of leading corporate worship, or that there may be profound and interlocking theological structures that undergird certain decisions about corporate worship. It is to say that the New Testament does not provide us with officially sanctioned public "services" so much as with examples of crucial elements. We do well to admit the limitations of our knowledge.

d. There is no mention of a lot of other things: drama, "special" (performance) music, choirs, artistic dance, organ solos. Many churches

---

43. It is at this point that I have most trouble with Robert E. Webber, *Blended Worship: Achieving Substance and Relevance in Worship* (Peabody: Hendrickson, 1994). Webber usefully describes the corporate worship practices of a great breadth of traditions and appreciates them all, movingly writing of his own participation in many of them. Unfortunately, he offers very little biblical or theological justification for his choices and recommendations, other than that he felt God was disclosing himself through this or that service. The theological rootlessness and subjectivism of the book are stunning, even though they are partially hidden behind transparent piety. In some ways his later book, *Planning Blended Worship: The Creative Mixture of Old and New* (Nashville: Abingdon, 1998), is better. What a lot of people mean by "blended worship" is not so much a blend as a lumpy stew. Webber is helpful in moving us beyond our narrow horizons without succumbing to painful dissonance.

are so steeped in these or other traditions that it would be unthinkable to have a Sunday morning service without, say, "special music"—though there is not so much as a hint of this practice in the New Testament.[44] Some preferences are conditioned not only by the local church but by the traditions of the country in which it is located. The overwhelming majority of evangelical churches in America, especially outside the mainline denominations, offer performance music almost every Sunday. The overwhelming majority of denominationally similar churches in Britain never have it.[45]

Occasionally attempts have been made to justify a "bells and smells" approach to corporate worship on the basis of some of the imagery in the Book of Revelation. In Revelation 5, for instance, incense is wafted before God by the elders, and the incense is identified as "the prayers of the saints." Granted that this is an instance of the rich symbolism of the Apocalypse, does it not warrant us to introduce similarly symbol-laden realities as aids to corporate worship? But this reasoning is misguided on several fronts. So much of the symbolism of this book's apocalyptic is deeply rooted in the Old Testament world. In this case, it calls to mind passages such as Psalm 141:2: "May my prayer be set before you like incense; may the lifting up of my hands be like the evening sacrifice." In other words, the comparison is drawn between David's private prayers and the central institutions of the tabernacle

---

44. By "special music" I am including not only the solos and small groups that a slightly earlier generation of evangelical churches customarily presented but also the very substantial number of "performance" items that current "worship teams" normally include in services. These are often not seen by the teams themselves as "special music" or "performance music," but of course that is what they are.

45. There are many entailments to these cultural differences beyond the differences in the corporate services themselves. For example, Britain, without much place for "special music" in corporate worship, does not have to feed a market driven by the search for more "special music." Therefore, a great deal of intellectual and spiritual energy is devoted to writing songs that will be sung congregationally. This has resulted in a fairly wide production of new hymnody in more or less contemporary guise, some of it junk, some of it acceptable but scarcely enduring, and some of it frankly superb. By contrast, our addiction to "special music" means that a great deal of creative energy goes into supplying products for that market. Whether it is good or bad, it is almost never usable by a congregation. The result is that far more of our congregational pieces are dated than in Britain, or are no more than repetitious choruses.

(and later temple)—which is precisely what is done away under the new covenant. One avoids the obvious hermeneutical quagmires by patiently asking the question, "So far as our records go, did Christians in New Testament times use incense during corporate worship?"

e. Historically, some branches of the church have argued that if God has not forbidden something, we are permitted to do it, and the church is permitted to regulate its affairs in these regards in order to establish good order (the Hooker principle, mentioned above). Others have argued that the only things we should do in public worship are those that find clear example or direct prescription in the New Testament, lest we drift from what is central or impose on our congregations things that their consciences might not be able to support (the Regulative Principle, also mentioned above).

To attempt even the most rudimentary evaluation of this debate would immediately double the length of this chapter. Besides, these matters will surface again in later chapters. But four preliminary observations may be helpful. First, historically speaking, both the Hooker principle and the Regulative Principle have been understood and administered in both a stronger and a more attentuated way, with widely differing results. Some have appealed to Hooker to support changes far beyond the appropriateness of prescribing or forbidding vestments and the like; others have appealed to Hooker in defense of a church-ordered prayer book. Some have appealed to the Regulative Principle to ban all instruments from corporate worship and to sanction only the singing of psalms; others see it as a principle of freedom within limits: it recognizes that we are not authorized to worship God "as we please" and that our worship must be acceptable to God himself and therefore in line with his Word. In short, both the Hooker principle and the Regulative Principle are plagued by complex debates as to what they mean, today as well as historically.[46] For many of the

---

46. For example, the Regulative Principle, well articulated by the Westminster divines, opposed the introduction of new *observances* in worship but does not deny culturally appropriate arrangements of the *circumstances* of worship—which has generated no little debate on what is meant by "circumstances." See the discussion in Clowney, "Presbyterian Worship," 117ff.; and John M. Frame, *Worship in Spirit and*

protagonists, their interpretations are as certain, as immovable, and as inflexible as the Rock of Gibraltar. Second, it must be frankly admitted that both the Hooker principle and the Regulative Principle have bred staunch traditionalists. Traditionalists who follow Hooker argue that according to this principle the church has the right to *regulate* certain matters, and endless innovation is a denial of that right. So stop tampering with the Prayer Book! Traditionalists who follow the Regulative Principle not only tend to adopt the simplest form of public worship but tie it to traditional forms of expression (e.g., they will always find fault with psalms set to contemporary music, preferring the metrical psalms sung centuries ago).[47] Third, both camps have also bred pastors who are remarkably contemporary, thoroughly evangelical in the best sense of that long-suffering term, and innovative in their leading of corporate worship. In the Anglican tradition, for instance, one thinks of John Mason's duly authorized "experimental service" in Sydney, which deserves circulation and evaluation among evangelical Anglicans;[48] in the Presbyterian tradition, one thinks of Tim Keller in New York (but here I will say little for fear of embarrassing a fellow contributor). Fourth, for all their differences, theologically rich and serious services from both camps often have more common *content* than either side usually acknowledges.

f. There is no single passage in the New Testament that establishes a paradigm for corporate worship. Not a few writers appeal to 1 Corinthians 14. Yet the priorities of that chapter are set by Paul's agenda at that point, dealing with *charismata* that have gained too prominent a place in public meetings. There is no mention of the Lord's Supper and no mention of public teaching by a pastor/elder—even though other passages in Paul show that such elements played

---

Truth (Phillipsburg: Presbyterian and Reformed, 1996), though on the latter, cf. the review by Leonard R. Payton in *Reformation and Revival* 6/3 (1997): 227–35.

47. On these and related points, see John Frame, *Contemporary Worship Music: A Biblical Defense* (Phillipsburg: Presbyterian and Reformed, 1997). See also Lee Irons, "Exclusive Psalmody or New Covenant Hymnody?" at http://members.aol.com/ironslee/private/Psalmody.htm.

48. John Mason, *A Service for Today's Church* (Mosman: St. Clement's Anglican Church, 1997).

an important role in the corporate meetings of churches overseen by the apostle.

g. First Corinthians 14 lays considerable stress on intelligibility. The issue for Paul, of course, is tongues and prophecy: his concern is to establish guidelines that keep undisciplined enthusiasm in check. Frame[49] applies the importance of intelligibility to the music that is chosen. Although that is scarcely what the apostle had in mind, I doubt that he would have been displeased by the application. Nevertheless, there are complementary principles to bear in mind. Paul speaks of "psalms, hymns, and spiritual songs." We may debate what is the full range of musical styles to which this expression refers, but psalms are certainly included—whether they are judged intelligible for our biblically illiterate generation or not. Corporate meetings of the church, however much God is worshiped in them, have the collateral responsibility of educating, informing, and transforming the minds of those who attend, of training the people of God in righteousness, of expanding their horizons not only so that they better know God (and therefore better worship him) but so that they better grasp the dimensions of the church that he has redeemed by the death of his Son (and therefore better worship him)—and that means, surely, some sort of exposure to more than the narrow slice of church that subsists in one particular subculture. The importance of intelligibility (in music, let us say) must therefore be juxtaposed with the responsibility to expand the limited horizons of one narrow tradition.[50] Incidentally, the punch of this observation applies both to churches trying to be so contemporary that they project the impression that the church was invented yesterday and to churches locked into a traditional slice that is no less narrow but rather more dated.

---

49. *Worship in Spirit and Truth*, passim.

50. One wishes, for instance, that more leaders were aware of a work such as Andrew Wilson-Dickson, *The Story of Christian Music: From Gregorian Chant to Black Gospel. An Illustrated Guide to All the Major Traditions of Music in Worship* (Minneapolis: Fortress Press, 1996). This is not to suggest that every church should try to incorporate every tradition: there is neither adequate time for, nor wisdom in, such a goal. But if we are to transcend our own cultural confines, we ought to be making a significant attempt to learn the traditions of brothers and sisters in Christ outside our own heritage.

11. Numerous matters cry out for articulation in greater detail—the various functions of the Lord's Supper in the New Testament, for example. But the primary focus of this section is to demonstrate and illustrate ways in which the body of believers in corporate worship strives "to align all the forms of their devout ascription of all worth to God with the panoply of new covenant mandates and examples."

Properly understood, this takes place "to bring to fulfillment the glories of antecedent revelation." In other words, the richest conformity to new covenant stipulation is not some Marcion-like rejection of the Old Testament but the fruit of a biblical-theological reading of Scripture that learns how the parts of written revelation interlock along the path of the Bible's plotline. The result is a greater grasp of what God has revealed and, ideally, a deeper and richer worship of the God who has so wonderfully revealed himself.

12. At the same time, such worship is an "anticipation of the consummation." The climax of the massive theme of worship in the book of Revelation lies in chapters 21–22. The New Jerusalem is built like a cube—and the only cube of which we hear in antecedent Scripture is the Most Holy Place. In other words, the entire city is constantly and unqualifiedly basking in the unshielded glory of the presence of God. There is no temple in that city, for the Lord God and the Lamb are its temple. God's people will see his face.[51]

But we must conduct ourselves here in the anticipation of this end. Biblically faithful worship is orientated to the end. Even the Lord's Supper is "until he comes" and thus always an expectation of that coming, a renewal of vows in the light of that coming. As Larry Hurtado has put it:

> More specifically, Christian worship could be re-enlivened and enriched by remembering the larger picture of God's purposes, which

---

51. Cf. N. T. Wright, *For All God's Worth: True Worship and the Calling of the Church* (Grand Rapids: Eerdmans, 1997), 7: "The great multitude in Revelation which no man can number aren't playing cricket. They aren't going shopping. They are *worshipping*. Sounds boring? If so, it shows how impoverished our idea of worship has become. At the centre of that worship stands a passage like Isaiah 33: your eyes will see the king in his beauty; the LORD is our judge, the LORD is our ruler, the LORD is our king; he will save us. Worship is the central characteristic of the heavenly life; and that worship is focused on the God we know in and as Jesus."

extend beyond our own immediate setting and time to take in all human history and which promise a future victory over evil and a consummation of redeeming grace. Apart from a hope in God's triumph over evil, apart from a confidence that Jesus really is the divinely appointed Lord in whom all things are to find their meaning, Christian acclamation of Jesus as Lord is a stupid thing, refuted and mocked by the powerful, negative realities of our creaturehood: the political and economic tyrannies, religious and irreligious forces, and social and cultural developments that make Christian faith seem trivial and our worship little more than a quaint avocation.[52]

Some Practical Conclusions

The brief list in this concluding section is suggestive rather than comprehensive. Much more practical wisdom is provided in the remaining chapters of the book.

1. If the line of argument in this chapter is biblically faithful, we ought to avoid common misunderstandings of worship. Ferguson identifies four of them: an external or mechanical interpretation of worship, an individualistic interpretation, an emotional uplift interpretation, and a performance interpretation.[53] We might add interpretations that restrict worship to experiences of cultus and, conversely, interpretations of worship that are so comprehensive that no place whatsoever is left for corporate worship.

2. Hindrances to excellent corporate worship are of various sorts. For convenience, they may be broken into two kinds. On the one hand, corporate worship may be stultified by church members who never pray at home, who come to church waiting to be entertained, who are inwardly marking a scorecard instead of participating in worship, who love mere tradition (or mere innovation!) more than truth, who are so busy that their minds are cluttered with the press of the urgent, who are nurturing secret bitterness and resentments in the dark recesses of their minds.

---

52. Larry W. Hurtado, *At the Origins of Christian Worship: The Context and Character of Earliest Christian Devotion* (Grand Rapids: Eerdmans, 1999), 116.
53. *The Church of Christ*, 227–29.

On the other hand, corporate worship may be poor primarily because of those who are leading. There are two overlapping but distinguishable components. The first is what is actually said and done. That is a huge area that demands detailed consideration, some of which is provided in later chapters. But the second component, though less easily measurable, is no less important. Some who publicly lead the corporate meetings of the people of God merely perform; others are engrossed in the worship of God. Some merely sing; some put on a great show of being involved; but others transparently worship God.

It is worth pausing over this word "transparently." By asserting that "others transparently worship God," I am indicating that to some extent we can observe how well we are being served by those who lead corporate worship: their conduct is "transparent." The way they lead must in the first instance be marked by faithfulness to the Word of God: that is certainly observable, in particular to those who know their Bibles well. But the way they lead can be measured not only in terms of formal content but also in terms of heart attitudes that inevitably manifest themselves in talk, body language, focus, and style. Some pray with strings of evangelical clichés; some show off with orotund phrasings; others pray to God out of profound personal knowledge and bring the congregation along with them.[54] Some preach without punch; others speak as if delivering the oracles of God.

What is at stake is authenticity. Some wag has said that Americans work at their play, play at their worship, and worship their work. But sooner or later Christians tire of public meetings that are profoundly inauthentic, regardless of how well (or poorly) arranged, directed, performed. We long to meet, corporately, with the living and majestic God and to offer him the praise that is his due.

3. The question of authenticity in corporate worship intersects with some urgent questions of contemporary evangelism. *First*, one of the passions that shapes the corporate meetings of many churches (especially in the "seeker-sensitive" tradition) is the concern for evangelism, the concern to tear down barriers that prevent particular people

---

54. I am referring now, of course, not to a particular style, but to a Spirit-anointed authenticity that in large part transcends matters of style.

groups from coming and hearing the gospel. The "homogeneous unit" principle, at one time associated with particular tribes, has now been extended to generations: busters cannot be effectively evangelized with boomers, and so forth. But somewhere along the line we must evaluate what place we are reserving in our corporate life for tearing down the barriers that the world erects—barriers between Jew and Gentile, blacks and whites, boomers and busters. How does our corporate life reflect the one new humanity that the New Testament envisages? Is there not some need for Christians from highly different backgrounds to come together and recite one creed, read from one Scripture, and jointly sing shared songs, thereby crossing race gaps, gender gaps, and generation gaps, standing in a shared lineage that reaches back through centuries and is finally grounded in the Word? This does not mean that everything has to be old-fashioned and stodgy. It *does* mean that those in the Reformed tradition (for instance) do well to wonder now and then what would happen if John Calvin were an "Xer."[55]

Second, one of the most compelling witnesses to the truth of the gospel is a church that is authentic in its worship—and here I use the word *worship* in the most comprehensive sense but certainly including corporate worship. A congregation so concerned not to cause offense that it manages to entertain and amuse but never to *worship God* either in the way it lives or in its corporate life carries little credibility to a burned-out postmodern generation that rejects linear thought yet hungers for integrity of relationships. Because we are concerned with the truth of the gospel, we must teach and explain; because we are not simply educating people but seeking to communicate the glorious gospel of Christ, the authenticity of our own relationship with him, grounded in personal faith and in an awareness not only of sins forgiven and of eternal life but also of the sheer glory and majesty of our Maker and Redeemer, carries an enormous weight.

4. Not every public service can fruitfully integrate everything that the New Testament exemplifies of corporate meetings. Not every meeting will gather around the Lord's Supper, not every meeting will

---

55. That line comes from Scot Sherman, "If John Calvin Were an 'Xer'...., Worship in the Reformed Tradition," *re:generation* 3/1 (Winter 1997): 22–25.

allow for the varied voices of 1 Corinthians 14, and so forth. But that means that, in order to preserve the comprehensiveness of New Testament church life, we need to plan for different sorts of meetings.

5. In every tradition of corporate worship, there are many ways in which a leader may greatly diminish authentic, godly, biblically faithful worship. Those in more liturgical traditions may so greatly rely on established forms that instead of leading the congregation in thoughtful worship of the living God, the entire exercise becomes mechanical and dry, even though the forms are well-loved and well-known expressions that are historically rooted and theologically rich. (Consider the pastor who, right in the middle of holy communion, interrupts his flow to tell the warden to shut a window.) Those in less liturgical traditions may retreat into comfortable but largely boring clichés: the freedom and creativity that is the strength of the "free church" tradition is squandered where careful planning, prayer, and thought have not gone into the preparation of a public meeting. Indeed, such planning may borrow from many traditions. I recently attended a Christmas service in a Reformed Baptist church in which there were not only the traditional Christmas Scripture readings and Christmas carols, but the corporate reading, from the prepared bulletin, of the Nicene Creed, the prayer of confession from Martin Bucer's Strasbourg Liturgy, and a prayer of thanksgiving from the Middleburg Liturgy of the English Puritans.

6. Small ironies surface when the essays in this book are read together. Sometimes churches that have the strongest denominational heritage of liturgies and prayer books, aware of the dangers of mere rote, and newly alive to the demands of biblical theology, become the vanguard that warns us against mere traditionalism. Knowing how Old Testament terminology has so often been abused when it has been unthinkingly applied to the church, they become nervous about using the term "sanctuary" when referring to the biggest room in the church building and will never speak of a "service." Conversely, churches from the most independent traditions, aware of the dangers of open-ended subjectivism and spectacularly undisciplined corporate meetings, and newly alive to the glories of public worship as a reflection of entire lives devoted to the living God, incorporate increasing solemnity, liturgical

responses, corporate readings, and the like. They do not hesitate to use terms like "sanctuary" and "service"—not because they associate such terms with either Old Testament structures of thought or with sacramentarianism, but (rightly or wrongly) out of respect for tradition.[56]

But perhaps the most intriguing irony is how much the best of the corporate meetings of *both* traditions, matters of terminology aside, resemble each other in what is actually said and done. Nowadays, the actual shape of a Sunday morning "service" (meeting?) varies more *within* denominations (from the seeker-sensitive party to the charismatic party to the more Reformed party) than *across* denominations when comparing similar parties. For those (like the writers of this volume) committed to "worship under the Word," minor differences in terminology and strategy surface here and there, while the fundamental priorities are remarkably similar, as is also the shape of their Sunday morning meetings.

7. Not long ago, after I had spoken on the subject of biblical worship at a large metropolitan church, one of the elders wrote to me to ask how I would try to get across my main points to children (fourth to sixth graders, approximately ages ten to twelve). He was referring in particular to things I had said about Romans 12:1–2. I responded by saying that kids of that age do not absorb abstract ideas very easily unless they are lived out and identified. The Christian home, or the Christian parent who obviously delights in corporate worship, in thoughtful evangelism, in self-effacing and self-sacrificing decisions within the home, in sacrificial giving for the poor and the needy and the lost—and who then explains to the child that these decisions and actions are part of gratitude and worship to the sovereign God who has loved us so much that he gave his own Son to pay the price of our sin—

---

56. One correspondent pressed further and asked what would happen if we could somehow put all our histories and traditions to one side and begin from scratch and then tried to label and speak of our corporate life, judging only by the terminology and theology of the New Testament. I take his point—but that is precisely what we cannot do. All of us speak and think and interact within a historical context, a context that needs reforming by the Word but that cannot be ignored. Moreover, I wonder if my interlocutor would like to construct all of his theology without benefit of historical insight, good and bad.

will have far more impact on the child's notion of genuine worship than all the lecturing and classroom instruction in the world. Somewhere along the line it is important not only to explain that genuine worship is nothing more than loving God with heart and soul and mind and strength and loving our neighbors as ourselves, but also to show what a statement like that means in the concrete decisions of life. How utterly different will that child's thinking be than that of the child who is reared in a home where secularism rules all week but where people go to church on Sunday to "worship" for half an hour before the sermon.

> "Come, let us bow down in worship, let us kneel before the LORD our Maker; for he is our God and we are the people of his pasture, the flock under his care. Today, if you hear his voice, do not harden your hearts" (Ps 95:6–8).

Chapter 2

FOLLOWING IN CRANMER'S FOOTSTEPS

MARK ASHTON WITH C. J. DAVIS

*F*our hundred and fifty years ago the work of one man went a long way toward bringing a whole nation to a Bible-centered Christian faith. The English Reformation of the sixteenth century and the origin of the Church of England are a much more complicated story than that, but the influence wielded by Archbishop Thomas Cranmer and his *Book of Common Prayer* on the history of world Christianity has been enormous.

Has that influence now finally come to an end? Is there anything still to learn from the Anglican tradition for those who want to put the Bible at the center of their church services? In much of the denomination the situation today is grim. Malcolm Muggeridge once commented, "Words cannot convey the doctrinal confusion, ineptitude and sheer chicanery of the run-of-the-mill incumbent [minister], with his *Thirty-Nine Articles*[1] in which he does not even purport to believe,

---

1. The *Thirty-Nine Articles* are a set of doctrinal formulae first issued by Convocation in 1563 in an attempt by the Church of England to define its dogmatic position

with his listless exhortations, mumbled prayers and half-baked confusion of the Christian faith with better housing, shorter hours of work and the United Nations."[2] The poor quality of the average Anglican church service has led many to the conclusion that the church is the dullest experience in the country.

The gospel continues to save men and women, however, as it always has. What gave Cranmer's Prayer Book the power to change lives and to introduce people to the living God still exercises the same power today. His aim in the *Book of Common Prayer* was "that the people by daily hearing of holy Scripture read in church might continually profit more and more in the knowledge of God, and be more inflamed with the love of his [i.e., God's] true religion."[3] He put the Bible at the center of church services in order to change lives. It is the task for latter-day Anglicans to follow in the footsteps of Cranmer by creating church services that reach out to our contemporaries as effectively as his services did.

This chapter will discuss how that can be done. We hope that it will interest those who are not Anglicans to see how the Bible is applied within this denomination and that it will encourage those who are Anglicans to follow authentically in Cranmer's footsteps.

The End of Common Prayer

Cranmer's work, enshrined in the *Book of Common Prayer,* played a central role in defining Anglicanism until the twentieth century, keeping the Bible at the heart of the nation's life. John Wesley's verdict on the Prayer Book was: "I know of no liturgy in the world, ancient or modern, which breathes more of solid, scriptural piety than the Common Prayer of the Church of England." But it would never have been Cranmer's wish to freeze Anglican liturgy for centuries to come so that it lost its cultural relevance and reintroduced into church services the obscurity that he labored so hard to remove.

---

in relation to the controversies of the sixteenth century. There had been many earlier stages (*Ten Articles,* 1536; *Bishops' Book,* 1537; *Six Articles,* 1539; *King's Book,* 1543; and *Forty-Two Articles,* 1553).

2. Quoted in Bernard Levin, *The Pendulum Years* (London: Pan Books, 1970), 91.

3. *The Book of Common Prayer,* "Preface: Concerning the Service of the Church."

Neither would he have welcomed many of the influences that led to liturgical revision in the twentieth century. It was the rise of Anglo-Catholicism in the nineteenth century that led to the publication of a Prayer Book with more Catholic options in 1928. Parliament refused to legitimize it, but the bishops published it. The publication of that 1928 Prayer Book (with liturgical influences from less Protestant parts of the Anglican Communion and from a church hierarchy that was redefining historic Anglican comprehensiveness in terms of theological relativism) led to a Liturgical Commission determined to produce a theologically broader Prayer Book than the *Book of Common Prayer*. It was their stated policy regarding disputed issues to use "forms of words which allow of different interpretation." The result was the "studied ambiguity" of the *Alternative Service Book* (1980), which had moved far from Cranmer's doctrinal moorings. This doctrinal change was not admitted at the time, but it has since been recognized that the *Alternative Service Book* was not just an attempt to put the church's services into modern English. The Archbishop of York, in a speech to the General Synod in November 1985, said, "I think it is fair to complain that not enough explicit attention was given to doctrine in the last round of revision; and, in particular, we did not really face openly enough the major shift in doctrinal emphasis in the new services."[4] We will see shortly just how far this process has moved the Church of England from its origins.

There is no longer one Prayer Book common to the Anglican Communion. There is an abundance of new liturgy, but no doctrinal consensus at its heart. This has created an identity crisis for Anglicanism. Our task must be the creation of services that are not only truly Anglican (in the historic sense) but that are also contemporary. If we would follow Cranmer faithfully, we must identify the principles upon

---

4. *Proceedings of the General Synod of the Church of England,* vol. 16, no. 3, p. 1045. The shift in doctrinal emphasis continues with each round of liturgical revision. The 1998 report by the Liturgical Commission on the Proposed Funeral service, for example, stated, "The current work of the Liturgical Commission both starts much further back from the Reformation and is set in a wider pastoral and theological context, in which the discussion about prayer and the departed can be seen from a different perspective" (GS 1298, p. 5, para. 16). In other words, the work of the Liturgical

which he worked. We will find that they reflect the teaching of the New Testament about Christians meeting together.

New Testament Teaching

This book has already dealt with what true Christian worship is and what it is not. Don Carson has made clear in Chapter 1 that the direction of a church service is both God-ward and man-ward.

Adoration and action go hand in hand in the worship of God. Hebrews 13:15–16 provides a definition of Christian worship: "Through Jesus, therefore, let us continually offer to God a sacrifice of praise—the fruit of lips that confess his name. And do not forget to do good and to share with others, for with such sacrifices God is pleased." On the one hand, there is "a sacrifice of praise" (adoration), and on the other, there is doing good and sharing with others (action). We make a mistake if we think the church service is confined to the first element here (adoration). In order to be true Christian worship, it must include the second element (action) as well. And so, of course, it does—which is why evangelism, ministry to one another, and the collecting of gifts of money are all essential parts of church services. Indeed, evangelism may well be implied in "the fruit of lips that confess his name," in which case adoration and action are even more closely intertwined, and there is even less distinction to be made between what happens in the service and what happens in the rest of the lives of those attending the service.

Edification, evangelism, and worship are not opposed to each other. Edifying one another (so that we build up and encourage each other's faith) is one essential way we worship God in our meetings. We must beware of "the common assumption that church services should be designed primarily to facilitate and encourage a private communion with God, either by spiritual exercises or ritual."[5] The most extended

---

Commission is set in a theological context where prayer for the dead is acceptable, a context very different from the biblical perspective of the Reformation.

5. David G. Peterson, "Worship in the New Testament," in *Worship: Adoration and Action,* ed. D. A. Carson (Carlisle: Paternoster, 1984), 79.

treatment of the Christian gathering in the New Testament is in 1 Corinthians 11–14. It is clear from these chapters that Paul's main concern was how the Corinthian Christians were treating one another and outsiders when they met, not how they were treating God—because how they were treating one another *was* how they were treating God! To concentrate on getting so absorbed with God that we cease to notice those around us during a church service is not perhaps as spiritual as it might seem. This was the very thing against which Paul warned the Corinthians. The more truly they focused on God, the more aware they would actually become of one another.

In the middle of those chapters comes the famous passage on love in 1 Corinthians 13. Paul placed it there as a deliberate contrast to the way the Corinthians were treating one another when they met together. It is applied in practical terms to the Christian meeting in the chapter that follows (1 Cor 14:1: "Follow the way of love. . . ."). In other words, what is it to make love our aim in a church service? It is to do everything for edification (vv. 12, 26). The church is edified as individuals are instructed and encouraged (vv. 19, 26) and the presence of the outsider is taken seriously. Hence Paul's emphasis in the chapter is on intelligibility, order, clarity, and corporateness.

The church service provides a special foretaste of the experience of heaven. In Hebrews 12:18–29, the way Christians experience the presence of God is contrasted with what the Israelites experienced at Mount Sinai. Significantly, it is a corporate experience. So when we come together, we can know God and relate to God and worship God in ways that we cannot do when we are alone. But that special corporate encounter with God should not cause us to forget one another. The vertical and horizontal dimensions of a church service are not at odds with each other. Christians can gather for church services with an eager expectation of being dealt with specially by God in that context. But it is a corporate context—and God's Word will direct us up to heaven and out to one another as we meet: "Let the Word of Christ dwell in you richly as you teach and admonish *one another* with all wisdom, and as you sing psalms, hymns and spiritual songs with gratitude in your hearts *to God*" (Col 3:16; emphasis added).

However, a large gap has clearly opened up in the two thousand years between the teaching of the New Testament and what we customarily do in church Sunday by Sunday. How can we read Matthew 23:1–10 and still think that special titles, special clothing, and special seats have any place in the Christian gathering? The human urge to worship, which is common to every culture in human history, has largely succeeded in conforming Anglican worship to the pattern of non-Christian religions. Some of what happens in Anglican churches on a Sunday is closer to a pagan understanding of worship than to Christianity. And one reason for that is because we have spent too much time praising the wonderful language of the *Book of Common Prayer* and given too little attention to the real source of its spiritual power.

Cranmer's Achievement

To discover where that power lies, we must consider what Cranmer's Prayer Book actually did. Roger Beckwith summarizes it like this:

> When compared with the state of liturgy at the beginning of Henry VIII's reign, Cranmer's Prayer Books show the following significant changes: the language has been altered from Latin to English; a many-volume service book has been reduced to one; . . . the rubrics have been pruned . . .; the lectionary has been reformed; preaching has been revived; the congregation has been given a considerable part in the service; the cup has been restored to the laity . . .; an impressive new structure has been given to the Communion service; the eight daily offices have been combined into two; the biblical content of most services has been greatly increased; and traditional doctrines and practices which Cranmer judged to be in conflict with biblical theology (notably the sacrifice of the Mass, transubstantiation, reservation, the confessional, petition for the departed and the invocation of saints) have been reformed or entirely removed.[6]

Cranmer's aims were "to attain intelligibility, edification, and corporateness." He achieved them "by producing . . . a single, simple liturgy

---

6. In *The Study of Liturgy,* ed. C. Jones, G. Wainwright, and E. Yarnold (London: SPCK, 1978), 73–74.

in the vernacular, in which the Scriptures are read and expounded in an orderly way, biblical teaching is incorporated throughout, all that is misleading or meaningless is excluded, words are audible, actions visible, and congregational participation in speaking, singing, and reception of the sacrament (in both kinds) is encouraged."[7]

Faced with the complexity and obscurity of the liturgy of the medieval Western church, Cranmer was determined to create a liturgy that was accessible to ordinary church members. It had to be in a language they could understand. "Whereas St. Paul would have such language spoken to the people in the church, as they might understand, and have profit by hearing the same," he wrote, "the service in this Church of England these many years hath been read in Latin to the people, which they understand not; so that they have heard with their ears only, and their heart, spirit and mind, have not been edified thereby." Moreover, the liturgy had to bring them to the Bible in an orderly manner. Of the lectionary he wrote, "These many years passed, this godly and decent order of the ancient Fathers hath been so altered, broken, and neglected, by planting in uncertain stories, and legends . . . that commonly when any book of the Bible was begun, after three or four chapters were read out, all the rest were unread."[8]

It is possible to see three principles running through Cranmer's work. He aimed at and achieved a rare combination: being *biblical*, *accessible*, and *balanced*. All three principles are driven by the Bible, but the first refers specifically to Cranmer's content, the second to his communication, and the third to his attitude.

1. Biblical

Cranmer made sure that the texts of his services did not just avoid conflict with the Bible, but that they positively expressed the ideas of the Bible, often in the very language of the Bible. Being biblical is not just a matter of including Bible readings and extracts (as the work of the Liturgical Commission does), but of faithfully reflecting the Bible's

---

7. Ibid.

8. All the preceding quotations are drawn from *The Book of Common Prayer*, "Preface: Concerning the Service of the Church."

message, which interprets and draws them together.

So for example, Morning and Evening Prayer were to begin with the reading of one or more Bible verses, followed by, "Dearly beloved brethren, the Scripture moveth us in sundry places to acknowledge and confess our manifold sins and wickedness." If we contrast this with the *Alternative Service Book* equivalent—"We have come together as the family of God in our Father's presence to offer him praise and thanksgiving"—we note a significant shift in emphasis away from the biblical insistence on divine initiative (grace: God's word calling us to repentance) to human initiative (our coming together to offer something to God). David Peterson has written, "The structure of the 1552 Communion service gave the English church a liturgical expression of the great doctrine of justification by faith only. As such it is unique among liturgies, Eastern or Western, and heads a new liturgical family."[9]

Cranmer was driven by biblical imperatives and principles. Where they were involved, he was thoroughly inflexible. When faced by opponents of reformation like Bishop Gardiner who claimed they could still find the Mass in Cranmer's 1549 Prayer Book, Cranmer reworked the material.[10] The result was the 1552 Prayer Book, in which every detail that Gardiner had used as a loophole for the Mass was altered. For example, instead of a prayer for the elements (the bread and the wine) in the Communion service, a prayer for the recipients was substituted. The 1549 reference to making a "memorial" (which could be interpreted to mean the offering of a memorial sacrifice of the body and the blood of Christ, the essence of the Mass) was omitted in 1552. (The *Alternative Service Book* started to reverse both of these examples.)

The structure of Cranmer's services reflects his biblical theology. For instance, the importance of putting confession near the beginning of the service is not that we should feel more sinful then and all clean again afterwards, but that we need to be reminded that we are gospel people. The invitation to God's people to rejoice when they come

---

9. David G. Peterson, *The Moore Theological Correspondence Course: Prayer Book* (Kingsford: St Matthias Press, 1992), 78.

10. He was helped by the strongly Protestant John Hooper, and both Hooper and Cranmer took into account the views of Martin Bucer in his *Censura* (an invited critique).

together (so frequent in the Psalms and in many Christian hymns) is not because we are excited to see one another. It is because we are coming together as forgiven people: God's grace has dealt with our sins and brought us back into relationship with him. So it is the gospel that brings us together, confessing our sins and rejoicing in God's forgiveness. A church service that starts in that way is starting in the right place theologically.

Another example is the structure of Cranmer's Communion. Because Jesus' words "This is my body. . . . This is my blood" (Luke 22:19, 20) were words of administration when he spoke them and not words of consecration, Cranmer put the distribution of the bread and wine immediately after the prayer of thanksgiving (with no "fraction," "elevation," or "adoration" in between). His structure emphasized our grateful acceptance of something God has done for us and resisted any sense of a specially "holy" moment at that point in the service, which easily becomes a loophole for magic and superstition. (Predictably, the *Alternative Service Book* again began to revert to a pre-Cranmer pattern.)

The *Book of Common Prayer* is full of sensible, common-sense provisions like these for communicating Bible truths. Cranmer was not a "nomenclature purist," but he does not use the word *worship* to refer to church services. The Communion table was to be called a "table," and never an "altar." Anglicans have lost more than we realize by allowing a stone altar to take the place of a moveable wooden table. Cranmer saw that such a detail had important theological implications: we meet around a *table* for the Lord's Supper or Holy Communion (where we commemorate Christ's death), but an "altar" suggests a reenactment of the sacrifice that was made once for all on Calvary. Even so small a change of terminology diminishes the work of Christ and misleads people as to how human beings relate to God.

2. Accessible

Cranmer was also concerned that the services of the church should be *accessible* to all the people. Biblical content would not edify unless it was clearly communicated. He achieved this primarily by putting the services into English. It is hard for us to imagine what a significant change that would have been for the majority of people, who had never before fully understood what was happening in church.

Cranmer also took care to write prayers that expressed Bible truths in language and thought forms appropriate to his own age and culture. Indeed, he did the job so well that his "collects" have communicated effectively to many other ages and cultures. The Collect for the Second Sunday in Advent is a good example:

> Blessed Lord, who hast caused all holy Scriptures to be written for our learning: grant that we may in such wise hear them, read, mark, learn, and inwardly digest them, that by patience and comfort of thy Holy word, we may embrace, and ever hold fast the blessed hope of everlasting life which thou has given us in our Saviour Jesus Christ. Amen.

Cranmer's aim to write in language clearly understood by the people suggests that he would have been horrified to think of people still using his sixteenth-century language for church services four centuries later. (What, for example, does the word "wise" in the Collect above mean today to someone with no interest in the history of the English language?)

Accessibility was also furthered by his work of simplification. Cranmer's single book replaced a range of pre-Reformation books so complicated that a separate book of instructions for priests (called *The Pie*) had to be used. The congregation had not expected to understand what was going on. Cranmer produced a single book for the whole congregation with clear instructions (rubrics) to explain what was happening at any given point (by contrast, note the rapid proliferation of liturgical texts today).

Another aspect of Cranmer's desire for church services to be accessible was his emphasis on corporateness. The significant parts of medieval services happened in the chancel with the congregation as observers rather than participants, in accordance with medieval Catholic theology. By comparison, Cranmer's services had a huge amount of congregational praying and involvement. Even today, modern informality and freedom compare poorly with Cranmer on this point. His liturgy has a much more corporate emphasis than some informal services today (where many individuals may make their own contribution, but people do less together).

3. Balanced

Cranmer's commitment was not just to biblical content and to clear communication but also to a biblical attitude that is encapsulated in the Bible's proportion, its nuances, and its silences. It is hard to think of a single term for this aspect of Cranmer's work. There was a maturity and moderation about Cranmer that kept him from being an extremist or a bigot. There was a fair-mindedness and a common sense about him that gave his work humility and perspective. He knew where to be flexible and where to be inflexible. He was sympathetic to human weakness and fallibility. He could recognize the authentic demands of rival viewpoints and was concerned not to go beyond God's Word or to argue it into being clearer than it is on some issues. This level-headed restraint and sensitivity would have been encouraged by his German mentor Martin Bucer, who had written in 1549, "Flee formulae, bear with the weak. While all faith is placed in Christ, the thing is safe. It is not given for all to see the same thing at the same time."[11]

For want of a better word, we are using "balance" to denote this Cranmerian attitude, but it is used in a much wider sense than mere compromise between the claims of the new and the traditional. While balance was not the most important of Cranmer's principles, it was probably the most distinctive aspect of the Anglicanism he helped to found. It created the attitude that J. I. Packer has described as "Anglican unwillingness to shape the Church in a way that either needlessly cuts loose from the past or needlessly cuts out Christians who would be part of it in the present."[12]

So Cranmer brought about his revolution at a controlled pace in order to include as many as possible and to exclude as few as possible. The development of his different Prayer Books showed that he accepted that change must be gradual. He endeavored to take from

---

11. Martin Bucer, *Scripta Anglicana fere omnia* (Basiliae: Pernae officina, 1577), 686.

12. J. I. Packer, *A Kind of Noah's Ark: The Anglican Commitment to Comprehensiveness,* Latimer Study 10 (Oxford: Latimer House, 1981), 20.

the Fathers, and indeed from the medieval church, anything that was edifying in the light of the biblical insights of the Reformation. He did not change as quickly as many would have liked him to, and he defended this policy on the grounds that Paul insisted on order in the churches and wanted all to agree, including the weak. Cranmer was concerned to distinguish between primary and secondary truths and to retain a sense of proportion as well as to exercise "charitable assumption" wherever appropriate.

Concerning "ceremonies" (rituals such as Processions, Creeping to the Cross, etc.) he wrote of removing those which "because they have much blinded the people, and obscured the glory of God, are worthy to be cut away, and clean rejected"; while retaining others "which although they have been devised by man, yet it is thought good to reserve them still, as well for a decent order in the church, (for the which they were first devised) as because they pertain to edification, whereunto all things done in the Church (as the Apostle teacheth) ought to be referred."[13] Cranmer saw that in a time of reformation some were bound to make novelty their authority rather than the Bible. But Cranmer himself had a biblical humility that recognized that he was not the first person since the apostles to have wisdom.

Cranmer's balanced attitude provided a natural context for the development of the "Hooker principle": that where the Bible is silent (for example, on the precise pattern for a church service), the church is free to regulate its life for the sake of good order.[14] Where the Bible gives us freedom, Cranmer endeavored to be flexible in his application of biblical principles to achieve the best results.

So the value of Cranmer's work for us today lies not just in its faithfulness to Bible doctrine, but in the example it provides of how to work Bible doctrine out in liturgical practice. There are many aspects of what Cranmer did that are not obligatory for Anglicans today. But they are nevertheless very helpful to us, and they are part of the Anglican heritage.

---

13. *The Book of Common Prayer,* "Preface: Of Ceremonies."

14. Richard Hooker (c. 1554–1600) defended the Elizabethan Settlement of 1559 in the masterly English prose of his *Treatise on the Laws of Ecclesiastical Polity* (1594 and 1597).

Cranmer's Legacy

So Cranmer's legacy is a sound biblical theology, combined with a moderate and common-sense theological pragmatism expressed in a liturgical tradition that has frequently strayed from its founder's ideals, particularly in recent years, but is still relevant. The spiritual power of the *Book of Common Prayer* lay in the fact that it expressed the teachings of the Bible in a form accessible to those for whom it was intended. It is not liturgy per se that is distinctively Anglican (if Cranmer and the *Book of Common Prayer* are to be allowed their true place in the origin of Anglicanism); it is liturgy based on the Bible and directed to expressing a biblical doctrine of worship. Nor is Cranmer's liturgy, in its original form, any longer workable (because its sixteenth-century language now contradicts his own principle of accessibility). But the doctrine expressed in the *Book of Common Prayer* (along with the *Thirty-Nine Articles* and the *Ordinal*)[15] determines what is and what is not Anglican today. Canon A5 of the Church of England states clearly:

> The doctrine of the Church of England is grounded in the Holy Scriptures, and in such teachings of the ancient Fathers and Councils of the church as are agreeable to the said Scriptures. In particular such doctrine is to be found in the *Thirty-Nine Articles of Religion, Book of Common Prayer* and the *Ordinal*.[16]

The clear direction of that Canon can be contrasted with the tone of modern liturgical revision:

> Part of the task of liturgy is to create resonances with people's experience and to identify with people where they are. That is why we sometimes need a mix of ancient and modern, as well as vibrant images in

---

15. The Ordinal is the ordination services to the offices of Deacon and Priest (Presbyter), written by Cranmer and bound in the same book as his *Book of Common Prayer*. These services have their own preface and were therefore technically a different book despite being bound in one volume with the *Book of Common Prayer*.

16. The Canons of the Church of England are the ecclesiastical laws promulgated by the Church of England to regulate its own life. They have a long history dating back to the beginning of the seventeenth century and are now reviewed by a Standing Canon Law Revision Committee to endeavor to keep them from becoming out of date.

the text. The next task of the liturgy is to take people from where they are on a journey towards God—a journey for both Christians and those as yet uncommitted. So the new liturgy is dynamic, moving people towards God himself, and therefore a powerful tool for both mission and spirituality.[17]

The human-centered perspective of such liturgical revision is obvious: the direction is now from us to God (in contrast to the from-God-to-human direction of the gospel and of Cranmer's services). There is no reference at all here (nor anywhere else in that particular pamphlet) to expressing the truths of the Bible through liturgy.

It is not possible to claim that liturgy now provides any sort of unity for the Church of England. To try to find some modern form of Anglican unity in the Church of England's "practice of prayer" is like pursuing a will-o'-the-wisp or nailing a jelly to the wall. The doctrine of the Church of England is no longer protected by its liturgy because that liturgy no longer expresses a uniform doctrine. Cranmer's clarity and simplicity have been abandoned, and obscurity and ambiguity have been intentionally brought back into Anglican liturgy (in order to achieve agreement among the revisers), with the result that real disunity (over what is believed) is concealed by apparent unity (over the form of words that are used in church).

Our Responsibility

Anglicans have received a precious legacy from Cranmer. If it is not to be squandered, there needs to be resolute and urgent action, for already much of it has gone.

There are some who are struggling with the processes of liturgical revision, seeking to stem the tide that has flowed right through the twentieth century and eroded the Bible from the services of the Church of England, while others are working to create good practice in local churches. The latter maintain that the Liturgical Commission may not

---

17. Preface to *Revising The Church of England's Liturgy,* Bulletin 3 (June 1998), written by the Bishop of Guildford, Chairman of the Liturgical Publishing Group, and the Bishop of Salisbury, Chairman of the Liturgical Commission.

dictate the precise form of Anglican services. The Liturgical Commission does not comply with Canon A5 (see above). It does not accept the Bible as the authority for what should or should not be included in Anglican services. So if the General Synod of the Church of England sees fit to act in this way with regard to the Canons, local churches are entitled to seek to stay in line with those Canons even if that means using forms of service that have not been authorized by the Synod.

In fact, the Canon Law of the Church of England allows its ministers considerable freedom in developing service patterns. Canon B5:1 reads, "The minister may in his discretion make and use variations which are not of substantial importance in any form of service authorised by Canon B1 according to particular circumstances." Canon B5:3 defines what constitutes a variation "of substantial importance": "All variations in forms of service and all forms of service used under this Canon shall be reverent and seemly and shall be neither contrary to, nor indicative of any departure from, the doctrine of the Church of England in any essential matter." A variation "of substantial importance" is a variation that affects doctrine. Variations are not forbidden by the Canon when they are not *culturally* Anglican (so long as they are "reverent and seemly"), but only when they are not *doctrinally* Anglican.

So the Canons allow freedom for variety within the authorized services of the Church of England in order to create services that are best suited for the congregations for which they are intended, that will teach that group of people Anglican doctrine most effectively, and that will edify them in their faith. When it was written, the *Book of Common Prayer* represented an attempt to make culturally relevant and accessible the uniform truth of the Christian faith. Modern Anglicanism is in danger of reversing that, trying to express a variety of "truth" in a uniform culture.

Fortunately, in theory at least, the doctrinal cornerstone of Anglicanism remains the *Book of Common Prayer,* the *Ordinal,* and the *Thirty-Nine Articles.*[18] And they, in turn, point us back to the Bible. So our first task in devising forms of church service for Anglican

---

18. See Canon A5, quoted above (p. 76) and explained by n. 14.

churches today should be to place the Bible at the very center of them (because in that way we will be putting Christ at the center).

Next we need to take seriously a culture as far removed from Cranmer's as his was from that of the first century. It is less familiar with Christianity; it is more diverse; it is more technologically sophisticated (so we can easily produce fresh service formats each week); it is, in some ways, more participatory, immediate, and democratic. (For example, many people are less at ease with a fixed liturgy—just as they would be with having one of the Homilies[19] read to them instead of hearing a sermon preached.) It is not a culture in which communal singing is common, except in churches and sports stadia.

Thus, we need to make edification and evangelism major goals of the meeting, reawakening congregations to the evangelistic opportunities of church services and using liturgy and festivals to serve these aims. We will want to maximize the intelligibility and develop the corporateness of the service. Like Cranmer, we will learn from the past and will not value the new merely because it is new. But we will be prepared for constant change, because in the gospel God calls us to change (both as individuals and as the church). We will want a clear center but fuzzy edges to the congregation, making it easy for those on the outside to find their way in. We will want to avoid making distinctions that God does not make.

If we are to follow in Cranmer's footsteps, we must be as determined as he was to put the Bible at the center of our church services; we must be as committed as he was to making Christianity accessible to ordinary people; and we must have the common sense he had in judging between primary truths and secondary truths, knowing where to be inflexible and where to be flexible.

---

19. The Homilies were the standard sermons published first in 1547 and then with a second part in 1563. Cranmer seems to have written the major part of the first book, and Bishop John Jewel (1522–71) the second. The Homilies were published "to avoid the manifold enormities, which heretofore by false doctrine have crept into the Church of God," and because "appointed ministers" in the early days of the Reformation did not necessarily have "the gift of preaching sufficiently to instruct the people." The Homilies are significant today, in particular, because various of the *Thirty-Nine Articles* refer to them for fuller explanation of various doctrines, showing that one of their purposes was to put flesh on the bones of the *Articles*.

In Practice

If our church services are going to match these criteria, Anglicans have a formidable task ahead, and we need to consider their practical implementation. It is important to say that the more practical the discussion becomes the less respect it should be accorded. There is a huge diversity in the Anglican Church, and therefore there are many variants that will affect the application of Cranmer's principles. The size and prosperity of a congregation will affect its resources, as will its spiritual maturity, its general ethos, and the varying confidence and ability of the members. The history of the congregation, its setting (urban, suburban, or rural), and the time available to its leaders will all play their part. The practical discussion that follows is not about achieving a uniform liturgical pattern, but about the varied applications of the same principles. Nor is it concerned to achieve a particular standard, but rather to maintain a particular direction.

If we are going to follow Cranmer conscientiously today, whether we stick to a set service pattern or use liturgical material more flexibly Sunday by Sunday, we will need to ponder, to pray for, and to plan our services every week. A set liturgy can provide a sound framework of biblical doctrine. It can also provide sufficient familiarity with the proceedings to allow a comfortable balance between the old and the new and to help with that sense of decency and order that Paul deemed necessary for the Corinthians' meetings (1 Cor 14:40). But it should not stifle creativity and innovation. Nor should it be the excuse for avoiding fresh thinking. The Church of England has suffered greatly from the way a set liturgy has encouraged clergy to lead services without thought and without preparation (particularly now that the most common form of that set liturgy is no longer firmly grounded in biblical doctrine). Good services require planning, and that requires time.

Service Planning

It is helpful to have a meeting to plan and review services in order to learn from mistakes and to develop good practice. Obviously some churches do not have this opportunity, but where the person responsible for the Bible teaching and the person responsible for the music can confer and pray together, it will raise the quality of the services. If such a meeting can be weekly and can include one or two others, with draft outlines of the service prepared and circulated in advance, it will be better still. It is particularly important to assess the sermon and to consider how the rest of the service relates to it. Sermons should not be divorced from the context in which they are delivered. Every preacher benefits from hearing his sermons reviewed, and every service benefits from the preacher playing a part in its preparation.

Careful preparation need not rule out spontaneity. Open prayer, impromptu testimony, a "flow" of singing, and other forms of unscheduled congregational participation may be appropriate according to the culture of the congregation. It was to regulate rather than exclude such activity that Paul wrote 1 Corinthians 14. The planning group will want to weigh how such participation fits with the collective temperament of their congregation and how outsider-friendly it will be. The preacher will be able to suggest what will be the best congregational response to his next sermon: a time of silence, a time of open prayer, a time for repentance, discussion groups, questions to the preacher, an after-meeting for those in need of an opportunity to respond to the gospel, or a time of counseling or prayer. Then the service leader will need to have the freedom to change what has been planned when the time comes, within whatever prearranged guidelines are appropriate.

Together with planning, prayer is an important purpose of this meeting. If we believe that we are involved in planning something God has ordained (the gathering of Christians), for God's purposes (winning and building up disciples), and that this is his work (in which we are simply co-workers), we will make prayer a priority as we plan. It is a way of acknowledging the importance of church services and our dependence on God as the One who alone can build his church.

Every occasion when believers gather in the name of Christ is too precious an opportunity to be allowed to go by without care being taken over it. For those in isolated ministry positions with no colleagues to pray or plan with, it is a high priority to find someone who will share in this task. The best services are normally team efforts, demonstrating the corporateness of the Christian life. But a mistake we often make is to draw others in to help with the execution of the service rather than with the planning and preparation of the service. The isolated vicar will be more helped by hearing someone else's assessment of his last sermon and service than by someone leading next week's intercessions for him. It is the difference between asking someone to do something *for* us and to do something *with* us. Some ministers never manage to establish teams because they never allow anyone alongside them to become a genuine yoke-fellow, sharing both encouragement and criticism. It will be much easier to prevent services from being doctrinally off-beam or dull if we draw in others to help.

But what are the guidelines for planning a service? If any service today is to fit into the Anglican heritage we have received from Thomas Cranmer, it will have to pass these three tests: (1) Is it biblical? (2) Is it accessible? (3) Is it balanced?[20]

1. Is It Biblical?

We will not have Jesus Christ at the center of our church services if we do not have his Word at the center. It is the Word of God that brought the Church of God into existence, and it is the ministry of the Word of God that is the wellspring and center of the church's life. The church in its local manifestation is the group of people who assemble around the ministry of the Word in a particular place. Our weekly meetings are for us to meet one another under the ministry of the Word of God. We often underestimate how much we all need the encouragement of the weekly gathering around the Word to go on believing in God for one more week.

So the service should not just contain extracts from the Bible. It should be Bible-driven. The great Bible doctrines should give it shape. Cranmer placed confession at the beginning to remind us that we are gospel people, brought together by God's grace (remember the start to Morning Prayer: "Dearly beloved brethren, the Scripture moveth us in

---

20. The term "balanced" is being used here to convey that characteristic of Cranmer's work that was discussed on pp. 74–75, above. It is not only a balance between new and old, but a whole attitude of moderation, broadmindedness, humility, and sensitivity.

sundry places to acknowledge and confess our manifold sins and wickedness. . . .")). We start from God's call to us in his Word, and we respond to him on his terms by confessing our sins and then rejoicing in his forgiveness. The reading of Bible verses and passages, the singing of psalms, prayers based on Scripture (for example, regular prayer for the government: 1 Tim 2:1–2), a confession of systematic biblical faith in the Creed, the provision of Bible-based homilies for those who could not preach, and the demand for preaching from those who could—all of these kept the Word of God at the center of Cranmer's services.

In our day we must do the same but by appropriate means. If it is no longer appropriate to chant psalms, we must find other ways to incorporate them into our services. Psalms are the main biblical medium for the expression of human emotion. (Expressions of sorrow and joy, confidence and despair, anger and elation, abound in the Psalter.) As the psalms have disappeared from our church services, so other expressions of human emotion have welled up, some of which are much less healthy than the psalms, and almost all of which are less biblical. But the psalms can still be used—as frameworks for prayer, as antiphonal readings, for meditation.[21]

If a service is to pass this biblical test, then it must edify. We meet to build one another up as individuals and together as a church. However far we have each individually traveled in the Christian life, we need the help of meeting together regularly under the Word of God, because our faith is sustained by his Word.

Church services do not exist primarily for the precise statement of Christian doctrine. They are for edification. But edification comes through doctrine—through the faithful teaching of the Word of God. So good doctrine must be safeguarded at church services. We must ask about every aspect of the service: Will this edify those who come? Will it help them to go on believing that there is a God who loves them? Will it encourage them to live holy lives and to serve other people this coming week? Is there anything here that will tend to discourage and

---

21. For example, *Psalms for Today* and *Songs from the Psalms,* both edited by David Iliff, Michael Perry, and David Peacock (London: Hodder and Stoughton, 1990), contain much helpful psalm-based material for singing.

dismantle faith? The great Bible truths—stated, explained, discussed, applied, prayed over, sung, meditated upon, responded to—are what build the congregation together in faith and each of us up as individual members of the Body.

Evangelism is part of building up the Body. In fact, there is no sharp distinction to be drawn between edification and evangelism in church services. The same Bible truths that strengthen the faith of the Christian challenge the lack of faith of the non-Christian. The church service should be one of the most effective means of evangelism. It must be an occasion to which Christians can easily invite their friends, during which those friends will not be embarrassed, and at which they will be able to come to grips with the Christian faith. What we do will not necessarily be familiar to them: how common an activity is community singing these days? But it should be apparent to a guest that we are in earnest. There should be no doubt that we take the Word of God seriously and that we want them to take it seriously as well.

David Peterson has written, "Those who are concerned about God-honouring worship will be preoccupied with bringing people to Christ."[22] That is a truth that should govern the whole life of the Christian, and it should also shape the way we plan our church services. They must be "outsider-friendly."

Cranmer revised the Lectionary to be sure that every local church went systematically through the Bible. We will want to achieve the same end, but we may want to use different means. Modern lectionaries, shaped by liberal theology, which sits in judgment on God's Word and deems certain parts of it unsuitable for modern ears, will not be satisfactory. A vicar may well feel that the responsibility for deciding what passages his congregation should hear is his alone; it is too important to be left to anyone else. But he will need to beware of his own hobby-horses. Aiming to work systematically through all the major Bible books, passage by passage, Sunday by Sunday, over a ten-year period provides a balance between freedom and system so that the present needs of the church can be weighed against the long-term responsibility to teach the whole counsel of God. All too few churches

---

22. Peterson, "Worship in the New Testament," 65.

today benefit from regular teaching by the same pastor from the same book of the Bible, carefully and faithfully expounded week by week. Those that do are often the most healthy.

The first question to ask of a church service, then, is: Is it biblical? Does it have the Bible at the heart of it? Is it shaped by Bible truths? Does it fulfill the twin New Testament aims for the Christian meeting of edification and evangelism? The second question to ask is: Is it accessible?

2. Is It Accessible?

It was Cranmer's great achievement to bring biblical truth close to ordinary people. Our services must do the same. We must take seriously the gap between what happens in church and what happens everywhere else. Cranmer was determined to remove obscurity from the services of the church and to put simplicity and clarity in its place. So language and behavior that needlessly alienate the outsider must be avoided. On the other hand, there are Christian terms that cannot be avoided (e.g., faith, grace, holiness, glory, sin); they can only be explained. Similarly, prayer, hymn-singing, saying a creed together, listening to a sermon—these are not everyday experiences for the nonchurchgoer. They have a place in our services, but we will need to introduce them in a way that allows those who are not familiar with a church culture to cope. It may be appropriate, for example, to allow a congregation a moment to read through a creed or a prayer of confession and ponder it for themselves before inviting them to say it.

Embarrassment is a great enemy of edification and evangelism. Will this greeting, this song, this prayer, this acclamation, this drama, this testimony, this time of open ministry, this collection, these notices, embarrass anyone? Will someone be feeling uncomfortable if we do things this way? Comfort is not a goal we seek for itself—the Word of God has a way of creating disequilibrium in the human heart in order to lead us to reassessment and repentance—but if we want to maximize the effectiveness of the service to edify and evangelize, we must minimize unnecessary embarrassment. And this will be a matter for discernment and sensitivity to the particular group of people for whom the service is intended. For most congregations today, a time for them to greet one another informally in the service is appropriate. But there will be some congregations for whom such informality is too threatening. It will do more harm than good, and the embarrassment factor will prove too great.

Of course, we are all different and are all embarrassed by different things. No service will ever suit all tastes and respect all sensibilities. But an attitude of sensitivity on the part of those responsible for the service will be eloquent, as will an attitude of seriousness and of trying to do things well. Even though an item in a service may not suit a particular individual's taste, the better it is done, the less uncomfortable that individual will feel about it.

We cannot suit every taste present in our congregations in everything we do, nor should we: it could be a bad sign if someone leaving at the end of a church service remarked, "Every aspect of that service was exactly how I would have wanted it to be." Every church service ought to be a mixture of tastes, challenging all of us to make greater allowances for the tastes and preferences of others present. It ought to widen our "comfort zones" without getting to the point where we find the mixture too threatening.

But if we cannot suit every taste, we can try to do everything we do to the best of our ability. That will honor God, it will emphasize the importance of our meeting together as a Christian fellowship, and it will minimize embarrassment. We want to honor God by doing things as well as we can for his sake. We are not trying to impress people with our own standards but to communicate to them what we think about God.

If our services are to be accessible, then even though an outsider may not agree with the Christian faith, he or she must be able to see that it matters to us, that we take it seriously, and that we are talking about it in terms that are intelligible. The congregation must be encouraged to *expect* non-Christians to be present. This will include those among their number who are professing but not converted. But it will also open the congregation up to the possibility of bringing non-Christian friends and family to church.

Non-Christians must not be made to feel like interlopers eavesdropping on a meeting of an esoteric sect. They must be reassured that it is all right to be there, that they are welcome as people who have not yet decided about Jesus Christ for themselves. At certain points in the service there may need to be a "let-out" clause: "Not all of us present will be able to say the Creed yet. If you prefer, please just think about these statements of belief as others of us say them aloud." Or the preacher may want to indicate that the application of a particular point will be different according to the spiritual state of the hearer.

"Is it accessible?" is a key question for deciding the appropriateness of different parts of the service. Wisdom is needed to judge these matters aright. Once again, the value of a second (and a third, and a fourth) opinion cannot be overstated. Without some sort of "service planning group," church services will tend to become the victim of one individual's tastes and cultural prejudices. And as a consequence, their capacity for edifying and for evangelizing will be severely limited.

3. Is It Balanced?

The question "Is it biblical?" pointed us to Scripture. The question "Is it accessible?" pointed to the people. A third feature of Cranmer's work was his sensitive pragmatism. It will make us ask the question, "Is this service balanced?"

That will lead us to ask of our services: Is this service sensitive to the people we expect to attend it? How can we do things better? How can we learn from the past? Have we introduced any change recently? Have we introduced too much change recently? Is there a balance of music in this service (perhaps between standard well-known hymns and more modern songs)? Is there a balance of emotional mood in the service (to speak to both the carefree and the depressed)? Is there content here that will stretch the intelligent as well as scope for encouraging the simple? Will this service help both to break the hard heart and to heal the broken heart? Will it speak to both the unconverted and the converted?

Of course, Cranmer's theological pragmatism amounted to much more than just a balanced form of service. It caused him to distinguish between primary and secondary issues. We will want to be sure that our services pronounce clearly on the foundational truths of Christianity: the deity of Christ, salvation by grace alone, the centrality of the cross, the authority of the Bible, and so forth (and we must always ensure that moral exhortation does not take the place of the doctrine of grace at the heart of our services). But we will not want our services to focus on denominational distinctions or the issues that divide believers from one another. So long as the center is clear, the edges can be fuzzy. It is not our task to preempt God's work of dividing sheep from goats.

A balanced approach will encourage us to assess what we do as well as what we say. The way we behave inside a church building will convey theological messages. If a part of the building is treated with special awe, we need to check whether that attitude is actually consistent with our theology. If all the seats face in one direction, we need to ponder what that is saying about the nature of a church service. Body position, tone of voice, clothing, movement, and symbols all preach—and if we are not careful, they may well be contradicting what we are saying with our lips. Cranmer's attitude to church furnishings and rituals was one of moderate change. We too may want to work gradually toward a greater degree of theological consistency. But this is a sensitive area: a congregation must first be taught why a change is theologically desirable. Only then will they be ready for that change. Change without theological justification will sooner or later split a congregation.

Is it biblical? Is it accessible? Is it balanced? We will now consider how these three Cranmerian tests might apply to a range of issues.

Variety of Services

Some churches offer a variety of services on Sunday: 8:00 A.M. *Book of Common Prayer* Holy Communion; 10:00 A.M. Family Service; 11:30 A.M. *Common Worship* Morning Prayer; 6:00 P.M. Evening Prayer; 8:00 P.M. Evening Praise. Each service is targeted to a particular clientele (such as a particular age group or ethnic group) and tries to operate in the culture with which that specific group is most familiar (formal/informal, etc.). Other churches have gone in the opposite direction, preferring to concentrate their resources on just one or two services in the day.

The former churches are opting for accessibility: providing services that are convenient and unthreatening to different types of people in the interest of evangelism (or perhaps, in some cases, to avoid criticism from church members who want a service that matches their particular taste). The latter churches are opting for the biblical test: as the gospel pulls down the barriers between human beings and brings them together in Christ, so the church as the gospel community should be bringing different types and races together and teaching them to sacrifice their own tastes and preferences for one another. This policy is hard work and means that, unlike choral "Matins" or informal "Evening Praise," the service will be always be something of a cultural compromise. However, cutting the number of services will allow more preparation to be focused on the one service, and a higher quality can perhaps be achieved. It will certainly display the church as a gospel community more faithfully, although it may not have the attractiveness to the outsider that the culturally homogenous service will have (so long as its culture is his or her culture).

Structure

We have already drawn attention to some of the ways that the structure of Cranmer's services reflected biblical truth. It is one of the values of set liturgies (both ancient and modern) that they provide a carefully considered structure for the service. We must ensure that the structure is *theologically sound*: it must begin with God's Word to us; we must then respond to God on God's terms (confession and repentance); and throughout, it must be God-centered and not human-centered, proclaiming grace and not works, telling us about God more than encouraging us to think about ourselves.

But it must also be an *accessible* structure. For example, where there is a mixture of musical tastes, it may be wise to start with the item that has the widest appeal (perhaps a well-known hymn), to confine the musical items with narrower appeal to the middle parts of the service, and to end with another hymn or song that is familiar to as many of the congregation as possible. Traditional hymns at the beginning and end can work as "sweeteners" for those who do not find modern songs congenial; but if carefully chosen, these hymns probably will not put off the person who does prefer modern singing.

The structure of the service will ensure balance. By working within a basic framework but omitting or including different parts of the structure on particular weeks, we can ensure a certain freshness while guarding against the danger of neglecting one element (like the Creed or the Ten Commandments) repeatedly. It will be the task of the service leader to "thread" the service together unobtrusively but theologically so that there is a spiritual logic in the way one part follows another. For example, "When we are reminded of God's forgiveness, Christians want to praise God, which we will now do by singing. . . ."

Music

The music at services must be controlled by the three Cranmer tests (biblical, accessible, and balanced). Because we are serious about what we are doing at our services, we can never take lightly the words we sing. In *The Barber of Seville*, Figaro sings, "If a thing is too silly to be said, it can always be sung."[23] As we know, some Christian songs merit that verdict. But John Wesley wrote (back in 1761), "Above all, sing spiritually; have an eye to God in every word you sing."[24]

So service planning ought to include surveying in advance the songs to be sung. Adjustments to their words may be necessary. Remember, the overriding purpose of the whole service is not the precise statement of doctrine; it is edification and evangelism. But if it is the Word of God that brings the church about, that builds it up, and that adds to its numbers, then it must be our task to be as faithful and as accurate as we can in communicating that Word, even when we sing.

Sometimes a careful introduction will be required to set a song in a correct theological framework. There used to be a children's song of which the second verse began, "You can be very sad, and I can be very

---

23. "Aujourd'hui, ce qui ne vaut pas la peine d'etre dit, on le chante" (Pierre-Augustin Caron de Beaumarchais, *Le Barbier de Seville*, Act I, Scene ii).

24. *The Works of the Rev. John Wesley, A.M.*, (New York: Carlton and Phillips, 1853), 7:580.

sad; but that's not the way it should be." Unless it was set in the context of our heavenly hope, that verse was open to misinterpretation and could be extremely hurtful to those in the fellowship who were troubled in spirit, for instance from a recent bereavement. (Those words have now been altered in later editions.) Another example is the song "Jesus We Celebrate Your Victory," which says in its second verse "And in his presence our problems disappear"—a line that requires qualification if it is not to be highly misleading.

Most of the great "classic" hymns have a history of adaptation and alteration over the years, as the footnotes in hymnals make clear. The original writers need to listen to the considered reflection of the church on the words they write. Writing to tell an author of a suggested emendation to a song is a helpful practice.

If the music at a church service is not controlled by these three tests, it will tend either to be embarrassingly bad or to dominate the meeting inappropriately. It is as dangerous to underestimate as it is to overestimate the part music plays in our meetings, but it should be no surprise that this is an area of the church's life that comes under frequent and intense spiritual attack.

Wisdom will be needed to encourage a congregation to be united over the music it uses. One result of the power of music is that people become deeply wedded to their personal preferences and find it difficult to recognize that the *style* of music is almost always a matter of no intrinsic theological importance. Training the congregation to recognize the difference between what is theological and what is cultural, and between where the Bible speaks clearly and where it does not, is an important part of training the congregation to be balanced in their biblical understanding. It has been wisely pointed out that many tussles over words and books are basically disputes about power in the life of a local church. Selfishness loves to dress itself in cultural clothes. Musical taste seems a lot more godly than self-interest, but all too often that is all a preference for one style of music over another amounts to!

We are all aware of the battles fought in this area. Ancient hymns won over modern songs in a BBC poll of church favorites. Peter Baker caricatured a well-known hymn for the occasion:

Dear Lord and Father of mankind,
Forgive our foolish ways;
For most of us, when asked our mind,
Admit we still most pleasure find
In hymns of ancient days,
In hymns of ancient days.

The simple lyrics, for a start,
Of many a modern song,
Are far too trite to touch the heart;
Enshrine no poetry, nor art;
And go on much too long,
And go on much too long.

O, for a rest from jollity,
And syncopated praise!
What happened to tranquillity?
The silence of eternity
Is hard to hear these days,
Is hard to hear these days.

Send thy deep hush subduing all
Those happy claps that drown
The tender whisper of thy call;
Triumphalism is not all,
For sometimes we feel down,
For sometimes we feel down.

Drop thy still dews of quietness
Till all our strummings cease;
Take from our souls the strain and stress
Of always having to be blessed:
Give us a bit of peace,
Give us a bit of peace.

Breathe through the beats of praise guitar
Thy coolness and thy balm;
Let drum be dumb, bring back the lyre,
Enough of earthquake, wind and fire,
Let's hear it for some calm,
Let's hear it for some calm. [25]

---

25. Peter Baker, quoted in *News of Hymnody*, Issue 59 of Grove Books (Cambridge: Ridley Hall, July 1996). Used by permission.

And, of course, criticisms can easily be made of ancient hymns as well. "Thine eye diffused a quickening ray" might conjure up a scene from a Star Wars film, but it is unlikely to be very helpful to an outsider to church life today. Continuing to sing what we love merely because *we* love it is not a practice in line with the Cranmer tests.

The person who controls the music at the church service plays a very powerful role in its life, often on a par with the power wielded by the person who controls the church's finances and beyond that of any churchwarden.[26] It is as well to recognize this fact and to pray for a mature, godly, humble person with a servant heart, who wants to use music in the service of the gospel and not for his or her own ends. Let's hope that we will never have to face what happened at Hayes Parish Church on 18 March 1749: "The Clerk gave out the 100th Psalm, and the Singers immediately opposed him, and sang the 15th and bred a disturbance."[27]

Prayers

There is more prayer in church services than is generally recognized. For example, many songs and hymns are actually prayers, and the confession is a prayer. Often a service leader will say, "Let us pray . . ." when the congregation is actually already praying. It always strikes a discordant note, as it suggests a lack of awareness of what is going on in the service.

Cranmer's collects are among some of the finest prayers ever written. But sadly, if we would be true to Cranmer, we cannot simply repeat them today. The onus is on us to write prayers for today that are as full of Bible teaching and as carefully constructed as his were. Cranmer's prayers customarily begin with Bible truth about God ("Almighty God, unto whom all hearts be open, all desires known, and from whom no secrets are hid . . .") before laying before him our requests ("Cleanse the thoughts of our hearts by the inspiration of thy

---

26. A churchwarden is one of two appointed lay leaders in a Church of England parish.

27. Hayes Parish Register.

Holy Spirit, that we may perfectly love thee, and worthily magnify thy holy name"). Our prayers would do well to follow that pattern.

It is biblical, too, for our prayers to be corporate. This is partly achieved by set-text prayers in a service sheet. In many congregations there are also some with a special gift for leading intercessions. They will often be those who take most trouble over their preparation. When such a person leads the congregation in pleading with God to fulfill his promises to his people, all of us learn better how to pray according to God's will. We need to learn to distinguish between things for which the Bible tells us to pray and things God has not said he will give us. That does not mean that we should not sometimes pray for the latter, but we need to learn to focus on praying prayers based upon God's nature and God's promises. Sometimes such prayers come spontaneously, but more often than not they require preparation.

There is a place for spontaneous prayer in services as well. But rarely is it as helpful to the whole congregation as well-led, well-constructed, carefully prepared, and biblically based praying. There may be problems of audibility with open prayer. It is more prone to being introverted and repetitive; and it is not possible to *ensure* that it is biblical, accessible, and balanced. But these may be minor considerations if spontaneous prayer allows the congregation to respond immediately to God's leading through his Spirit and his Word.

Drama and Testimony

Drama is a powerful medium to employ in a church service, too powerful to be used without careful thought. It may leave a more striking image in the memory of the congregation than anything else in the service. Drama needs to be carefully linked to the Bible passage and to the sermon. It will be more effective in illustrating than in explaining the Word. It needs to be vetted by the preacher, and sometimes the preacher will have to insist on its exclusion if he realizes it is going to negate or dilute his Bible message.

There can also be a high "cringe factor" with drama if it is not well performed. If it will embarrass the congregation more than edify them, it needs to be left out—even at the last moment. This will require humility and godliness on the part of actors and producer. They will need the same servant spirit as musicians do, placing the good of the congregation and the glory of God before their own ego needs for self-expression and acclaim. Choir items and solo music items need to pass the same test. We should be very grateful for the organist or choir leader who has the courage and godliness to omit a rehearsed item at the last minute when it is clear that it will not help the service.

Testimonies and interviews also have a part to play. They involve fresh people and may have wider appeal to the congregation when it is clear that this is an "ordinary" person rather than a "professional." Indeed, sometimes it is inexperience and lack of fluency that are so moving about a testimony; for example, when someone with a speech impediment tells what God has done for him, and everyone is sharply aware how much it has cost that person to stand up and address them. Where an individual is too nervous to give his own testimony unsupported, it may be possible to interview him. Well-chosen and well-timed questions by the interviewer remove some of the embarrassment and help to keep the testimony moving.

Regular opportunities for interview or testimony will be provided by the imminent departure (or recent return) of a member of the congregation for Christian work elsewhere, or by a baptism (with the parents, in the case of an infant baptism!). We may well want to incorporate this sort of contribution into our services on a more ad hoc basis, giving members the chance to share what God is doing in their lives. But it will require good judgment to distinguish between those who want to contribute in this way for the sake of others, and those who wish to do it primarily for their own ego needs. It will do more harm than good if it detracts from the reading and explanation of the Bible.

Leading the Service

The role of the service leader becomes more significant as more careful planning goes into the service itself. Well-prepared leading can make the difference between outsiders feeling welcome or not. It can help the congregation to grasp the theme of the service. But over-preparation can lead to dullness, and there is a place for spontaneity, impromptu humor, and off-the-cuff remarks as well.

The person leading the service must seek to achieve a balance between gripping the interest and attention of the congregation, and communicating the seriousness of what is happening. Some service leading is good at holding attention but communicates a sense of superficiality. It may be characterized by humor and quick wit but convey the flippancy of a TV chat show. Another style of leading is minimalist (often the refuge of the person who has spent little or no time in preparation). It may be justified on grounds of "not drawing attention to the personality of the leader," but it misses a valuable opportunity to edify the congregation. The bare announcement of a hymn or song number with no reference to the meaning of the words we are about to sing usually indicates that this is one part of the service that the service leader has not bothered to prepare. Recall David's "I will not offer to the LORD my God burnt offerings that cost me nothing" (2 Sam 24:24). All too often Anglican church services have amounted to "sacrifices of praise and thanksgiving" that cost very little, certainly in terms of time spent in preparation by the person who leads them. No wonder they have been so ineffective for edification and evangelism and so monstrously dull for those who come (or prefer, perhaps wisely, not to come)!

If service leading is kept mainly in the hands of one person, it has the advantages of continuity, familiarity, and (so long as that person is suitably gifted) a uniformly high standard of leading. If the service leader is also the main Bible teacher in the church, the service leading will be another way he is able to teach doctrine to the congregation.

On the other hand, where service leading is a team ministry, the individuals involved may be able to prepare their own (smaller) part of the service in greater detail, with closer attention to its different aspects. A team ministry also publicly displays the corporate nature of the church's ministry and provides an opportunity for new individuals to be drawn into the role. Wherever possible, we should avoid giving the impression that Christian ministry is a one-man show.

In this matter it is probably best to try to have our cake *and* eat it, hard though that may be to achieve! We need the example of strong, theologically astute service leading to set the standard, but we also need to make clear that this role is not restricted to some priestly caste. It is healthy to see a new face and to hear a new voice fulfilling this ministry from time to time. But it must be done as well as possible, and that will mean training people to draw the best out of them by encouragement and criticism. Good leading draws less attention to the personality of the leader and focuses more attention on the purpose of the service.

The Notices[28]

These are often one of the dullest parts of a church service. But while the weekly services are the hub of the church's structured life, there will be other meetings radiating out like spokes from that hub, and the life of a church fellowship during the rest of the week is important. Ideally the church leadership will be checking very carefully that church activities do not grow and grow so as to invade and monopolize the leisure time of the congregation members and thus remove them from all normal social intercourse with the non-Christian world. But there will be some midweek meetings of the church that need to be advertised in the notices on Sundays.

So we should not be ashamed of the notices or try to stick them away in some corner of the service where they will do least damage. But neither should we let them become the opportunity for the minister to "have a go" at the congregation, heaping guilt onto them for past and possible future sins of omission, like failing to book for the Parish Weekend. No church should run on guilt, and the notice about an important meeting (like a monthly prayer meeting) must be carefully worded.

Once again, preparation is the key. The notices must be carefully prepared. They will not be well delivered if they are drawn from scraps of paper hastily assembled in the vestry just before the service begins. Careful preparation enables us to convey important information in the most efficient and concise way. Notices have a notorious tendency to

---

28. Or "Announcements" in much of the English-speaking world.

fill more and more time. They need to be pruned of all excess verbiage. Where a notice sheet can be provided, it will save valuable service time. Or attention may be directed to a notice board, where further details of an event are available for those interested. Larger churches will sooner or later discover the value of an Information Desk, where inquiries of all sorts can be dealt with individually and sensitively, and where publicity handouts and fliers can be available in quantity.

Size of the Congregation

The Bible does not encourage us to think that there is any spiritual significance in the size of our gatherings. A new spirituality has arisen in recent years that implies that God is specially present with his people when they assemble in large numbers. It has been called "a new doctrine of the Real Presence." The old doctrine claimed that Christ became uniquely present in the Mass at the moment of the consecration of the bread and the wine; but now it is when his people are "gathered for power" and "transported in praise." There is no Bible basis for either of these.

But neither is small necessarily beautiful when it comes to the congregation. What is certainly true is that different sizes of congregation work in different ways, and services must be planned accordingly. If the congregation is so small that it really only amounts to a cell group, then it ought to work toward developing its life in that way—perhaps by discussion of the Bible passage after a sermon or sharing prayer needs. It will be hard for such a group to come alive if it continues to behave with the formality appropriate to a congregation many times its size.

In smaller situations it may not be possible to think freshly about the services every week. It may be wise to rely on a set liturgical pattern (with a solid scriptural base) as the standard framework, with only the hymns, intercessions, notices, readings, and sermon varying from week to week. But it should be possible to review the services with one or two others on a monthly (or at least quarterly) basis. If that review meeting seeks God's will for the church services, it will be a source of new life and blessing for the services of the church. In many situations change can only come very slowly—but it can come. The New Testament urges patience and perseverance on us so frequently because God works on a time scale that is different from ours. We usually overestimate where we can get to in six months but underestimate where, under God's providence, we can get in five years (if we maintain our purpose).

At the other end of the scale, when several hundred or more people assemble for a service, it is hard for them to have a cell-group experience. Other arrangements will have to be made to provide them with the opportunity for sharing and intimacy. In a larger gathering it may be wise to concentrate on those things we can only do when we come together in numbers—like encouraging one another in our faith as we sing together and as we listen together to God's Word being expounded—rather than on things like silent or spontaneous prayer. That is not to suggest that there is no place for silence in the large gathering. Of course there is, just as there is also a place for spontaneous participation. But it is a matter of how we balance the service. What works best in a particular gathering will depend on the size of that gathering. We do not know what size the Corinthian church was, but it is clear from Paul's correspondence with them that he wanted their meetings to be conducted in a way that was appropriate for their size. Order and intelligibility were his concerns. There are bound to be limiting factors on what can be done in church services, particularly with a larger congregation.

Whether a congregation is large or small, the experience of listening to the Word of God being taught will always be similar. It will be a participatory experience. This is not to say that there must always be questions or discussion groups, but Bible preaching is not like an academic lecture or a performance. The Bible's own imagery suggests that the meal table is a better analogy for the sermon than the school lesson as we sit listening to the Word of God and "feed" on it together. That is why it is so important that, if at all possible, the members of the congregation have the Bible text open before them. It is why the most encouraging sight to see, while listening to a sermon, is not the preacher passionately gesticulating in the pulpit, but other members of the congregation listening attentively and poring over their Bibles to see "whether these things [are] so" (Acts 17:11 NRVS). It is why the preacher must make it clear to his congregation from time to time that his role is to teach the Bible faithfully and that it is their responsibility to check that he is doing so, "weigh[ing] carefully what is said" (1 Cor 14:29). It is why a preacher needs to be prepared to apologize to the congregation when further attention to a passage leads him to the conclusion that he has misrepresented Bible truth in some way in a previous sermon.

There are few more encouraging noises for the preacher than the rustle of Bible pages among the congregation when he announces his text. He should draw comfort from that, more than from sounds of approval for what he is saying during the sermon. A faithful congregation will draw faithful preaching out of their pastor. Conversely, it is very hard to persevere as a faithful teacher of the Word of God to a congregation that does not want to have it taught to them. To some extent congregations get the preachers they deserve, because preaching is a two-way process: the attitudes of preacher and congregation must unite in a humble hunger for God's Word. And because this is at the very center of every church service and is unaffected by whether a congregation is large or small, so it does not matter what size that church service is. What matters is that Jesus Christ should be present—and he will be if his Word is being heard and obeyed.

Length of Service

The appropriate length for a church service is a matter to be decided in terms of what is appropriate for the culture. If services are too long, we may make the gospel inaccessible to our contemporaries. But there are cultures where anything brief will not be taken seriously. It is another issue of accessibility. But beware—church services have a natural tendency to lengthen. They do not have a natural tendency to stay short.

Within the service, the proportion of time allotted to the sermon raises a biblical issue. Ours may be a culture of sound-bites and limited attention span, but we cannot evade our duty to take the Word of God seriously. Although the whole service may be Bible-driven, our attitude to the Bible will be clearly revealed by how long we spend lis-

tening to it being read and explained. It may be necessary to acclima-
tize a congregation gradually to increased sermon length. Accessibility will mean that a preacher will not equate length with quality and
will recognize that it is better to leave hearers wanting more rather
than exhausted and bored. Sermon length will vary from congregation
to congregation, but the absence of any control over length will usually lead to ill discipline and a poorer quality in preaching. The time
constraints we live under in the Western world today put a premium
on preparation both for the service and for the sermon: the more
preparation, the more that can be packed into a restricted time.

Whether we are right to allow ourselves to be enslaved to this
"tyranny of time" is a moot point: some church fellowships have broken free of it and thereby proclaim the Bible truth that the God who
is the Lord of time deserves better than to be squeezed by our over-
crowded time schedules. Others work within the culture in order to
be accessible to those who are locked into it. Our worship is not confined to the time we spend in church. It embraces the whole of our
lives. If there is sufficient time in church for effective edification and
evangelism, limiting service times does make sense, particularly when
we consider non-Christians who may well find unlimited service length
unappealing.

The Church Building, Furnishings, Clothing, and Movement

Most Anglican church buildings reflect medieval Catholic theology in
their architecture and therefore are not very helpful in reinforcing the
message of the gospel. The chancel at the east, if it becomes the preserve of clergy (and possibly choir) alone, very easily smacks of a holier
part of the church building. This is particularly a danger if Communion takes place at the east end and if the table is decorated and
treated as an altar. Cranmer did not institute a program for the full
reordering of the internal architecture of medieval church buildings,
but he made clear the theology of the Reformation by replacing the
medieval altar with a moveable table set up in the chancel—length-
ways, at right angles to the east wall. Communicants then moved into

the chancel and knelt around the table to receive the bread and the wine. This made it clear that the Communion is a meal. It is impossible to say how far church buildings would have been reordered if Cranmer had lived longer, if the magisterial Reformation had gone on unchecked, and if there had been no Restoration backlash from the Protestantism of the Civil War years.

Church furnishings, clothing, and movement as well as architecture are symbolic of convictions and attitudes. If we are not careful, they may well be contradicting the doctrines we are trying to teach. For example, the Anglican church today argues that none of the vestments it uses has theological significance and that any can be used by anyone from any theological position. This is to maintain the pretence that there are no real theological disagreements within the denomination. But those clothes that have always been "Mass vestments" are still used for Communion and other sacramental services by many Anglican clergy but not for Morning and Evening Prayer. It is clear that they are considered to be an indication of sacerdotal priesthood and are at odds with the doctrine of the *Book of Common Prayer*. Any clothes worn by the minister and not by the congregation will communicate a clericalism that sits ill with "the priesthood of all believers." In terms of accessibility as well, robes are unlikely to appeal to a population largely convinced that church is a matter of meaningless mumbo jumbo.

It also matters where clergy sit and stand. Cranmer's moving of the minister to the north side of the table for Communion has been noted as symbolic of the minister's instrumentality in the means of grace: he sets the table, reads the gospel, and declares Christ's words—no more than that. The details will be different today, but all steps should be taken to rid the congregation of any idea that the clergy are spiritually elevated above other members of the congregation. Neither special positions nor special clothing point in a biblical direction (see Matt 23:1–13).

But these are not issues of primary importance, and the wise church leader will handle them very sensitively. A congregation needs to be taught the right theological principles from the Bible before it is asked to accept changes in the way things are done. Change without an understood and accepted scriptural rationale will create heat but not bring any light.

The Church Year

At the Reformation, Cranmer greatly cut down on the number of saints' days and festivals in the Church Year. He maintained "red-letter" days which were a bare minimum from the medieval "sanctorale," and "black-letter" days stemming from the use of the Church's Calendar, for legal and commercial as well as religious purposes. He wrote in his "Preface" that his dislike of special days was due to their constant interruption of the consecutive reading of the Bible. At the same time, it is apparent that the Church Year was so imprinted in the consciousness of the nation that, because the Bible did not forbid it in principle, he considered it pragmatically useful to keep it in skeleton form.

Today, apart from Christmas and Easter, the Church Year has little place in popular culture. So to observe it closely may be damagingly disruptive to consecutive Bible reading and teaching. But Christmas and Easter (and other locally important festivals) may provide some of the best evangelistic opportunities of the year. Such festival services should be treated as Guest Services. Indeed, they may well be Family Services as well, in which case they present the double challenge of needing to be accessible to outsiders and friendly to children.

The same will apply to other festivals that have local importance. Mothering Sunday,[29] for example, brings the largest congregation of the year in some places; a Harvest Festival may do so in others. On such occasions the familiarity of what is sung may be as important as its doctrinal content. For example, people will come to Anglican churches at Christmas, not just expecting but *wanting* to sing traditional carols. If we disappoint that hope, we are unlikely to have increased their willingness to hear the gospel at the service. Even in churches that normally avoid "thees" and "thous," it may be appropriate to reinsert them for a carol service.

Other special days in the Christian year may, of course, provide the opportunity for services that major on one doctrine (Ash Wednesday, Good Friday, Pentecost, Ascension Day, etc.). What is sung and what is said can all be planned around a single focus in such services.

---

29. Or "Mother's Day" in many parts of the English-speaking world.

Particular Services

Holy Communion

Holy Communion is the most doctrinally sensitive of all services. We have already seen how far the revised Communion services have moved from the *Book of Common Prayer*. Because the Communion service was instituted by Jesus himself, the Devil has made sure that it has been a theological battleground all down the centuries. So the Communion service needs to be handled with particular sensitivity. It will be very easy to convey unbiblical messages through it. For example, the stipulation that the service should be led by an ordained person is a denominational requirement, not a biblical one. Similarly, there is no biblical reason for the administration to be regarded as a particularly holy or edifying moment in the service, and yet most Anglican Communion services treat it with special awe. If that awe is not actually edifying (but tends toward superstition instead), then we may want to abbreviate that part of the service by finding ways to administer the bread and the wine to the congregation more quickly.

A careful reading of 1 Corinthians 11 (the only specific reference to the institution of Holy Communion in the New Testament other than in Luke 22) will convince us that we do not get the emphasis of the service quite right in contemporary practice. "The Lord's Supper, which has so often throughout church history been understood as a means of deepening the personal communion of believers with their Lord, is clearly meant to focus the eyes of the participants on one another as well as on God," says David Peterson.[30] The Apostle Paul discussed the Lord's Supper against the background of divisions in the Corinthian church. Proclaiming "the Lord's death until he comes" is reminding one another of the significance of Jesus' death on the cross. If we disregard one another at a Communion service, we are negating the very point of that death. To keep our Anglican Communion services biblical, we will want to reassert their man-ward dimension as well as their God-ward dimension. And because the Communion service is inevitably less accessible to the outsider than other services, it should not be the dominant service in the life of our church.

---

30. Peterson, "Worship in the New Testament," 82.

Baptism

Baptism services are a joy. It is the practice of the Church of England to baptize all ages in all ways. The requirements for Anglican baptism are that it should be in the name of the Trinity, with water, and in the context of faith. The water is a sign that all ages, from the youngest to the oldest, need their sins forgiven and that forgiveness is available to all ages through the cross of Christ. Where a baby is born into a Christian family with Christian parents who have every intention of bringing that child up as a Christian, the Anglican assumption is, not that the child is an unbeliever until he or she chooses to believe for himself or herself, but that the child is a believer until (and the reverent hope is that this moment will never come) he or she chooses *not* to believe. Very many believers who have been brought up in a Christian family would say that they can never remember a moment when they did not believe. This approach is not a license for indiscriminate paedo-baptism. Clear profession of faith is required of parents and godparents (and the Anglican liturgy can be "filled out" on this point by testimony or interview).

Adult baptism services are a particularly good opportunity for explaining the gospel. Unlike Communion, baptism is accessible and, in an increasingly less Christianized society, the phenomenon of adult conversion is becoming more common and can have a strong evangelistic impact.

The manner of baptism is a matter for individual choice in the Anglican tradition. An increasing number of churches have baptisteries, allowing the freedom to sprinkle or immerse. (Cranmer's rubric was to "dip" the child "in the water discreetly and warily.")

If we would keep in step with our third Cranmer test, we will not allow the age or the manner of baptism to become a point of contention between Christian believers. We believe our Anglican practice to be in agreement with Scripture. But we certainly do not want to force it on other Christians who have different convictions.

Family Service

The value of the Family Service—when all ages (except infants) stay together throughout the service—should not be underrated. Although all parts of such a service must be child-friendly (it is not fair to keep the children in and then to ignore them), they do not have to be child-*ish*. A shorter simplified and illustrated sermon can edify and evangelize adults effectively. Indeed, it may be more effective because it is the medium and not the message that has been adjusted. Spiritual truth is not appropriated merely intellectually by human beings. It is not only well-educated adults who can feed in depth on the Word of God. But if a Family Service talk is going to edify the whole family, the preacher will need to prepare as seriously as he would for a full-length adult sermon. More time may have to go on the medium of communication, and more time will certainly have to go to the painful business of what to leave out; but we should never let ourselves think that it is "only a children's talk this week." Great simplicity requires great clarity of thought, and that will require the sort of deep understanding of the passage that comes only through hard preparation.

Adults sometimes learn more when they do not think they are being directly addressed. Their guard is down when they feel like spectators watching a speaker talk to children. Nevertheless, it is a mistake to encourage the congregation to think in those terms about a Family Service. The children have a greater need to know that the Bible is being taken seriously by their parents and the rest of the adults of the church than the adults have to watch the Bible being taught to the children. The Bible is not a book of morals for teaching our children how to behave properly; it is a book by which all believers live. So it is vitally important that the children of the church see the adults of the church being taught the Bible and bringing their lives under it. Therefore, preachers should speak directly and specifically to the adults from time to time in Family Services and let the children know they are doing so. In that way there can be no doubt in anyone's mind as to how seriously we *all* take the Bible.

The communication of the faith from one generation to the next is an important biblical concern (particularly in the Old Testament). While the Bible provides little warrant for evangelizing other people's children (despite all the Christian energies over the years that have gone into that form of evangelism), it does give us plenty of encouragement for edifying and evangelizing the whole family (the whole household) together. In our child-centered society, young parents are usually happy if their children are happy. A well-presented Family Service can be very effective evangelistically, but it will require more preparation than a normal service.

Guest Service

The same is true of a Guest Service. Here the test of accessibility will need to be applied ruthlessly. Anything unfriendly to the outsider will be carefully weighed up: should there be a collection? notices? the Creed? singing? (It is worth looking round a Guest Service congregation during a hymn and noting how many adult males are *not* singing.) On the other hand, items that are immediately accessible (like drama, testimony, a musical performance item) will be at a premium. Length of service and length of sermon will need to be carefully considered. The biblical content of the service will be restricted to the basic gospel truths. Routine parts of the service like the Confession and the Intercessions may need special explanation. There must be an appropriate opportunity for people to respond to the gospel—by attending an after-meeting, by taking a booklet, by meeting the speaker, by filling in a card, by coming forward. There must be information available about how they can take their interest in the gospel further (by signing up for a Christian Basics course, or by meeting with an individual for Bible study and discipling).

Conclusion

Guest services are a good topic with which to end a chapter about the church services of a denomination that once shaped the national life of the English people but has now lost its hold. The Church of England was begun, and has always defined itself, by the work of Archbishop Thomas Cranmer, enshrined in the *Book of Common Prayer,* the *Thirty-Nine Articles of Religion,* and the *Ordinal.* These are reformed, evangelical documents, written under the authority of the Bible and expressing the great biblical truth of justification by grace alone. But along the way, the Church of England has "lost the plot."

The liturgical revision of the twentieth century was motivated by a praiseworthy desire to increase the accessibility of Anglican services so that they could be understood by, and be culturally relevant to, ordinary English people. But the Bible was no longer regarded as authoritative, and justification by grace alone was either not understood or not accepted by the majority of the revisers. Consequently, the revised services have not been successful in attracting people back to the church; and with every year that passes, the Church of England plays a less and less significant role in the country. But it was actually the Bible that gave the *Book of Common Prayer* its spiritual power. It was not some innate power in Cranmer's wonderful skill with the English language, nor in the wisdom and balance of his approach to change and to other inflammatory issues.

If it is ever to play a part in English national life again, the Church of England has to recover its spiritual reason for existing. God has promised to bless the preaching of Jesus Christ. He has not promised to bless denominational distinctives. If Anglicans continue to preach Anglicanism and not the gospel, Anglicanism will continue to die. But if as Anglicans we preach the gospel, the Church of England may yet have a future in the purposes of God.

Church services are the shop window of the church. They are too important to be left to the experts of the Liturgical Commission. All church members must understand what they are for and why Christians gather in church. And then we must recover Anglican church services for the gospel. Reformation and renewal in church life usually come up from below, starting at the grass roots. So Anglicans should not look to the Synods and wait for the Canons to be changed to reorient our services around the Word of God. The Canons of the church have always been adjusted to accommodate what has already happened in the local church. They exist to resolve conflict within the church, not to regulate (or strangle!) life. It is our responsibility to be truly Anglican (in the sense of Canon A5, as quoted above) and to create services that are as true to the Bible and as accessible to the ordinary person as Cranmer's were. We should do it for the glory of God and for the sake of all who do not yet know that glory.

Appendix

Putting the Principles into Practice

It would not be in keeping with the rest of this chapter to provide "model" service outlines. One of the weaknesses of the use of the *Book of Common Prayer* over the centuries has been the way it has encouraged the clergy of the Church of England to lead church services without thought and without preparation. So this appendix is not an attempt to provide modern equivalents for Morning and Evening Prayer. Nevertheless, in many situations it is not possible to redesign church services each week. Liturgical patterns are unavoidable. While the day of a national liturgy may have gone, there is still the need for good local liturgy.

So for what they are worth, three "real" services are included here with a parallel commentary about the material used. They have been selected at random to provide examples (not models) of how the principles of this chapter might be put in to practice. The dominant criteria in the planning were to provide appropriate services for different occasions which were driven by the Bible, were friendly to outsiders, and were short. (The decision had been taken at this particular church to endeavor to keep services to approximately one hour, with "family" services aiming to be nearer 45 minutes. See the discussion of service length on pages 100–101).

This book was written at the time when the *Alternative Service Book* of the Church of England came to the end of its life. The current state of Anglican liturgical revision allows the local congregation considerable freedom to fashion service patterns that suit their own particular needs and that are thoroughly biblical. New resources for church services are being published all the time, although few of them express a thoroughgoing reformed theology. The challenge is to discover good liturgical material in the available books and to fit it into a service pattern that balances familiarity with freshness and that is appropriate to the congregation concerned.[1]

---

1. Any list of resources will date rapidly, but some works useful in planning services (in addition to hymnals and song books) are given on page 135 at the end of this appendix.

First Sample Service Outline

**10:30 A.M.   18 October 1998
with Crèche[2] and Trekkers (3–10)**

[Welcome]

HYMN   **Sing to God new songs of worship—**
all his deeds are marvellous;
he has brought salvation to us
with his hand and holy arm:
he has shown to all the nations
righteousness and saving power;
he recalled his truth and mercy
to his people Israel.

Sing to God new songs of worship—
earth has seen his victory;
let the lands of earth be joyful
praising him with thankfulness:
sound upon the harp his praises,
play to him with melody;
let the trumpets sound his triumph,
show your joy to God the king!

Sing to God new songs of worship—
let the sea now make a noise;
all on earth and in the waters
sound your praises to the Lord:
let the hills rejoice together,
let the rivers clap their hands,
for with righteousness and justice
he will come to judge the earth.

[from *Cantate Domino* (Psalm 98)][3]
(© Michael Baughen/Jubilate Hymns) CCL Licence 1584

---

2. Infants and toddlers—i.e., nursery.

3. Admin. by Hope Publishing Company, Carol Stream, IL 60188. All rights reserved. Used by permission.

Commentary

Introduction—This was a normal Communion service at 10:30 A.M. with two nurseries (toddlers and babes in arms) running throughout the service and with children's work (called Trekkers, aged 3–10) starting after the Notices.

The Order of Service was produced on the inside of a folded A4 sheet, with the week's notices on the two outer pages. (The words for the hymns and songs were not actually printed on the Order of Service but projected onto two screens. A separate word sheet was offered to those who preferred to use it.)

The provision for children was highlighted at the beginning of the Order of Service because it was welcoming to those who were being drawn into the church through the families' work.

Welcome—A general welcome was given with particular reference to certain groups, such as international visitors. The outline of the service was mentioned. An opportunity was provided for members of the congregation to greet each other and to fill any gaps in the rows, while the word sheets were given out to those who indicated they would like one.

Following the time of greeting, the leader read a verse of Scripture that focused the congregation on the words of the hymn they were about to sing (Psalm 98:1).

Hymn—This modern hymn (based on Psalm 98) was chosen as a lively, moderately familiar start to the service. Its disadvantages were that it is not a traditional hymn (and so is less well known to the church outsider); that the words of the first line could reinforce the idea that worship equals singing, unless the New Testament meaning of the word is briefly explained when the hymn is introduced; and that there is no obvious link between the hymn and the main Bible passage of the service.

CONFESSION

[Together]   **Almighty God, our heavenly Father,
we have sinned against you in thought and word and deed,
through negligence, through weakness,
through our own deliberate fault.
We are truly sorry and repent of all our sins.
For the sake of your Son Jesus Christ, who died for us,
forgive us all that is past;
and grant that we may serve you in newness of life,
to the glory of your name. Amen.**

ASSURANCE OF FORGIVENESS

SONG   Jesus' love is very wonderful,
Jesus' love is very wonderful,
Jesus' love is very wonderful,
O wonderful love!

So high, you can't get over it,
so low, you can't get under it,
so wide, you can't get round it,
O wonderful love!

(H.W. Rattle © Scripture Union) CCL 1584[4]

NOTICES   [Collection]

(Trekkers leave)

PRAYERS

---

4. Reprinted here with permission.

Confession—The advantage of this confession is that it is God-centered (as opposed to focusing on how we hurt other people). However, it does not give much sense of God's anger at sin, and it may fall into the danger of many Anglican confessions: that people will think the gospel merely offers temporary, week-by-week forgiveness. Psalm 98:8, 9 could have provided a good Bible link between the first hymn and the act of confession.

Assurance of Forgiveness—The assurance of forgiveness was a spontaneous declaration of God's commitment to forgive those who come to him in humility and confession, based on a Bible verse. (Psalm 98:1 could have been used again, or 1 Corinthians 2:2). It is difficult to ensure that false assurance is not given to the unconverted, while at the same time declaring forgiveness clearly to the converted and penitent.

Song—At this point in the service the smaller children were invited to come and help with the musical accompaniment and a variety of tambourines, drums, cymbals, triangles, rattles, and other similar musical instruments were offered. The song had been chosen, therefore, both for its lively beat and because its words connect naturally with the assurance of forgiveness. (Sometimes, instead of the children's musical accompaniment, the whole congregation might be invited to join in the actions of a child-friendly song like this.)

Notices and Collection—The collection came at this point with a clear introduction to the effect that there was no need to participate. ("People give in many different ways to many different things; and if it is not appropriate for you to give in this particular way at this particular time, please just pass the bag along when it comes to you, as many will be doing.") The collection was taken in that way (by passing bags through the congregation) because it is one way of emphasizing that our worship is the whole of our lives and not just certain ritual acts like singing or praying.

The notices were given at this point so that the children and leaders of the children's work would hear them and so that there is a natural focus in the middle of the service on the church's life through the rest of the week. Listening to the notices is no less spiritual than anything else that happens in a service. At the end of the notices the children (Trekkers) left. The term "Sunday school" is avoided because it has many unhelpful connotations (particularly linking the communication of the faith too closely to the overdeveloped educational system of the Western world).

Prayers—Having the intercessory prayers at this point had the disadvantage that it was difficult to start them against the noise of the children and their leaders leaving. It had the advantage that they could be longer and more complex than would have been appropriate for the more child-friendly, first part of the service.

THEME SONG **Foolish the wisdom of the world,**
its certainties denied
by wisdom of God's foolishness
that is Christ crucified.

Christ is my strength, my righteousness,
who shatters worldly pride.
God grant that I should nothing know
except Christ crucified.

He chose the weak to shame the strong,
the fool to shame the wise,
he lifted high the humble things
philosophers despise.
Christ is my strength. . . .

This foolish message of the cross
we preach, though some deride.
We fools for Jesus cannot boast
save in Christ crucified.
Christ is my strength. . . .

(Hilary Jolly)[5]

READING   1 Corinthians 1:17—2:5   Page 1144

SERMON   *God's Power*

We cannot experience God's power,
while we cling to our own human "wisdom"

1. *God became weak: Christ crucified*   1:17–25

2. *God chose the weak*   1:26–31

3. *God used weakness*   2:1–5

The Result: A Faith Resting on God's Power 2:5

COMMUNION

(When the bread comes to you where you sit, if you wish to share it please take a
*piece, pass the plate to your neighbor, perhaps with the words **"Given for you,"***
and then eat your bread. When the cup reaches you, please take a sip, and then
*pass it to your neighbor, perhaps with the words **"Shed for you."** If you do not*
want to share the communion, please pass both on. During the administration
there will be some quiet singing. Please join in if you would like to.)

---

5. © Jubilate Hymns Ltd. Admin. by Hope Publishing Company, Carol Stream, IL
60188. All rights reserved. Used by permission.

Theme Song—This song had been written especially by two members of the congregation to support the sermon series on 1 Corinthians. Both words and tune had been critically reviewed and commented on by others, and the song was sung each Sunday, with various verses being added and others removed, as the sermons progressed through Paul's letter (e.g., an alternative verse for 1 Corinthians 5):

Let not the yeast of sin and shame
work in the bread of Christ.
Jesus, the spotless lamb of God
for us was sacrificed.

Reading—The theme song had already focused the congregation on the passage in Paul's letter to the Corinthians that was to be preached on. The reading overlapped with the previous week (which had ended at 1 Corinthians 1:25) in order to help the congregation grasp the flow of the letter.

The reader encouraged the congregation to follow the reading in the copies of the New International Version of the Bible that were already on the seats.

Sermon—The title of this sermon had been changed from the original version on the church's program. As the preacher grappled with the text in his preparation, he had decided that the planned title was not appropriate. The sermon endeavored to pick up on the previous week's sermon (point 1). It was a straightforward exposition of the verses, but it was directed specifically to the non-Christian present as well as to the Christian. It was approximately twenty minutes in length because this was a communion service (and there was a specific reference to communion contained in the sermon).

Communion—The long paragraph in brackets and italics was necessary to explain to visitors and outsiders how the administration of communion would take place so that they would not be anxious about being taken by surprise or about being embarrassed. The leader gave a warm welcome to the Lord's Table to all believers, while warning the congregation of the serious consequences of receiving the bread and the wine inappropriately. He tried to do this in a friendly and well-reasoned way.

A disadvantage of this service was the abrupt shift from the end of the sermon into the communion. The leader tried to lessen that sense of abruptness by allowing a brief time of silence and using a Bible verse to focus the congregation on the Lord's Supper.

PRAYER OF HUMBLE ACCESS

[Together]

We do not presume
to come to this your table, merciful Lord,
trusting in our own righteousness,
but in your abundant and great mercies.
We are not worthy even
to gather up the crumbs under your table.
But you are the same Lord who delights in showing mercy.
Grant us therefore, gracious Lord,
so to eat this bread and drink this wine
that our bodies and souls
may be made clean by Christ's body and blood
and that we may evermore dwell in him, and he in us. Amen

PRAYER OF THANKSGIVING

[Together]

Almighty God, our heavenly Father,
we thank you that in your tender mercy
you gave your only Son Jesus Christ
to suffer death upon the cross for our redemption;
he made there a full atonement for the sins of the whole world,
offering once for all his one sacrifice of himself;
he instituted, and in his holy gospel commanded us to continue,
a perpetual memory of his precious death until he comes again.

In the same night that he was betrayed,
he took bread and gave you thanks;
he broke it, and gave it to his disciples, saying,
"Take, eat; this is my body which is given for you;
do this in remembrance of me."
In the same way, after supper he took the cup and gave
you thanks;
he gave it to them, saying, "Drink this, all of you;
this is my blood of the new covenant, which is shed for you
and for many for the forgiveness of sins.
Do this, as often as you drink it, in remembrance of me."
Amen.

THE ADMINISTRATION

SONG

It's your blood that cleanses me,
it's your blood that gives me life.
It's your blood that paid the price
in redeeming sacrifice;
and washes me whiter than the snow, than the snow,
Lord Jesus, God's precious sacrifice.

Prayer of Humble Access—He then invited the congregation to join together in a Prayer of Humble Access, slightly adapted to strengthen the theology. The prayer served as a valuable reminder of the basis on which we receive the bread and wine at communion.

Between the Prayer of Humble Access and the Prayer of Thanksgiving, the leader used some of the verses known as the **"Comfortable Words"** from the Anglican communion service (Matt 11:28; John 3:16; 1 Tim. 1:15; 1 John 2:1).

Prayer of Thanksgiving—The leader invited the congregation to join him in saying this prayer (the *Alternative Service Book* 1980s modern version of Cranmer's prayer). It was said together to avoid suggesting that the leader is a "priest" who turns the bread and wine into the body and blood of Christ by his words. The aim was to focus solely on the atonement rather than on various other parts of the ministry of Christ and works of God or on what we offer to God.

The Administration—At the end of the Prayer of Thanksgiving, the leader used an invitation to the Lord's Table: *"Draw near with faith; let us eat and drink in remembrance that Jesus died for us, and feed on him in our hearts by faith with thanksgiving,"* during which the stewards came forward and distributed the bread and wine throughout the building. A large number of stewards were used in order to abbreviate the administration as much as possible.

Song—During the administration this song was sung, at first very softly by the musicians, starting a few minutes into the administration. The words focused the congregation on the meaning of communion, and the verse was repeated until everyone had received the bread and wine. Gradually more members of the congregation joined the musicians in singing it.

PRAYER

[Together]   **Almighty God, we offer you our souls and bodies,
to be a living sacrifice, through Jesus Christ our Lord.
Send us out into the world in the power of your Spirit,
to live and work to your praise and glory. Amen.**

HYMN   **To God be the glory! Great things he has done;**
so loved he the world that he gave us his Son
who yielded his life an atonement for sin,
and opened the life-gate that all may go in.

> Praise the Lord, praise the Lord!
> let the earth hear his voice;
> praise the Lord, praise the Lord!
> let the people rejoice;
> O come to the Father
> through Jesus the Son
> and give him the glory;
> great things he has done.

O perfect redemption, the purchase of blood!
to every believer the promise of God;
the vilest offender who truly believes,
that moment from Jesus a pardon receives.
> Praise the Lord . . .

Great things he has taught us, great things he has done
and great our rejoicing through Jesus the Son:
but purer and higher and greater will be
our wonder, our gladness, when Jesus we see!
> Praise the Lord . . .

FINAL PRAYER

[Coffee and tea will now be brought to you where you sit.]

Prayer—This prayer was said together at the end of the administration because it focuses on our right response to the Lord's Supper: worship in the world.

Hymn—This familiar and traditional hymn made a good conclusion to the service. It has a rousing tune; it refocused the congregation both on the truths of the sermon ("so loved he the world that he gave us his Son") and on the communion ("who yielded his life an atonement for sin"), as well as on the invitation to respond ("O come to the Father through Jesus the Son, and give him the glory; great things he has done").

Final Prayer—The final prayer was a blessing on the same theme as the sermon.

After a silent pause, during which one of the service leaders and the preacher went to the door of the church, the musicians began to play quietly and tea and coffee were brought out on trays by the stewards to the congregation where they were sitting. (This allows a quicker distribution of the drinks and seems to encourage more conversation among the congregation than inviting them to go to collect tea and coffee themselves from a trolley or a kitchen hatch. It is also more effective in encouraging the congregation to stay and talk to one another.)

Conclusion

While it could clearly have been better in places, the service seemed to work well. It was a bit over an hour long (and the sermon had to be limited to 20 minutes to allow that).

It was led by four different people (including the preacher), the first of whom was a female member of staff (curate), who gave the welcome at the beginning and led through to the children's song ("Jesus' love is very wonderful"). A male member of staff gave the notices and invited the Trekkers to leave; the prayers were led by a young woman in the congregation, who also introduced the theme song and read the passage from 1 Corinthians; the vicar preached the sermon and led the communion through to the administration; the post-communion prayer and final hymn and prayer were led by the female curate. Having different leaders for various parts of the service allowed more concentrated and careful preparation than would have been the case had one person done all (or most of) the leading.

One weakness of the service was the difficulty experienced in holding all its various parts together, particularly with the emphasis on being child-friendly before the notices, then focusing on adults during prayers and the sermon, followed by the communion. The careful but brief links between different items provided continuity and "spiritual logic" that would otherwise have been missing.

Second Sample Service Outline

5:00 P.M.   8 November 1998

Guest Service with Pathfinders (11–14) and crèche facilities

[Welcome]

HYMN **My song is love unknown,**
my Saviour's love for me;
love to the loveless shown
that they might lovely be:
but who am I, that for my sake
my Lord should take frail flesh and die?

He came from heaven's throne
salvation to bestow;
but they refused, and none
the longed-for Christ would know:
this is my friend, my friend indeed,
who at my need his life did spend.

With angry shouts, they have
my dear Lord done away;
a murderer they save,
the Prince of life they slay!
Yet willingly he bears the shame
that through his name all might be free.

Here might I stay and sing
of him my soul adores;
never was love, dear King,
never was grief like yours!
This is my friend in whose sweet praise
I all my days could gladly spend.

(S. Crossman © in this version Jubilate Hymns) CCL Licence 1584[7]

CONFESSION Lord the only God,
compassionate and gracious,
slow to anger and full of love:
be with us now.

---

7. Admin. by Hope Publishing Company, Carol Stream, IL 60188. All rights reserved.
Used by permission.

Commentary

Heading—This was the first Sunday in a week of evangelistic events. The pattern of the service was not radically different from normal, but the leading was geared to outsiders.

The evening service time of 5:00 P.M. had proved good in the life of this particular church, although it had been discovered providentially, owing to a need to relieve pressure on the morning service by persuading more of the congregation to attend in the evening.

Crèche facilities meant a room with toys (rather than a staffed crèche). There was a loud-speaker in the room transmitting the service and the sermon. This was not a satisfactory arrangement for newcomers to the church who came with a small baby, although it was sufficient for some of the regular mothers.

Welcome—The vicar began leading this service and led through to the Assurance of Forgiveness. The instructions for leading stressed the need to "keep everything outsider-friendly and jargon-free."

Hymn—This hymn was a mistake for the start of a Guest Service. It was too subjective and pushed guests to sing words of faith they may not have believed. It is, however, a classic, which is outsider-friendly. Only four of the six verses were sung: the overall aim at the Guest Service was to keep well within an hour.

Confession and Assurance of Forgiveness—This had the same problems as all general confessions when non-Christians are present; and it needed to be introduced carefully, discouraging people from praying it without faith and indicating that confession is a great benefit for God's people.

Judge of the guilty,
we have been stubborn,
we have rebelled against you:
forgive our wickedness and sin,
and receive us as your own;
through Jesus Christ our Lord. Amen.

(From *Bible Praying,* Michael Perry, Fount. # 69)

ASSURANCE OF FORGIVENESS

SKETCH   "Do Not Touch"

NOTICES   *[Collection]*

(Pathfinders leave)

SONG   **How deep the Father's love for us,**
                how vast beyond all measure,
                that he should give his only Son
                to make a wretch his treasure.
                How great the pain of searing loss:
                the Father turns his face away
                as wounds which mar the chosen one
                bring many sons to glory.

                Behold the man upon the cross,
                my sin upon his shoulders;
                ashamed, I hear my mocking voice
                call out among the scoffers.
                It was my sin that held him there
                until it was accomplished;
                his dying breath has brought me life—
                God knows that it is finished.

                I will not boast in anything,
                no wealth, no power, no wisdom;
                but I will boast in Jesus Christ,
                his death and resurrection.
                Why should I gain from his reward?
                I cannot give an answer,
                but this I know with all my heart,
                his wounds have paid my ransom.

                (Stuart Townsend © 1995 Kingsways Thankyou Music) CCL Licence 1584[8]

PRAYERS

---

8. All rights reserved. Reprinted here by permission.

Sketch—This sketch was a mime: an actor passed by a chair with a notice on it saying DO NOT TOUCH. She returned, intrigued, touched it tentatively, and found her hand stuck to it. She got increasingly stuck to it and was eventually sitting in the chair unable to move. Another actor saw her predicament, pointed her to God's Word, and she was released. It was far stronger in performance than it sounds on paper! The preacher referred to it in the sermon.

Notices—A male member of staff began to lead at this point and led through to the prayers. He was particularly aware of outsiders present and therefore of the need to be brief and not to use names or expressions that were unintelligible to the nonmember. There was a collection at the beginning of the notices. Despite a disclaimer (that there was no need to participate in the collection), it was probably a mistake to include this in a Guest Service.

Song—This starts as a good, objective, modern song in the first verse, although it becomes more subjective toward the end and was another unusual choice for a Guest Service. With regard to the second verse, it is not strictly true that "my sin" held Jesus to the Cross "until it was accomplished"—it was actually the wrath and justice and mercy of God "that held him there," and an appropriate adjustment to the words might have been made here.

Prayers—Just three prayers were prayed, each short and outsider-friendly. They included prayer for the needs of the world and matters outside the life of this particular church so that they were outward-looking and easily understood.

INTERVIEW / TESTIMONY

SONG   **The Lord my shepherd rules my life**
and gives me all I need;
he leads me by refreshing streams,
in pastures green I feed.

The Lord revives my failing strength
he makes my joy complete;
and in right paths, for his name's sake,
he guides my faltering feet.

Though in a valley dark as death
no evil makes me fear;
your shepherd's staff protects my way,
for you are with me there.

While all my enemies look on
you spread a royal feast;
you fill my cup, anoint my head,
and treat me as your guest.

Your goodness and your gracious love
pursue me all my days;
your house, O Lord, shall be my home—
your name, my endless praise.

To Father, Son, and Spirit, praise!
to God whom we adore
be worship, glory, power and love,
both now and evermore.

(from Psalm 23)
(© in this version Christopher Idle/Jubilate Hymns)[9]

READING   Genesis 3:14–24

SERMON   *Paradise Lost*

HYMN   **I cannot tell why he whom angels worship**
should set his love upon the sons of men,
or why as shepherd he should seek the wanderers,
to bring them back, they know not how or when.
But this I know, that he was born of Mary
when Bethlehem's manger was his only home,
and that he lived at Nazareth and laboured;
and so the saviour, saviour of the world, has come.

---

9. Admin. by Hope Publishing Company, Carol Stream, IL 60188. All rights reserved.
Used by permission.

Interview / Testimony—This was one of a series of testimonies during the week of evangelistic events, and in this case it was from a young woman in her twenties who had recently been converted. The testimony had been prepared in quite considerable detail, and she had been encouraged to be sharply focused both theologically and in terms of time.

Song—This is a modern version of the 23rd Psalm, which was sung to "Brother James Air," a secular folk tune, rather than to the somewhat churchy "Crimond." It was a mistake at a Guest Service, because although folk tunes can make a new hymn/song seem familiar, it is disconcerting when the words or tune of something familiar are tampered with. The 23rd Psalm sung to "Crimond" is one of the very few pieces of church music very widely known outside the church. Any newcomer or guest who saw the song on the order of service would have assumed it was "Crimond" and been put out to discover that both words and tune had been changed.

Reading—This passage fitted into a sermon series on the early chapters of Genesis in which the church was engaged. It also fitted the evangelistic nature of a Guest Service. It was read by a young woman, which may have tipped the gender balance of the service slightly too far toward women.

Sermon—The visiting speaker for the week was prepared to fit into the sermon series, but he handled the passage in a way that drew out its gospel appeal. Enclosed in every order of service was a response slip, inviting individuals to indicate whether they wished to pursue matters further by joining one of a number of "Discovering Christianity" courses that were about to start in the church. The preacher suggested that people complete the cards and leave them in bins at the back of the church as they left. He also suggested that there might be those who would like to pursue things further that same night and would like to stay for a brief after-meeting, at the end of the service.

Hymn—At this point the vicar took over to finish leading the service. This hymn was a good choice because it rehearsed the gospel again in traditional hymn form to the familiar "Londonderry Air" ("Danny Boy"). The hymn is helpfully agnostic in the first half of each verse but clearly objective about the facts of the gospel in the second half of each verse. We sang only the first, second, and third verses—it would have been too long for the end of a Guest Service had we sung all four.

I cannot tell how silently he suffered
as with his peace he graced this place of tears,
nor how his heart upon the cross was broken,
the crown of pain to three and thirty years.
But this I know, he heals the broken-hearted
and takes our sin and calms our lurking fear,
and lifts the burden from the heavy-laden
for still the saviour, saviour of the world, is here.

I cannot tell how he will win the nations,
how he will claim his earthly heritage,
how satisfy the needs and aspirations
of east and west, of sinner and of sage.
But this I know, all flesh shall see his glory,
and he shall reap the harvest he has sown,
and some glad day his sun will shine in splendour
when he the saviour, saviour of the world, is known.

(W. Y. Fullerton) CCL Licence 1584

FINAL PRAYER

AFTER-MEETING

[Coffee and tea will now be brought to you where you sit.]

Final Prayer—This prayer focused on the gospel truths with the undecided in mind.

After-Meeting—This was held in a corner of the church, starting fairly promptly after the end of the service. Chairs were turned in a semicircle with their backs to the rest of the building, and the preacher spoke to a small group for a further ten minutes, explaining how they could respond to the gospel there and then, and praying a model prayer for them to follow.

Conclusion

This service did not work particularly well. The planning was over-hurried, and the principles that should govern a Guest Service were frequently ignored. It is always hard to detect this in advance, but the experience of a badly planned service confirms the need to take the principles seriously and work them out carefully in practice.

Third Sample Service Outline

10:30 A.M.   3 January 1999

United Family Service with Young People's Orchestra and crèches

[Welcome]

HYMN
> **As with gladness men of old**
> did the guiding star behold,
> as with joy they hailed its light,
> leading onward, gleaming bright:
> so, most gracious Lord, may we
> evermore your splendour see.
>
> As with joyful steps they sped
> to that lowly manger bed,
> there to bend the knee before
> Christ whom heaven and earth adore:
> so with ever-quickening pace
> may we seek your throne of grace.
>
> Holy Jesus, every day
> keep us in the narrow way,
> and when earthly things are past,
> bring our ransomed souls at last;
> where they need no star to guide,
> where no clouds your glory hide.
>
> In the heavenly city bright
> none shall need created light—
> you, its light, its joy, its crown,
> you its sun which goes not down;
> there for ever may we sing
> alleluias to our king.
>
> (W. C. Dix © in this version Jubilate Hymns) CCL Licence 1584[10]

---

10. Admin. by Hope Publishing Company, Carol Stream, IL 60188. All rights reserved. Used by permission.

Commentary

Heading—This was a service attended by all ages throughout with the exception of the crèches (one for babes in arms and one for toddlers). Such a service is necessary approximately once a month to allow those who teach in the children's work of the church to have a break.

The aim is to provide a service that is child-friendly but not childish and that lasts around 45 minutes.

Welcome–The vicar began the service. He also mentioned at this point the "Welcome Card" that could be filled in by any who had begun to come to the church regularly but had not yet been identified and welcomed by the staff. The word *Welcome* was not put on the order of service because it can seem forced, but this service began with a customary introduction, pointing out that it was a "United Family Service" and explaining that it might be noisier than usual but that this was regarded as perfectly acceptable. A number of child musicians were involved, playing in what was known as the Young People's Orchestra, and they were welcomed at the outset as well as visitors and guests. The provision of the crèches was particularly emphasized.

Hymn—This hymn was appropriate for the season and fitted with the Bible passage. It was a familiar and appropriately up-tempo start for the service. It was introduced with a quotation from Matthew 2:1–2.

CONFESSION SONG

[Together]

**For the things that I've done wrong,
things that I remember long,
hurting you and those I love,
I am very sorry, God.**

**Help me Father now I pray,
take all sin and guilt away,
cleanse the secrets of my heart,
fill my life in every part.**

ASSURANCE OF FORGIVENESS

CAROL

It's not the bright light but it's the starlight
that showed the shepherds where the baby lay.
It's not the presents but it's the giving
of the Lord to us on Christmas day.
He gave Jesus, Jesus, let's stand up for Jesus;
He's the reason we celebrate this season.
Jesus is the Saviour we've been waiting for.

Jesus the Saviour of the world is the way,
so I'll follow the Saviour of the world.
With all the rushing and all the worry
that's in our busy lives from day to day
Lord, may we shine out and may we burn bright
as lamps that point to you always.
Jesus, Jesus, give your heart to Jesus,
He's the reason we celebrate this season
Jesus is the one we worship and adore.

(Anita Davidson)

NOTICES   *[Collection]*

PRAYERS

CAROL

We three kings of Orient are,
bearing gifts we travel afar—
field and fountain, moor and mountain—
following yonder star.

> O star of wonder, star of night,
> star with royal beauty bright:
> westward leading,
> still proceeding,
> guide us to your perfect light!

Confession Song—This song had been written some years previously by a member of the congregation to meet the need for a serious but child-friendly form of confession. It was sung sitting down. The tune was very easy for those who had never heard it before.

Carol—This was a new carol written by a member of the congregation. It is valuable to sing songs written by members of the church because it encourages all church members to think what talents they have that they might use to the benefit of others.

Notices—At this point the wife of a staff member took over leading the service. The notices began with birthday cards being given out to children whose birthdays came in that week. (Had any of their birthdays actually fallen on the Sunday, a special birthday song would have been sung to them:

A happy birthday to you,
a happy birthday to you,
every day of the year
may you know Jesus near.
A happy birthday to you,
a happy birthday to you,
And the best one you've ever had.)

Prayers—The prayers were led by a parish assistant. There were just three prayers, and they were short and simple.

Carol—This carol again fitted the passage for the sermon. Its familiarity compensated for the obscurity of some of its words. It was sung by the whole congregation throughout (with no solos for the three kings). The fact that there is no biblical basis for there being three visitors, all of them kings, was pointed out in the sermon, but it is a point of minimal spiritual significance.

Born a king on Bethlehem's plain—
gold I bring to crown him again:
king for ever, ceasing never,
over us all to reign.

   O star of wonder . . .

Frankincense to offer have I—
incense tells of Deity nigh;
prayer and praising all are raising:
worship him—God most high!

   O star of wonder . . .

Myrrh is mine—its bitter perfume
breathes a life of gathering gloom:
sorrowing, sighing, bleeding, dying,
sealed in the stone-cold tomb.

   O star of wonder . . .

Glorious now behold him arise—
king and God and sacrifice!
Heaven sings "Alleluia!"
"Alleluia!" the earth replies.
   O star of wonder . . .

READING   Matthew 2:1–12

            (Printed out in full from the *Good News Bible*)

CAROL   **The virgin Mary had a baby boy,**
the virgin Mary had a baby boy,
the virgin Mary had a baby boy
and they say that his name is Jesus.
   He come from the glory,
   he come from the glorious kingdom;
   (Yes!) he come from the glory,
   he come from the glorious kingdom:
      O yes, believer!
      O yes, believer!
   He come from the glory,
   he come from the glorious kingdom.

The angels sang when the baby was born,
the angels sang when the baby was born,
the angels sang when the baby was born
and they sang that his name is Jesus.
   He come from the glory . . .

Reading—Because this was a United Family Service, the passage was read from the *Good News Bible* and printed out in full on the order of service. No reference was made to the NIV Bibles on the seats.

Carol—This was an appropriately familiar carol to be easily sung at this service and yet has a beat that was suitable for the younger children to come forward and join in with the orchestra by beating tambourines, cymbals, castanets, drums, triangles, and so forth. (It would have been possible to add or substitute a verse—"The wise men came where the baby was born"—to match the theme of the service.) The children then stayed up front for the sermon.

The shepherds came where the baby was born,
the shepherds came where the baby was born,
the shepherds came where the baby was born
and they say that his name is Jesus.
He come from the glory ...

(West Indian © collected Boosey & Hawkes) CCL Licence 1584

SERMON   *The Star in the East*

CAROL   **The first nowell the angel did say**
was to Bethlehem's shepherds in fields as they lay;
in fields where they lay keeping their sheep
on a cold winter's night that was so deep:
    Nowell, nowell, nowell, nowell,
    born is the king of Israel!

Then wise men from a country far
looked up and saw a guiding star;
they traveled on by night and day
to reach the place where Jesus lay:
    Nowell, nowell ...

At Bethlehem they entered in,
on bended knee they worshipped him;
they offered there in his presence
their gold and myrrh and frankincense:
    Nowell, nowell ...

Then let us all with one accord
sing praises to our heavenly Lord;
for Christ has our salvation wrought
and with his blood our life has bought:
    Nowell, nowell ...

(© in this version Word and Music/Jubilate Hymns) CCL Licence 1584[11]

FINAL PRAYER

[Coffee and tea will now be brought to you where you sit.]

---

11. Admin. by Hope Publishing Company, Carol Stream, IL 60188. All rights reserved. Used by permission.

Sermon—This was preached by a male member of staff (the student worker), who spoke for 12 minutes, explaining the story of the Magi and applying it in ways appropriate both to the small children, who were gathered around his feet, and to the rest of the congregation. He used colorful pictures on a Velcro board to keep the attention of the young (along with other visual aids, like a large silver star hanging from the rafters of the church). The sermon focused particularly on the contrast between the reaction of King Herod and "everyone else in Jerusalem" (v. 3) and that of the visitors from the East. It interpreted a familiar post-Christmas passage but avoided being predictable.

Carol—Once again the familiarity of this carol outweighed the obscurity of its language (few church members know what "nowell" means!). It was introduced by the preacher.

Final Prayer—This was led by the staff member's wife who had given the notices. It was a simple prayer, easily followed by young children.

Conclusion

This service came at a fairly quiet time in the life of the church, and it also came after the church had had a number of United Family Services in succession (the children's work having had a break over the Christmas period). Nevertheless, it worked well, lasting 45 minutes, with a nice blend of familiarity and freshness, and a fast and lively pace maintained throughout. Leading that was up-tempo without being flippant played an important part in helping the service to work well.

Resources for Planning Services:

The *Book of Common Prayer*

An English Prayer Book, ed. Church Society (Oxford: Oxford University Press, 1994)

John Mason, *A Service for Today's Church* (Mosman: St. Clement's Anglican Church, 1997)

Michael Perry, *Bible Praying* (London: Harper Collins Religious, 1992)

Michael Perry, ed., *Church Family Worship* (London: Hodder and Stoughton, 1986)

A Service of the Word and Affirmations of Faith (London: Church House Publishing, 1994)

Patterns for Worship (London: Church House Publishing, 1995)

Chapter 3

FREE CHURCH WORSHIP

The Challenge of Freedom

R. KENT HUGHES

*U*nlike the Anglican Mark Ashton and the Presbyterian Tim Keller, I came to my Reformed convictions and theology of worship apart from a defined denominational tradition.

My earliest religious memories extend back to 1949 when my Southern Baptist grandmother, Rose Hughes, took me as a six-year-old to a huge tent on the corner of Washington and Hill Streets in Los Angeles to hear a young evangelist named Billy Graham. The dressed-up crowd, the young evangelist's blue eyes radiating in the spotlights, and cowboy Stuart Hamblin singing "Just a Closer Walk With Thee" are etched on my memory.

During the following years my family trekked in from the suburbs to worship at Vermont Avenue Presbyterian Church. It was there, hushed and seated next to my mother along with other reverent worshipers in the dark, Scottish-kirk ambience of that old church, that I began to sense the transcendence of God and to be drawn to Christ.

But it wasn't until I was a teenager in the mid 1950s that I came to Christ—and then it was through the ministry of mission-minded evangelical Quakers who had recovered their gospel commitments in the Wesleyan revivals of the late nineteenth century. In retrospect, I see that their corporate worship was an eclectic mix of Methodist, Nazarene, and Baptist traditions—decidedly Free Church. Aside from a thirty-second time of silence (a vestige of the old silent meetings), the services were indistinguishable from those of our Baptist and other Free Church neighbors. Sunday mornings were a warm blend of gospel songs and choruses, perhaps a hymn, a choir number, and a sermon.

Quite frankly, "worship" was never a concern; it was evangelism that was important. So apart from my regular attendance at services, my considerable energies were devoted to youth work and the outreach of Youth for Christ for which, after graduation from high school, I worked as a club director. I have searched my memories of those years, and I cannot recall having a single reflective thought about corporate worship. I certainly never gave any thought as to the purpose of our Lord's Day gatherings, other than as a venue for preaching.

It wasn't that as a young man I didn't think theologically. Quite the contrary. As a teenager my soul was so ravished by the book of Romans and the truth of God's sovereignty that "the doctrines of grace" became the backbone of my theology—as they remain today. My newfound Calvinism enhanced my love for God and his Word and fueled my evangelistic fervor. But in regard to corporate worship? I simply made no connection.

My seminary and youth pastoring years coincided roughly with the 1960s, the tie-dyed, bell-bottomed, guitar-toting, and (for Christians) Bible-toting decade. My students carried immense New American Standard Bibles covered with fluffy rabbit skins! Positively, on the one hand, fresh winds swept across the church, so that everything was questioned and subjected to the painful tests of authenticity and relevance. Much of the effect was salutary as vapid old gospel songs were dropped and unadorned Bible teaching replaced homiletical discourse. And in some quarters, music and corporate worship focused more on God.

On the other hand, irreverence became widespread. Congregational prayers were often a mindless stream-of-consciousness offered in a "kicked-back" cannabis tone. Mantra-like music was employed to mesmerize worshipers, and preachers were replaced by "communicators" who offered bromides strung together with a series of relational anecdotes.

It was in the midst of this as a youth pastor that my theology began to kick in with questions relevant to this chapter: What do the Scriptures have to say about corporate worship? What does our sovereign, holy God think of our gathered worship services? How is Jesus Christ (our Creator, Sustainer, and Redeemer) glorified by this? Is this meeting Word-centered? How, then, is the Word read and preached and sung? What is this song actually saying? Are the lyrics biblical? Does the music support the lyrics? Is this entertainment or authentic worship?

These elementary questions took on special urgency for me in the 1970s when my wife and I were called to plant a church. Everything was new. There were no traditions other than the experiences that our varied congregation brought with them. And experiment we did! My Reformed convictions were the only constant.

During the 1980s and 90s, my philosophy and practice of worship underwent a continual tweaking in the congenial environment of College Church. This has produced some firm convictions and deep concerns about corporate worship in today's Free Church tradition. But before I express these, a brief profile of the church I have pastored for the last two decades is in order. College Church was founded by Jonathan Blanchard, an abolitionist and the first president of Wheaton College. He was a friend and disciple of New England's famous Beecher family, so the church was congregational—College Church of Christ. Naturally, College Church stands proudly in the Free Church tradition. In fact, its logo is a profile of the Mayflower, which celebrates its Puritan roots. In the 1930s, after many congregational churches had become Unitarian, the church severed its association with the denomination, and presently it has no affiliation other than with the National Association of Evangelicals. Free indeed!

Though College Church has always been separate from Wheaton College, its proximity to the campus has given it a significant ministry to students and faculty over the years. But today the bulk of the congregation is "thirty-something," and the church overflows with babies.

On one recent Sunday there were one hundred three-year-olds in the nursery! The church has been in an extended springtime. Some 117 missionaries have been commissioned by the church in the last decade, and nearly half of the church's budget goes to missions. Eleven short-term mission teams were sent out from the church this last year. Evangelism and missions are alive and well at College Church.

Sunday morning corporate worship at College Church is bibliocentric and traditional. The congregation is noted for its singing and hearty declaration of the Apostles' Creed. Music, prayers, Scripture reading, and testimonies are designed to increase congregational participation and edification under the unifying theme of the morning exposition. The evening corporate gathering is more casual and less structured, and the music is more eclectic in its service of the unifying scriptural theme.

I relate this positive picture to give weight to what I say. I fear that many in the Free Church tradition may be giving away the very heart of an effective ministry as they uncritically enfold seeker-sensitive corporate worship patterns.

Worship Is More Than Sunday

In recent years biblical theology has exercised a profound effect on my thinking with its nuanced emphasis on the order of biblical revelation in respect to the history of redemption. The writings of William Dumbrell and Graeme Goldsworthy have been particularly helpful in this respect.[1] For some time I have been in implicit agreement with Don Carson's assertion that New Testament worship encompasses all of life and that it is misleading to imagine it as only a corporate activity of the assembled church.

The biblical evidence is conclusive. Jesus' coming fulfilled the Scripture's promise of a new covenant (cf. Jer 31:31–34). And it is most significant that the entire text of this substantial prophecy is recorded in Hebrews 8:7–13, in the midst of a section (Heb 7–11) which asserts

---

1. Graeme Goldsworthy, *Gospel and Kingdom* (Sydney: Lancer, 1992), idem, *According to Plan* (InterVarsity, Lancer, 1991); W. J. Dumbrell, *Covenant and Creation* (Carlisle: Paternoster, 1984).

that there is no longer *sacrifice, priesthood,* or *temple* because all have been fulfilled in Christ.

The worship language of the Old Testament is now transmuted in the New Testament so that "worship" is a broader phenomenon, encompassing all of life. There is, as Carson says, a de-sacralization of space and time and food—or better, a re-sacralization of all things for the believer. There are no longer any sacred times or sacred spaces. Under the new covenant Christians are thus to worship all the time—in their individual lives, family lives, and when they come together for corporate worship. Corporate worship, then, is a particular expression of a life of perpetual worship.

The New Testament "cultus" is expressed in terms of our lives being living "holocausts," whole burnt offerings: "Therefore, I urge you, brothers, in view of God's mercy, to offer your bodies as living sacrifices, holy and pleasing to God—this is your spiritual act of worship" (Rom 12:1). This is what worship is: day-in-day-out living for Christ, the knees and heart perpetually bent in devotion and service.

The understanding that new covenant worship is centered in Christ, who is at once temple, priest, and sacrifice, argues for the Protestant and Free Church tradition over against the Orthodox, Roman Catholic, and Anglo-Catholic traditions. Since Christ is the temple, "sacred spaces" and consecrated grounds are a delusion. Since Christ is high priest according to the order of Melchizedek, the priesthood is superseded and obviated. Likewise, priestly vestments and clerical dress are out of date. Since Christ is the Lamb of God slain once for our sins, there is no justification for the Mass or for sacrificial accoutrements such as an altar or chasuble. These superseding new covenant realities should also serve as a warning to those in the Reformed tradition whose devotion to the "Regulative Principle" inclines them to draw from the cultus of the old covenant.

As to everyday living, the fact that Christian worship is to be coextensive with all of life suggests that care must be taken in the way we speak of it. To call our public meetings "worship" can unwittingly install a re-sacralization of time and space. It is better to employ terms like "corporate worship." Other unwieldy expressions can sometimes work—"believers worshiping together" or "Christians assembled in worship" or "the worship of gathered believers" or "the congregation assembled in worship"—but "corporate worship" or "gathered worship" works best for me.

Because worship is a way of life, you cannot worship corporately on the Lord's Day if you haven't been worshiping throughout the week—apart from repentance! Christians don't have a Sunday "worship switch," despite what is sometimes portrayed on television. Neither must we be allowed to think that "worship" is only a part of the service—as if singing and praise were worship in contrast to the preaching. And "worship leader?" What an odd term! Does the worship end when his or her part is done?

Certainly it is true that mutual edification is the hallmark of corporate worship, as David Peterson argues.[2] And edification must not be understood to be merely the cognitive reception of biblical truth through preaching. Of course, it is true that mutual edification takes place through preaching. But congregational singing, sitting together under the Word as it is read, contemplating God's Word sung, uniting in Word-centered congregational prayer, corporately confessing our faith, and rebuke and exhortation—all these edify.

Here we must understand that the togetherness of corporate worship aids edification. As Robert Rayburn explains:

> When there are a number of worshipers present, there is a participation in worship which is more intense than is the individual passion of any one of them when he is by himself. It is common knowledge that a mob is more cruel than any individual in it would be by himself. Similarly, the enjoyment of an elite company of music lovers at the symphony is more intense than that of a single music lover sitting by himself listening to the same music. God has so created man that there are deeper delights and more intense inspiration in the worshiping congregation than in individual devotion.[3]

---

2. David Peterson, *Engaging With God* (Leicester: Apollos, 1994), 114: "Although the edification of the church is a principle that should govern the thinking and behaviour of Christians in all circumstances, Paul normally employs this notion with reference to the activities of Christian assembly. When Christians gather together to minister to one another the truth of God in love, the church is manifested, maintained and advanced in God's way."

3. Robert G. Rayburn, *O Come, Let Us Worship* (Grand Rapids: Baker, 1984), 29, 30.

This intensifying effect of corporate worship enhances edification. In fact, edification will not flourish as it ought apart from it, because hearing God's Word amidst the corporate assent of a congregation intensifies the mind's engagement and reception of the truth. Likewise, participation in the community of belief intensifies taking the truth to heart. And then the example of the truth lived out moves the believer to live out the radical truth of God's Word. Corporate worship is essential to edification.

Thus, I have come to see that while all of life is worship, gathered worship with the body of Christ is at the heart of a life of worship. Corporate worship is intended by God to inform and elevate a life of worship. In this respect, I personally view how we conduct gathered worship as a matter of life and death.

The Irony of Freedom

There was a time when the Free Church tradition was the poor, outcast relative of the established Church of England; but today this is no longer the case, especially in North America, where the majority of Protestants (and the overwhelming majority of evangelicals) attend churches that conduct corporate worship in the Free Church tradition. More than fifty million American Protestants corporately worship in one of the variations of the Free Church tradition.[4] A cause for rejoicing? I think not.

There is no doubt about the principled beginnings of the Free Church tradition in early-seventeenth-century England as a protest against the ecclesiastical demand that they use the *Book of Common Prayer*. The designation "free," in fact, records the desires of both Separatists and Puritans to be free to order corporate worship according to God's Word.[5] The name "Puritan" recalls the closely parallel desire

---

4. James F. White, "The Missing Jewel of the Evangelical Church," *Reformed Journal* 34/6 (June 1986): 11.

5. The distinction between the Puritans and the Separatists is that the Puritans remained within the state church in the hope of effecting reform, while the Separatists pursued immediate reformation apart from the established church.

to reform Prayer Book worship according to the *"pure* Word of God."
The Separatists and Puritans were largely in agreement except for their
marked differences in attitude toward the established church. Indeed,
Horton Davies, the renowned authority on Puritan worship, includes
Presbyterians, some evangelical Anglicans, Congregationalists, and
Baptists under the Puritan rubric.[6] Significantly, the famous Puritans
of Cambridge University became a diverse lot. William Perkins and
Thomas Cartwright became Presbyterians; Thomas Goodwin and John
Cotton, independents; John Preston, a nonconforming Anglican; and
Richard Sibbes, a conformist.[7]

The penetrating critiques offered by Puritan and Free Church
leaders in their historical contexts were both substantial and salutary.
The seven points that follow are necessarily broad brush strokes and
lack the qualifications and subtleties of a detailed portrait; nevertheless, they do convey the essence of the critique.

1. Preaching

At the heart of the critique was the nature of preaching. The Anglican
preference for Prayer Book homilies was countered by the Puritan
insistence on weighty exposition of Scripture. The typical Puritan or
Free Church sermon was part of a continuous serial exposition of a
book or section of the Bible.

William Ames, whose *Marrow of Divinity* became the indispensable Puritan theological text, decried topical preaching. He insisted that
the sermon be drawn from the text.[8] Plain exposition was the Puritan
preachers' goal. "The plainer the better," wrote William Perkins in his
Arte of Prophecying. In the use of ostentation, he said, "we do not paint
Christ, but ... our own selves."[9] Because communicating the Word was
such a priority, their sermons were models of order, with clear headings and discernible skeletons that enhanced memorization.[10]

---

6. Horton Davies, *Christian Worship—Its History and Meaning* (New York:
Abingdon, 1959), 65.

7. J. I. Packer, *A Quest for Godliness* (Wheaton: Crossway, 1990), 280.

8. Leland Ryken, *Worldly Saints* (Grand Rapids: Zondervan, 1986), 98.

9. Quoted in ibid., 105.

10. Packer, *Quest for Godliness,* 285.

Application was taken to a new level by Perkins's classification of the types of people the minister must keep in mind for application and then by the catalog of types of application listed in the *Westminster Directory for Publick Worship*.[11] Such preaching was aimed to penetrate like arrows into the hearers' hearts. And such sermons were lengthy, prolix, passionate, and exhaustive—full of prophetic zeal and fire.

Because the Puritan and Free Church clergy took the sermon to new levels, an educated clergy became a must. The reason for the founding of Harvard College only a few years after the Puritans' coming to America was the fear of leaving "an illiterate ministry to the churches, when our present ministers shall lie in the dust."[12]

Notwithstanding the likes of John Donne and Lancelot Andrewes, this Word-centeredness gave the Puritans a massive intellectual and spiritual ascendancy over the typical Anglican clergyman who read his service from the Prayer Book.[13]

2. Scripture

The main Puritan/Free Church objection to the lectionary in the *Book of Common Prayer* was the joining together of brief disparate texts, which they contemptuously called "pistling and gospelling." In contrast, the Free Church tradition gave itself to the reading of full chapters of the Old and New Testaments.

3. Prayer

The Prayer Book's collects were rejected by the dissenters as "short cuts," and its responsive prayers were dismissed as "vain repetitions" or "tennis playing." In contrast, lengthy prayers offered extemporane-

---

11. Quoted in ibid., 287.

12. *New England's First Fruits,* the first history of Harvard College (1640).

13. Ryken, *Worldly Saints,* 95–96: "No doubt there are many exceptions to Samuel Johnson's linking of an age of ignorance with an age of ceremony, but it is indisputable that the Anglican practice of reading services from the Prayer Book instead of preaching sermons fostered an alarming ignorance among clergymen. John Hooper's inquiries uncovered 171 (out of 311) Anglican clergymen who could not recite the Ten Commandments, 33 of whom did not know where they were to be found. Thirty could not tell where the Lord's Prayer appears in the Bible, 27 could not name its author, and ten could not recite it."

ously or from a book became the practice in the Free Church tradition.[14] Ministers were encouraged to prepare well for such prayers.[15]

4. Singing

The Free Church tradition came to stress the need for the congregation to express their praise in hymns rather than leaving it to a professional choir as was typical among the Anglicans. It is a matter of record that most of the ten most often sung hymns in America between 1737 and 1960 have been from the Free Church tradition.[16]

5. Sacraments

Free Church advocates faulted the Prayer Book's "Order for Holy Communion" for: (a) not employing the Dominical words of institution (cf. 1 Cor 11:23–25), (b) its emphasis on individual participation as contradictory to the Lord's command, and (c) its allowing of unworthy reception of the Lord's Supper by not requiring an examination of the communicants. Kneeling at Communion was rejected as promoting the adoration of the elements and the doctrine of transubstantiation.[17]

Baptism was seen to be encrusted with unscriptural additions: crossing the child, private baptism, baptism by women, questions to the child, and the presence of godparents. (And of course the English

---

14. Davies, *Christian Worship—Its History and Meaning,* 67–69.

15. Ibid., 68.

16. Edith Blumhofer and Mark Noll, eds., *Singing the Lord's Song in a Strange Land: Hymnody and the History of Denominations and Religious Movements* (Champaign: University of Illinois Press, forthcoming), provide the database used by Stephen Marini, "The Evangelical Hymns Database," working paper, Institute for the Study of American Evangelicals, Wheaton College, 2000. The ten hymns most frequently published in the United States between 1737 and 1960 are (1) *Jesus Lover of My Soul,* (2) *Come We (Ye) That Love the Lord/We're Marching to Zion,* (3) *All Hail the Power of Jesus' Name,* (4) *How Firm a Foundation,* (5) *Alas and Did My Savior Bleed/At the Cross,* (6) *Am I a Soldier of the Cross,* (7) *Come Thou Fount of Every Blessing* (8) *There Is a Fountain Filled with Blood,* (9) *Rock of Ages Cleft for Me,* (10)—a five-way tie—*Blest Be the Tie That Binds; Guide Me O Thou Great Jehovah; Joy to the World; Just As I Am; Love Divine All Loves Excelling.* All but the ninth came from the Free Church tradition.

17. Horton Davies, *Worship of the English Puritans* (repr., Morgan, Pa.: Soli Deo Gloria Publications), 61, 70, 71.

Anabaptists understood the Scriptures to teach only believers' baptism by immersion.) Such were the convictions of the Pilgrim Fathers when they came to America.

6. Simplicity

The Separatists' radical opposition to set forms of worship and their example of liturgical simplification greatly influenced the Puritans and other Free Church expressions toward simplicity in corporate worship. This simplicity moved them away not only from the Anglican tradition but also from the practices of the continental Reformed churches. This movement to simplicity was so profound that it fostered a distinctive church architecture, as is seen in the meetinghouses of New England.

7. Vestments

The Free Church tradition rejected vestments as being Aaronical and unsuitable for ministers of the new covenant.[18]

Free Indeed!

When these Free Church distinctives (about preaching, Scripture, prayer, singing, sacraments, simplicity, and vestments) were carried to North America by their English and Scottish forebears, the effects on corporate worship were largely beneficial. Pastors were free to dress like their congregations, perhaps donning a simple black Geneva gown for preaching. They were free to order their Lord's Day meetings with biblical simplicity. They were free to structure their God-centered worship around the centrality of the Word of God, publicly reading extended passages from the Bible, preaching weighty sermons from the text. Devout preachers who knew their Bible and their people were free to offer extemporaneous prayer from their hearts with an immediacy that set prayers rarely attain. They were free to administer communion and baptisms with chaste simplicity according to the theological dictates of Scripture as they understood them.

---

18. Ibid., 26, 47, 48, 55, 48, but especially pp. 59, 60, which give a trenchant summary of the radical Puritan critique.

At its best, the corporate worship of the Free Churches was radically biblical, ever more scriptural and authentic. Certainly there was some regrettable iconoclasm, and sometimes they went too far and abused their freedoms. Who today can read the 1662 *Book of Common Prayer* and not appreciate its excellencies?[19] Who with Bible in hand can defend the radical Separatists' extremes? But the Puritans and their Free Church friends reached a certain consistency. They were energized by the unshakable belief that the Word of God is the sole guide for directing corporate worship. Free Church worship was patterned on the Bible and nothing but the Bible.

Free-fall to Pragmatism

For more than 150 years the Free Church tradition operated on the "Scripture only" principle. The last two centuries brought change. In America, where the Free Church tradition had once meant the freedom to order corporate worship according to the Scriptures, it came to mean the freedom to order such worship as one pleased or as one felt it would work best. As James White describes it, "The 'freedom' of the Free Church worship became not so much freedom to follow God's word, but freedom to do what worked."[20] In short, Free Church biblicism deteriorated into Free Church pragmatism. The great proponent of this was the nineteenth-century revivalist Charles G. Finney, who promoted the revival system of "new measures," which if followed, he promised, would bring a harvest of souls.

The result of this de-biblicizing of corporate worship was that in many quarters it was reduced to "a revivalist message with opening

---

19. Notwithstanding the Puritan criticisms, the *Book of Common Prayer* of 1662 is saturated with Scripture. It is Thomas Cranmer's attempt to express Reformation theology in liturgical form so that the people would receive scriptural truth in their heads and hearts. It was meant to be a Protestant liturgy for a Protestant Church. Indeed, could any words be more "Protestant" than those prescribed for the minister as he administers the bread and the cup? "Take and eat this in remembrance that Christ died for thee, and feed on him in thy heart by faith with thanksgiving. . . . Drink this in remembrance that Christ's Blood was shed for thee, and be thankful."

20. White, "The Missing Jewel," 15.

exercises." The structure of corporate worship became: (1) the preliminaries, (2) the sermon, and (3) the invitation. This three-part organization became the order in most Baptist, independent, Methodist, and some Presbyterian congregations. Singing and musical selection were made in regard to their effect rather than their content. Gospel songs (celebrating experience) often supplanted hymns to God. Scripture reading was reduced so as not to prolong the "preliminaries." Prayers were shortened or even deleted for the same reason. As to the sermon, the careful interaction with the biblical text so treasured by the Puritans was in many instances replaced with a freewheeling extemporaneous discourse. After all, the Bible had become the optional resource for the sermon rather than the source for the whole of corporate worship.[21] Frontier Baptists, for example, would countenance no preacher who used notes.[22]

The descent from biblicism to pragmatism was also accompanied by a slide into anthropocentrism. Baptist historian T. R. McKibbens writes:

> Perhaps the hymns more than any other medium of worship reflect the shift from theocentrism to anthropocentrism. The Baptist hymnals published between 1784 and 1807 were notably theocentric, giving God the leading role in the drama of worship and salvation. Later hymnals, especially those published in the nineteenth century, were characteristically anthropocentric, with a tendency to define the drama of salvation more in terms of human response rather than divine initiative.[23]

The congenital twins of pragmatism and anthropocentrism have vastly influenced twentieth-century Free Church corporate worship. What McKibbens describes of Baptist practices has been generally true across the Free Church tradition. Corporate worship has taken the form of something done *for* an audience as opposed to something

---

21. James F. White, "Where the Reformation Went Wrong," *Christian Century*, (27 October 1982), 1074.

22. T. R. McKibbens Jr., "Our Baptist Heritage in Worship," *Review and Expositor* 80 (1983): 64.

23. Ibid., 65.

done *by* a congregation. And in many places it has come to be regarded as entertainment, as the egregious terms "stage," "program," and "musical number" suggest.[24] It is not too much to say that some preachers have debased the sermon to a form of mass entertainment.

Today the "seeker-sensitive" movement at its worst has *consciously* cultivated anthropocentrism and pragmatism. And my concern is that it could, given enough time or the same trajectory, lead to post-Christian evangelicalism. The issue of how corporate worship is to be conducted is of utmost importance. Because of this, I have discerned six distinctives that must inform and control Free Church corporate worship, and all of life as worship.

Christian Worship: Its Distinctives

The six distinctives of Christian worship anticipate and indeed demand one another. A full exposition of any one distinctive would necessarily touch upon the others. Here, as we move through the essential distinctives of corporate worship, their bouquet will become increasingly evident and, I think, compelling. Because all of life for the Christian must be worship, these distinctives must inform life in its totality. But here the emphasis is on how these distinctives must shape corporate worship, which is, of course, central to a life of worship.

1. Worship Is God-centered

It can be inaccurate to characterize any form of Christian worship as "human-focused" because if it is consistently so (avoiding any God focus), it cannot be Christian. But the term is appropriate for making distinctions regarding where modern churches begin when setting the trajectory of their corporate worship services.

The human-focused model begins with what its proponents consider to be the average person on the street and asks, "How can we design our corporate worship so that it will be least offensive and most inviting to the unchurched?" The motivation (and it is clearly noble) is evangelism. It must also be said that the human-focused trajectory may

---

24. Ibid., 66.

be accompanied by an emphasis that is more or less on God. It is the "less" that is of greatest concern.

The human-centered approach has some unfortunate characteristics. Preaching, for example, is often reduced to a fifteen or twenty minute homily, and Bible exposition is jettisoned as "too heavy" in favor of lighter, more topical fare. Some communicators have gone so far as to make a point of not carrying a Bible because they believe its presence will put off the unbelieving. And with this comes such overt attempts at relevance that any language, prayer, or music deemed to be out of sync with popular culture is consciously avoided. The end effect, to use Marva Dawn's term, is "a dumbing down" of the church—producing a people who are weak in their knowledge of the Scriptures as well as of the great writings and music of the church. Such people live with the unfortunate illusion that they have come from nowhere, *ex nihilo,* without heritage or roots.

There is an intrinsic downward gravity in human-centered worship. Among the greatest dangers is pragmatism, because where pragmatism becomes the conductor, the audience increasingly becomes humans rather than God. And when humanity is played to first, when what humanity wants becomes the determining factor, it will corrupt not only worship but theology.

God-centered worship begins with a focus on the awesome revelation of God, the God of Holy Scripture who is the *omnipotent* Creator who spoke everything into existence; who is likewise *omnipresent,* being above everything, below everything, in everything, but not contained; who is *omniscient,* even numbering the very hairs of his children and knowing their thoughts before they become words; who is transcendent and *omni-holy,* and who dwells in the unapproachable light of his own glory.

Because worship encompasses all of life, this awesome focus must perpetually be cultivated. When we meet for corporate worship, we must consciously begin with the question: How must we conduct our lives and shape our meeting so as to glorify God? This vision and this question are of the greatest importance for our generation, for these reasons: (1) Corporate worship that is informed and shaped by the Scriptures' vision of God will cast off idolatries and foster worship in truth and in spirit. (2) A stunning vision of God will promote holy living. (3) Such a vertical focus will enhance horizontal unity. As A. W. Tozer memorably explained:

> Has it ever occurred to you that one hundred pianos all tuned to the same fork are automatically tuned to each other? They are of one accord by being tuned, not to each other, but to another standard to which each one must individually bow. So one hundred worshipers met together, each one looking away to Christ, are in heart nearer to each other than they could possibly be were they to become "unity" conscious and turn their eyes away from God to strive for closer fellowship.[25]

(4) A massive vision of God and worship consonant with this vision will keep hearts from wandering. Many who have grown up in the desolate worship of evangelical churches have an unrequited need to worship, and as young adults they leave for traditions that have a reverent form of worship, even where the reality has long departed.

By insisting that corporate worship must be radically God-centered, I am not in any way suggesting a disregard for humankind and the lost world, but rather I insist that the proper approach to worship must first be God-focused and then human-sensitive. Only when the question of God's glory and pleasure is addressed can the second question, regarding humanity, be pressed. Again, my concern is that the second question is the dominant force today in many circles and that this has a pernicious effect. A persistent focus on humanity could lead to a post-Christian, human-centered evangelicalism.

Certainly the church must be culturally attuned and sensitive. It had better be in its preaching! Preachers must hold the Bible in one hand and the newspaper in the other. They must "understand the times" (cf. 1 Chr 12:32). The church must be creative and relevant in all aspects of worship—and appeal to the hearts of lost men and women. But at the root of all of this, it must be radically God-focused.

The ultimate question must be: What does God think of the way we worship him?

---

25. A. W. Tozer, *The Pursuit of God* (Wheaton: Tyndale, n.d.), 97.

2. Worship Is Christ-centered

The New Testament does not reveal a greater God than does the Old Testament, but the New Testament provides a greater revelation of that God. As the Apostle John so beautifully said, "No one has ever seen God, but God the One and Only, who is at the Father's side, has made him known" (John 1:18). The phrase "has made him known" is the single Greek word *exegesato*, from which comes our English word exegesis—so that, as Carson says, "we might almost say that Jesus is the exegesis of God."[26] Jesus explained (exegeted, narrated) God for us. As the Word, he is God's ultimate self-expression.

The early christological hymn, Paul's great hymn of the incarnation in Colossians 1:15–20, provides a mind-boggling revelation of God in Christ as the Creator, Sustainer, Goal, and Reconciler. The hymn first sings of Christ as *Creator:* "For by him all things were created: things in heaven and on earth, visible and invisible, whether thrones or powers or rulers or authorities; all things were created by him and for him" (Col 1:16). Jesus Christ created the invisible spirit world, for that is what "thrones ... powers ... rulers ... authorities" refer to. He created the vast visible world and universe. He created the fires of Arcturus and the firefly. He created the colors of the spectrum— aquamarine, electric blue, orange, saffron, vermilion. He created every texture, every living thing, every planet, every star, every speck of stellar dust in the most forgotten backwash of the universe. And he did it *ex nihilo,* from nothing.

The song goes on to celebrate Christ as *Sustainer:* "He is before all things, and in him all things hold together" (Col 1:17). There is a medieval painting that shows Christ in the clouds with the world of humans and nature below. And from Christ to every object is painted a thin golden thread. The artist was portraying this same truth in Colossians—that Christ is responsible for sustaining the existence of every created thing. The tense used in the Greek emphasizes that he continues presently to hold all things together; thus, apart from his continuous action all would disintegrate. Astounding! The pen I write

---

26. D. A. Carson, *The Gospel According to John* (Grand Rapids: Eerdmans, 1991), 135.

with, the book you hold, your very breath that falls upon this page are all held together by his powerful word (cf. Heb 1:3). And if he for one millisecond ceased his power, it would all be gone.

The majestic truths of his creatorship and sustaining power virtually demand this truth that Christ is the *Goal* of creation: "All things were created . . . for him" (Col 1:16)—an astonishing statement. There is nothing like it anywhere else in biblical literature.[27] He is the starting point of the universe and its consummation. All things sprang forth at his command, and all things will return at his command. He is the beginning and the end—both Alpha and Omega. Everything in creation, history, and spiritual reality is for him!

The hymn of the incarnation ends with Christ as *Reconciler:* "He is the head of the body, the church; he is the beginning and the firstborn from among the dead, so that in everything he might have the supremacy. For God was pleased to have all his fullness dwell in him, and through him to reconcile to himself all things, whether things on earth or things in heaven, by making peace through his blood, shed on the cross" (Col 1:18–20).

If you worship Christ as the *Creator* of everything, every cosmic speck across billions of light years of trackless space, the Creator of the textures and shapes and colors that dazzle our eyes; if you worship Christ as the *Sustainer* of all creation, who by his word holds the atoms of your body and this universe together; if you worship him as the *Goal* of everything, that all creation is for him; if you further worship Christ as the *Reconciler* of your soul—then you worship the God of the Bible. Anything less than this is reductionist and idolatrous.

We also have it from Jesus' lips that he himself is the focus of the Old Testament Scriptures. As he explained to Cleopas and his companion after the resurrection: "'How foolish you are, and how slow of heart to believe all that the prophets have spoken! Did not the Christ have to suffer these things and then enter his glory?' And beginning with Moses and all the Prophets, he explained to them what was said in all the Scriptures concerning himself" (Luke 24:25–27, cf. vv.

---

27. Peter T. O'Brien, *Colossians, Philemon,* Word Biblical Commentary 44 (Waco: Word, 1982), 47.

44–47). Luke's descriptive "in all the Scriptures" indicates that it was not just the prophecies, not just the sacrificial system, not just the tabernacle, but the entire Old Testament that speaks of Christ.

Christ, of course, is not found in the specious pietistic typology that sees Rahab's red cord as the blood of Christ, but rather in the great salvific events and personages of Israel's history, as well as in the classic prophetic texts. Israel's history points to the kingdom and to the coming King. The epic sagas of Genesis articulate the theme. The Exodus foreshadows the great deliverance wrought by Christ, a salvation that is by grace alone. The stories of the judges—of people such as Ehud, Gideon, and Samson—are stories of mini-salvations that point to the ultimate work of grace through Christ. The lives of the great leaders, such as David and Moses and Joshua, foreshadow Christ. God would work a sovereign deliverance through the son of David even as he had sovereignly done through young David. David prefigures the saving person and work of Christ. So wherever you turn in sacred Scripture, whether to the Psalms or to the Prophets, you come to Christ. Could there be any grander, more scintillating theme in all history than Christ? What joy to search the Scriptures and repeatedly find Christ (cf. John 5:39–49).

The Old Testament, of course, is matched by the consuming Christocentricity of the New Testament. The writer of Hebrews argues in chapters 7–10 that believers no longer need a priesthood, a sacrifice, or a temple because Christ is at once their priest, their sacrifice, and their tabernacle.

Because Christ is the ultimate revelation of God, because he is the great epicenter of the New Testament, he must be the central focus of New Testament worship. This is worship that embraces all of life. Christians must focus on Christ every second of their lives. And when they come together for corporate worship, they must set their hearts to join together in radical Christocentricity. To this end, E. V. Hill, pastor of Mount Zion Missionary Baptist Church, told of the ministry of an elderly woman in his church whom they all called "1800" because no one knew how old she was. On unsuspecting preachers "1800" was hard because she would say, "Get him up!" (she was referring to Christ). After a few minutes, if she didn't think it was happening, she would again shout, "Get him up!" If a preacher did not "Get him up!" he was in for a long, hard day. Dear old "1800" was no theologian, but her instincts were sublime. True worship exalts Jesus. It cannot fail to "Get him up!" because both Testaments lift him up.

There is nothing more important, and more salutary for the church, than Christ-centered worship.

3. Worship Is Word-centered

In the sixteenth century the Scottish church, flush with the Reformation, began a beautiful ritual for opening and closing its services. When the people were seated for worship, the doors to the nave opened and the presiding ministers were led to the pulpit by a parish officer who bore before them the large pulpit Bible, held high so that all the congregation might see it. And as the elevated Bible passed by, the people reverently rose to their feet. They did this, not in worship for the book, but in respect for its divine author.

As the Bible was carefully placed on the pulpit, the parish officer (the beadle in Scottish parlance) opened it to the lesson of the day. This symbolized that the preacher had authority only as he stood behind the book and preached from its riches. At the completion of the service, the beadle once again ascended the pulpit, closed the Bible, and elevated it. As he did this the people again reverently rose to their feet, and the Word of God was carried out with the ministers again trailing in procession. This beautiful tradition evokes deep resonance in my soul because corporate Christian worship, and indeed all of life, must be radically Word-centered from beginning to end.

(a) *Old Testament.* The necessity of life-encompassing, Word-centered worship has substantial roots in the way God's Word was regarded under the old covenant. A particularly defining instance occurred early in Israel's history at the end of Moses' life when, after Moses finished writing the law, he commanded the Levites to place it beside the ark of the covenant, called for Israel to assemble, sang his epic song, and then immediately declared, "Take to heart all the words I have solemnly declared to you this day, so that you may command your children to obey carefully all the words of this law. They are not just idle words for you—they are your life" (Deut 32:46, 47;

cf. 31:9–13; 32:1–45). God's covenant people were called to a radical day-in-day-out absorption in God's Word.

Later the psalmist gave this call magisterial expression in the 176 verses of Psalm 119. There, in twenty-two stanzas (one stanza for each letter of the Hebrew alphabet) he repeatedly emphasized the sufficiency of God's Word as covering "everything from A to Z." Subsequently, the prophet Isaiah would record the divine declaration, "This is the one I esteem: he who is humble and contrite in spirit, and trembles at my word" (Isa 66:2).

Still later in Israel's history, when Nehemiah superintended the rebuilding of Jerusalem's wall and Ezra opened the newly recovered Book of the Law to read, all the people stood in reverent attention from daybreak to noon—some six or seven hours. It was an explicit gesture that the Word was to be central in Israel's existence. Indeed, it was their life. It would seem certain that the Scottish reformers had Israel's response to Ezra's reading of the Word in view when they stood for the entrance of the Word.

(b) New Testament. When we come to the New Testament, we discover a remarkable Word-centered continuity with the Old Testament. Jesus' summary response to the Tempter was like a corresponding bookend to Moses' declaration that the Scriptures are "your life." Jesus insisted that they are the soul's essential food: "It is written: 'Man does not live on bread alone, but on every word that comes from the mouth of God'" (Matt 4:4; cf. Luke 4:4; Deut 8:3). The Scriptures were *life* to Moses and *food* to Jesus—which, in effect, mean the same thing: the Scriptures are essential and indispensable to life itself. In fact, Jesus' call to life in the Word is a quotation from Moses!

Jesus' preaching expounded Old Testament scriptures and concepts. The Sermon on the Mount is a prime example, as is his exposition of key Old Testament texts, not to mention the texts from Luke 24 already cited, which indicate that Christ preached himself from all the Scriptures. The book of Acts repeatedly demonstrates that apostolic preaching followed suit.

As we would expect, corporate worship in the early church centered on God's Word. Paul's order to Timothy was precisely this: "Until I come, devote yourself to the public reading of Scripture, to preaching *(paraklesis)* and to teaching *(didaskalia)* (1 Tim 4:13). Justin Martyr, writing toward the middle of the second century, provides a window as to how this worked out: "On the day called Sunday, all who live in cities or in the country gather together to one place, and the memoirs of the apostles and the writings of the prophets are read, as long as time permits; then, when the reader has finished, the president speaks, instructing and exhorting the people to imitate these good things."[28]

So we must see that corporate worship in the apostolic church and subapostolic church was Word-centered from beginning to end. This, of course, is consonant with Paul's bibliocentric instructions to Timothy regarding preaching (cf. 2 Tim 2:15; 3:14–17; 4:1–5). Thus, we conclude that Word-centered worship was rooted in the Old Testament and explicitly flowered in the New Testament.

(c) Word and Spirit. There is a further substantial reason why all corporate worship must be Word-centered: Word and Spirit cannot be separated. In a 1995 article in honor of the British preacher R. C. Lucas, Australian Old Testament scholar and pastor John Woodhouse makes a compelling argument for biblical exposition based on the inseparableness of the Word of God and the Spirit of God. He notes that the Hebrew *rûah* and the Greek *pneuma* can mean "wind" and "breath" as well as "spirit," and that in many biblical texts "the Spirit of God" can be well translated "the breath of God." Thus, "in biblical thought the Spirit of God is as closely connected to the Word of God as breath is connected to speech."[29]

Woodhouse shows that the connection of Word and Spirit begins in the opening words of the Bible: "In the beginning God created the heavens and the earth. Now the earth was formless and empty, darkness was over the surface of the deep, and the *Spirit (rûah;* read *breath)* of God was hovering over the waters. And God *said,* 'Let there be light,' and there was light" (Gen 1:1–3, italics added). Furthermore,

---

28. Quoted in John Stott, *Guard the Truth* (Downers Grove: InterVarsity Press, 1966), 121, citing *First Apology,* trans. A. W. F. Blunt, in *Cambridge Patristic Texts* (Cambridge: Cambridge University Press, 1911), 1.67.

29. In *When God's Voice Is Heard,* ed. David Jackman and Christopher Green (Leicester: IVP, 1995), 55.

the dynamic connection between *rûah* (Spirit) and speech ("God said") is often missed. But the psalmist made the connection:

> By the *word* of the Lord were the heavens made,
> their starry host by the *breath [rûah]* of his mouth
>   (Ps 33:6, italics added)

Again, Spirit and Word are as closely connected as breath and speech.

The prophet Isaiah affirms the connection with similar poetic parallelism: "For the mouth of the Lord has commanded, and his Spirit [*rûah;* breath] has gathered them" (Isa 34:16, RSV cf. Isa 59:21; 61:1). Dr. Woodhouse comments: "The logic is that where the Word of God is, there the Spirit (or breath) of God is also. For one's word cannot be separated from one's breath."[30]

This inseparable connection between Word and Spirit flows right on into the New Testament. Jesus says: "For the one whom God has sent speaks the *words* of God, for God gives the *Spirit* without limit" (John 3:34, italics added). And again Jesus says, "The *words* I have spoken to you are *spirit* and they are life" (John 6:63, italics added). Indeed, there are many statements in the New Testament in which "Spirit" and "Word" are virtually interchangeable (e.g., James 1:18; 1 Pet 1:23; cf. John 3:5).[31]

Thus, it follows that if we have any desire for the ministry of the Holy Spirit in our corporate worship services, those services must be radically Word-centered. Authentic worship is Word-centered because:

- God's Word is our life.
- God's Word is our food.
- God's Word is the centerpiece of New Testament corporate worship.
- Word and Spirit cannot be separated.

---

30. Ibid., 56. For other New Testament connections, see Acts 1:8; 5:30–32; 1 Thessalonians 1:4–5; 2:13.

31. Ibid., 58.

This means that our corporate worship must be Word-centered from beginning to end. We do not meet for "worship *and* the Word." It is *all* a ministry of the Word. This means that the preaching must be wholly biblical—in a word, *expositional*.

But installing exposition as the main event is not enough. God's Word must infuse everything. The careful reading of the Word must be central. Hymns and songs must be Word-saturated. Prayers must be biblically informed, redolent with biblical reality—often reflecting the very language and structure of Scripture. The preaching of the Word of God must be the Word of God. Such a service requires principled, prayerful thought and hard work. There may be no need to parade the Scripture in and out while God's people rise in reverence. But it must happen in our hearts. Corporate worship must be Word-centered if it is to glorify God as it ought.

This ought to give serious pause to many in the Free Church tradition who consciously minimize the Word of God in corporate worship.

4. Worship Is Consecration

There are those who argue that worship does not—almost cannot!— take place in church because hymn-singing and listening require so little of us in respect to how we live. They argue that authentic worship takes place when we live obediently Monday through Saturday amidst a hostile world. Certainly they have a point. Worship cannot be separated from consecrated service to God. The notion that you can come to church on Sunday and bend your knee in worship when in fact you have not done so during the week is a delusion. Such "worship" is a spiritual impossibility. Certainly no liturgical exercise performed in a putative "sacred space" can presume to be worship apart from week-long service of God.

Yet to limit the purpose of the corporate assembly of God's people on the Lord's Day to edification is needlessly restrictive and reductive. Properly understood and administered, corporate worship will strengthen authentic worship throughout all of life. Corporate worship regularly functions to intensify our consecration to service. Martin Luther said, "At home in my own house there is no warmth or vigor in me, but in the church when the multitude is gathered together, a fire is kindled in my heart and it breaks its way through."[32]

Was Luther an unconsecrated man? No. Did he serve God throughout the week? Yes. But his heart was joyously harrowed and fired for a life of worship by regular corporate worship. Indeed, this is one of the principal reasons for worshiping with the body of Christ—because through the reading and preaching of God's Word, through corporately singing the Word in hymns and spiritual songs (most hymns are intrinsically consecrational), through corporately praying for God's will, and through participating together in the Lord's Table, God's people will be encouraged and strengthened to live consecrated lives.

We must understand that it is often during corporate worship or as a result of such worship that many Christians come to deeper consecration—and so live daily lives of profound worship. The Apostle Paul was clear that consecration is essential to true worship: "Therefore, I urge you, brothers, in view of God's mercy, to offer your bodies as living sacrifices, holy and pleasing to God—this is your spiritual act of worship" (Rom 12:1). Corporate worship must always fuel the sacrificial fires of everyday worship.

To understand that worship is consecration means that the pastor must see to it that everything in gathered worship leads to Isaac Watts's conclusion: "Love so amazing, so divine / demands my soul, my life, my all."

5. Worship Is Wholehearted

Encompassing. Jonathan Edwards's treatise *The Religious Affections* is a brilliant exposition and application of 1 Peter 1:8: "Though you have not seen him, you love him; and even though you do not see him now, you believe in him and are filled with an inexpressible and glorious joy." Edwards employed this text as a lens through which to evaluate and authenticate true Christianity. He held that truly regenerate souls are characterized by such love, faith, and joy.

---

32. Quoted in Robert G. Rayburn, *O Come, Let Us Worship* (Grand Rapids: Baker, 1984), 29.

Unlike us, Jonathan Edwards didn't use the word *affections* to describe a moderate feeling or emotion or a tender attachment. By "affections" Edwards meant one's *heart,* one's *inclinations,* and one's *will.*[33] He wrote, "For who will deny that true religion consists in a great measure in vigorous and lively actings of the inclination and will of the soul, or the fervent exercises of the heart?"[34] Edwards then went on to demonstrate from a cascade of Scriptures that real Christianity so impacts the affections that it shapes one's fears, one's hopes, one's loves, one's hatreds, one's desires, one's joys, one's sorrows, one's gratitudes, one's compassions, and one's zeals.[35] Thus, he offers these conclusions:

> For although to true religion there must indeed be something else besides affection, yet true religion consists so much in the affections that there can be no true religion without them. He who has no religious affection is in a state of spiritual death, and is wholly destitute of the powerful, quickening, saving influences of the Spirit of God upon his heart. As there is no true religion where there is nothing else but affection, so there is no true religion where there is no religious affections.[36]

> If the great things of religion are rightly understood, they will affect the heart. The reason why people are not affected by such infinitely great, important, glorious and wonderful things, as they often hear and read of in the Word of God, is undoubtedly because they are blind; if they were not so, it would be impossible, and utterly inconsistent with human nature, that their hearts should be otherwise than strongly impressed, and greatly moved by such things.[37]

Certainly, then, true worship is demonstrative: it pours from your heart, it infuses your inclinations to please God, and it directs your will

---

33. Jonathan Edwards, *The Religious Affections* (Edinburgh: Banner of Truth, repr. 1994), 24: "This faculty is called by various names; it is sometimes called the *inclination:* and, as it has respect to the actions that are determined and governed by it, is called the *will:* and the *mind,* with regard to the exercises of this faculty, is often called the *heart."*
34. Ibid., 27.
35. Ibid., 31–35.
36. Ibid., 49.
37. Ibid., 50.

to serve him. True worship is not the outcome of a moderate feeling or emotion. It galvanizes your whole being. In a word: it is encompassing! So much then for the Calvinist whose worship is neatly measured and conveniently interior—who references God in scholastic, Latinate categories but is embarrassed when others become enthusiastic about God's love.

Worship engages the whole being.

Passionate. Certainly we all understand that authentic worship cannot be dispassionate. But not all are comfortable with the assertion that worship must be passionate. Nevertheless, this is wholly true—with the proviso that we understand that passion is mediated through the uniqueness of our cultural backgrounds and God-given personalities. Some personalities are naturally baroque, while others are more "Bostonian" in nature. But when worshiping, both the effusive and the reserved must be passionately involved.

We must also allow that there may be times when our religious affections are stirred to extraordinarily passionate worship. Mary of Bethany's anointing of Jesus was a one-time worship event. Indeed, it was never repeated because his death followed so closely. Jesus said of Mary's worship, "She poured perfume on my body beforehand to prepare for my burial" (Mark 14:8).

Mary's heart erupted in a fervent expression of devotion as passionate as found anywhere in Scriptures. Snap went the bottleneck! Out poured a fortune of perfume! And down came her hair as she used it humbly, worshipfully, to wipe her Savior's feet (cf. John 12:3). It was a spontaneous outpouring of her love, and so very extravagant—scandalously so in the eyes of Jesus' disciples (vv. 4, 5). But Jesus placed his imprimatur on her passion: "Leave her alone," he said. "Why are you bothering her? She has done a beautiful thing to me. . . . I tell you the truth, wherever the gospel is preached throughout the world, what she has done will also be told, in memory of her" (Mark 14:6, 9).

We must leave room in our lives for such humbling extravagance if God so inclines our hearts. As King David said at another signal event in salvation history, "'I will celebrate before the Lord. I will become even more undignified than this, and I will be humiliated in my own eyes'" (2 Sam 6:21b, 22). Worship demands all our affections. It calls for passionate devotion.

> Heaven regrets the lore
> of nicely calculated less and more.[38]

Engaged. The point is, there is no room for detached, laid-back worship or cold intellectualized formality. We must be engaged.

The hymns and songs of the church demand radical engagement. John Wesley's "Directions for Singing" written more than 230 years ago in the preface to *Select Hymns* sets the standard:

> Above all sing spiritually. Have an eye to God in every word you sing. Aim at pleasing him more than yourself, or any other creature. In order to do this attend strictly to the sense of what you sing, and see that your heart is not carried away with the sound, but offered to God continually; so shall your singing be such as the Lord will approve here, and reward you when he comes in the clouds of heaven.[39]

Likewise, the reading of the Scriptures must be attended by close attention. The picture of all the people of Jerusalem standing from dawn till noontide as Ezra read from the Law conveys the idea (Neh 8).

Congregational prayers must be matched with interior and exterior "Amens" as our hearts resonate with what is prayed. True engagement in corporate prayer affords our souls the benefit of riding the prayers of others to places we might not otherwise go, and of expressing thoughts beyond our normal capacities.

And preaching? Inasmuch as it is true to the Word, it must be listened to as the Word of God.[40]

6. Worship Is Reverent

Here we must reflect on the two contrasting mountains of Hebrews 12 (Sinai and Zion) because together they provide the vision that must

---

38. William Wordsworth, *Ecclesiastical Sonnets,* Part 3, 43.

39. John Wesley, *Select Hymns with Tunes Annext: Designed chiefly for the Use of the People Called Methodists* (Bristol: William Pine, 1761, ed. 1770).

40. Second Helvetic Confession (1566): "The Preaching of the Word of God is the Word of God" *(praedicatio verbi Dei est verbum Dei).*

inform all New Testament worship. Briefly, the author's argument in Hebrews 12:18–29 is this: You have *not* come to Mount Sinai and the consuming fires of God (vv. 18–21); rather you have come to Mount Zion and the consummate grace(s) of God (vv. 22–24). Your graced standing requires two things of you: *obedience* (vv. 25–27), and *worship:* "Therefore, since we are receiving a kingdom that cannot be shaken, let us be thankful, and so worship God acceptably with reverence and awe, for our 'God is a consuming fire'" (vv. 28, 29).

So the paradox: though you are standing on Zion's graced slopes and not at fiery Sinai, the reverence with which you are to worship in all of life is informed and infused by Sinai's revelation that God is a consuming fire. How is this? Very simply, both mountains reveal God. The God of Zion is the same God as the God of Sinai. And though we can approach him because of his unbounded grace, he remains a holy consuming fire. Note well the tense: "our 'God is [not was!] a consuming fire'" (v. 29; cf. Deut 4:24). This is an abiding new covenant reality.

Mount Sinai. Sinai as it is memorably described in verses 18–21 provides a salutary background for a life of worship. We see a mountaintop blazing with "fire to the very heavens" (Deut 4:11), cloaked with deep darkness, lightning flashing arteries in the clouds, with the mournful blasts of trumpets baying through the thunder and the ground shaking as God's voice intones the Ten Commandments. The holy God radiates wrath and judgment against sin. He cannot be approached.

Mount Zion. Of course, the other mountain, Mount Zion of the New Testament, completes the picture. This mountain, with its sevenfold benefits, is eminently approachable. "But you have come": (a) to the *city of God,* Mount Zion, "the heavenly Jerusalem, the city of the living God"; (b) to *angels,* "to thousands upon thousands of angels in joyful assembly"; (c) to *co-heirs,* "to the church of the firstborn, whose names are written in heaven"; (d) to *God:* "You have come to God, the judge of all men"; (e) to the *church triumphant,* "to the spirits of righteous men made perfect"; (f) to *Jesus,* "the mediator of a new covenant"; (g) to *forgiveness,* "to the sprinkled blood that speaks a better word than the blood of Abel" (vv. 22–24).

What a vision we are bequeathed from Calvary. Here is God the Son with his arms nailed wide as if to embrace all those who come to him, his fallen blood speaking a better word than the condemning blood of Abel. Here is the consuming grace of God. Mount Zion, crowned by Golgotha, shows us God and his grace.

Both mountains—Sinai and Zion—reveal the God we worship. Neither can be separated from the other. God is not the God of one mountain but of both. Both visions must be held in blessed tension in our hearts. This massive dual revelation of the mountains is meant to shape how we live our everyday lives in worship. We must worship God according to his revelation, not according to our disposition. We must worship God with reverence and awe, for our "God is a consuming fire." This is an individual, domestic, and corporate necessity.

Not a few church leaders have failed to understand this. And the corporate folly here described probably indicates deficient worship in everyday life. While on vacation, one of my associates visited a church where, to his amazement, the worship prelude was the ragtime theme song from the Paul Newman/Robert Redford movie *The Sting*, entitled (significantly, I think), "The Entertainer." The congregation was preparing for divine worship while cinematic images of Paul Newman and Robert Redford in 1920s garb hovered in their consciousness! And that was just the prelude, for what followed was an off-the-wall service that made no attempt at reverent worship. The "high point" was during the announcements when the pastor (inspired, no doubt, by the rousing prelude) stood unbeknownst behind the unfortunate person doing announcements making "horns" behind his head with his forked fingers and mugging Bozo-like for the congregation. This buffoonery took place in a self-proclaimed "Bible-believing church" that ostensibly worships the holy triune God of the Bible.

But what was in the pastor's and people's minds? What did they really think of God? How could anyone do such things and understand who God is? They were unwitting evangelical Marcionites whose ignorance of both Testaments had so edited God that divine worship had become human-centered vaudeville.

Of course, the example is extreme. Such bathos is rare. At the same time, the unremitting horizontal trajectory of many Sunday services, the inattention to God's Word, both in reading and preaching, and the casual, unthought-through stream-of-conscious prayers have trivialized corporate worship.

Certainly, Christians ought to connect with each other, and they ought to have the best sense of humor on this planet. Christians ought to enjoy life to the fullest. But they must also know and understand that God remains a "consuming fire" and that acceptable worship takes place when there is authentic reverence and awe in all of life, not the least in corporate worship.

Summary

These six distinctives of worship are the controlling principles for how we conduct our corporate services at College Church. This is not theory, but practice.

Each of the six by themselves will, when taken to heart, exert a profound influence on gathered worship. And when they are purposefully mixed in bouquet—when worship is at once God-centered and Christ-centered and Word-centered and consecrated and wholehearted and reverent—the effect is all-controlling. Indeed, our experience is that these six essences, like a good perfume, augment each other in rich fragrance—a sweet aroma of worship to God.

The importance of these distinctives, even at the horizontal level, is immense, because corporate worship is where edification most effectively takes place. If the church-gathered effectively worships God, then the church-scattered will better worship God in all of life.

Corporate Christian Worship: Its Music

Before we move to the "how-to" of corporate worship, music must be given proper perspective as a medium of gathered worship. Music has validity in Christian worship only as it participates in, and contributes to, a service of the Word from beginning to end. That is why music must remain under constant scrutiny, and the ministry of music must be constantly reforming so as to be Word-centered. The historic examples of Ambrose and Luther, whose hymns brought people to the faith and taught them the Bible, are as important today as at any time in Christian history.[41]

1. Music Serves Preaching

In our setting, we understand music to be the servant of preaching. And because the entire service is built around the sermon, all the songs and hymns are made to relate to, or comment on, some aspect of the text. This may mean singing about the character of God as revealed in the text; it may highlight a teaching principle or application; or it may underline a commitment that the text emphasizes. Sometimes what is sung is related to a parallel Scripture passage or is a paraphrase of the text itself. So what the congregation sings and what it hears sung will flow from the central biblical text of the day.[42]

Likewise, instrumental music is often based on apt hymn tunes and their association with well-known texts. Many times the character of the sermon passage will suggest the musical character of nonvocal music—peaceful, martial, joyous, and so forth.

We believe that music must principally serve the text. Don Hustad (the "dean" of evangelical church music) describes music for worship as essentially "functional."[43] The words and actions of the people of God assembled for worship create the need for music, provide the environment for music-making, and must finally serve as the judge of how successfully it lifts up Christ and his Word.

---

41. J. McKinnon, *Music in Early Christian Literature* (Cambridge: Cambridge University Press, 1986), 132, quotes *Sermo contra Auxentium de basilicis tradentis* xxxiv; PL xvi, 1017–18, which is an apparent reference to the congregational singing of Ambrose's hymns: "They also say that the people are led astray by the charms of my hymns. Certainly; I do not deny it. This is a mighty charm, more powerful than any other. For what avails more than the confession of the Trinity, which is proclaimed daily in the mouth of all the people?" This also recalls the backhanded compliment to Luther: "He has damned more people with hymns than with his preaching."

42. We do observe the church calendar of Advent. On those Sundays, our music may relate to the "day" and not to the sermon. Even then, however, music relates to the Scriptures of Advent.

43. Donald Hustad, *Jubilate II* (Carol Stream: Hope, 1993), chapter 2: "Church Music: A Functional Art."

2. Music Develops Maturity

The very act of singing God's Word, or singing scriptural truth about God, is intrinsically edifying because music is so easily remembered. The immense scope of the five books of the Psalms testifies to music's power to edify. Because music is so naturally affective, great care must be taken to assure its biblical fidelity. Too often today the church serves up affective sentiments without much care for the discipline of the Word.

So we see music's role in its finest practice as obedience to the Word of God. Worship is elevated when music-makers (composers, directors, and all who sing or play instruments) and the congregation they serve bow the knee to God's glory and make music in obedience to God's Word.

3. Music Is Everyone's Responsibility

In the Old Testament music was a priestly function; in the New Testament it still remains a priestly matter. Jesus, our High Priest, says, "I will declare your name to my brothers; in the presence of the congregation I will sing your praises" (Heb 2:12, quoting Ps 22:22). And of course, as a kingdom of priests, God's people are enjoined to sing. The Apostle Paul commented on this musical responsibility when he instructed the church in Corinth about the public exercise of gifts. He said, "I will sing with my spirit, but I will also sing with my mind"—as he encouraged them to full mental engagement with the words they were singing (1 Cor 14:15). A few lines later he instructed them, "When you come together, everyone has a hymn, or a word of instruction, a revelation, a tongue or an interpretation. All of these must be done for the strengthening of the church" (v. 26). As God's people they were to employ their voices to build up the church. It remains everyone's responsibility.

In his letter to the Ephesian church, Paul charged his readers, in respect to the Spirit's filling, "Speak to one another with psalms, hymns and spiritual songs. Sing and make music in your heart to the Lord, always giving thanks to God the Father for everything, in the name of our Lord Jesus Christ" (5:19–20). Similarly in his exhortation to the Colossian church, the apostle demonstrates his grasp of the teaching and reforming role of music: "Let the word of Christ dwell in you richly as you teach and admonish one another with all wisdom, and as you sing psalms, hymns and spiritual songs with gratitude in your hearts to God" (3:16).

Paul understood the inseparability of Word and Spirit (they are as speech and breath) and commanded God's people to engage corporately in a mutual ministry by Word and Spirit as they sang. It is the responsibility of Christ's body whenever it assembles.

4. Musical Selection Is Important

The selection of appropriate worship music is not merely a matter of choice between traditional and contemporary Christian music. The decision must be made on principle. Whatever the genre of music, it must meet three criteria: text, tune, and fit.

Text. Evaluation of the music's text or lyrics comes first. Whoever selects music must do the biblical work required to conform all text-based music to the thrust of the sermon text. The music leader must work with a hymnal in one hand and the Bible in the other.

Are the lyrics biblical? Scriptural allusions, even abundant allusions, do not ensure this. Some lyrics conflate disparate allusions into confused montage. The well-known song "You Are My All in All" is a case in point. It goes in part:

You are my strength when I am weak,
You are the Treasure that I seek....

Seeking You as a precious jewel,
Lord, to give up I'd be a fool....

There can also be Scripture-based lyrics that do not represent what the Scripture means in its context. An example of this is the chorus:

This is the day
(This is the day)
That the Lord hath made.
(That the Lord hath made.)
We will rejoice
(We will rejoice)
And be glad in it.
(And be glad in it.)[44]

---

44. © 1967 Scripture in Song (a division of Integrity Music, Inc.)/ASCAP. All rights reserved. International copyright secured. Used by permission. C/o Integrity Music, Inc., 1000 Cody Road, Mobile, AL 36695.

The chorus's bouncy tune is evocative of believers exulting on a sunny day, and it is often used to begin morning assemblies. But the quotation is from Psalm 118:24, which is in the context of eschatological judgment. This sense is apparent when read with the preceding sentence: "The stone the builders rejected has become the capstone; the Lord has done this, and it is marvelous in our eyes. This is the day the Lord has made; let us rejoice and be glad in it" (Ps 118:22–24).

Indeed, Jesus quoted verse 22 in his temple discourse to confirm a parable of judgment: "Jesus looked directly at them and asked, 'Then what is the meaning of that which is written: "The stone the builders rejected has become the capstone"? Everyone who falls on that stone will be broken to pieces, but he on whom it falls will be crushed'" (Luke 20:17, 18).

Yes! This is the day that the Lord has made. And, yes, we will rejoice and be glad in it. But not *when* or *as* the popular tune suggests.

We must be aware that many popular new songs come from a hermeneutical environment that disconnects individual passages of Scripture from their contextual meaning. In a similar way, even a so-called "Scripture song" (that is, it is all Scripture) can be unscriptural because it is sung as a repetitious sound-bite and thus conveys a sense far from its biblical intent. The singing of Psalm 46:10a, "Be still and know that I am God" (three times) to a sweet, bucolic melody suggests a relaxed idyll with God. That is hardly consistent with its martial context (Ps 46:8–11). Better not to use a hymn or song at all if it misrepresents the textual meaning.

Tune. Next, the tune must support the meaning of the text. It is inevitable that a sentimental melody attached to a hortatory text will deflate the force of the text. Thus, the essentials for evaluating a tune are answered by the questions: Does its character fit the text? Does it have a melody capable of standing alone? These are not esoteric questions that can only be answered by the "experts." Anyone with some musical understanding, some common sense, and a willingness to think about it can make good decisions.

Here we must also note that the musical meter must be appropriate for the text. For example, a 3/4 meter, which is a waltz or skating meter, is not appropriate for certain theological truths. For example, the gospel song "Jesus Is Coming Again" has a big band waltz melody in a style popular in the 1940s; and while the Second Advent is certainly the Christian's "Blessed Hope," it will not be a waltz or an "All Skate."

Fit. Lastly, the task of hymn selection must be in the context of knowing the congregation. There is a cultural appropriateness that cannot be ignored in this matter. A hymn or song may be textually sound, its tune may be consistent with the text, but it may be either too formal or too informal for a certain congregation in its particular setting. Those leading worship must be attuned both to the Word and to the people who are served.

5. Musicians Must Be Prepared

After selection comes the need for spiritual preparation. Musicians must see themselves as fellow laborers in the Word and must lead with understanding and an engaged heart. Those who minister in worship services must be healthy Christians who have confessed their sins and by God's grace are living their lives consistently with the music they lead. The sobering fact is that over time the congregation tends to become like those who lead.

Musicians are also called to render their very best to God. Qualitative standards can be expressed classically (unity, clarity, proportion), and biblically (creativity, beauty, craft). In Christian worship, where music is a servant of the Word of God, musical standards are a requisite to clear communication. Church music must be judged by universal standards of musicianship: it must be good music, well performed, with due attention paid to intonation, rhythmic accuracy, articulation, and tone. Happy is the congregation led by godly, competent musicians!

6. The Congregation Is the Chief Instrument

The congregation must also be prepared for its ministry of music because the congregation is the chief instrument of praise, the one indispensable choir! Musicians and choirs serve a questionable function (entertainment?) if the congregation does not sing. At College Church our choirs understand that first among their ministry responsibilities is leading the congregation in singing. This is foremost a heart matter, then one of earnest example. Whenever we introduce new music, we make sure the choirs have it down first. This makes new hymns and songs less daunting. Great singing builds up God's people in his Word and also draws unbelievers to consider both the reality and the substance of the faith.

We have found that thoughtful exposure to new songs (timing, placement, pastoral considerations) and intentional training will build a congregation in its capacity for praise. In our own particular context, we begin instructing our children in the essentials of worship during the years of kindergarten through second grade with a program entitled Wonders of Worship (W.O.W.) in which an entire year is given to focusing on the who, where, when, why, and how of worship. (See Appendix B.)

The ministry of music is not ministry of a different sort. It is first, last, and always a ministry of the Word of God.

Appendix A

College Church Worship

1. Sunday Morning

Planning—For years I met on Thursdays with my executive pastor, part-time minister of music, and a spiritually and aesthetically minded member of the congregation to plan corporate services. After prayer, the first part of our time was spent evaluating the previous Sunday. Next we planned future services, and then we gave attention to any loose ends for the coming Sunday. This hands-on approach was for me an education in itself.

Now that we employ a full-time minister of music, the burden has shifted to his capable shoulders. His practice is to study the upcoming texts on his own to discover their themes or "melodic lines" (he consults me only if necessary) and then to mold the order of corporate worship around the biblical text. Weekly evaluation takes place first in the staff meeting and then by ourselves in a brief meeting.

In addition to keeping an eye on the six distinctives of worship, special attention is given to planning services that are unified around the biblical text from beginning to end. The services are characterized by creative excellence and joyous warmth. Generally, the congregation is unaware of the depth of unity as it worships. We like it this way. Self-conscious "unity" can be strained and distracting.

We vary the order of corporate worship from time to time. Below are two examples, listed side-by-side for comparison:

Prelude	Prelude
Welcome	Choral Call to Worship
Silence	Welcome
Introit	Silence
Apostles' Creed	Invocation
Hymn	Doxology
Congregational Prayer/Lord's Prayer	Apostles' Creed
Anthem	Hymn
God at Work	Anthem
Scripture Reading	Tithes and Offerings
Sermon	Scripture Reading
Hymn	Gloria Patri

Benediction
Postlude

Sermon
Hymn
Benediction
Postlude

Here we will confine our comments to the principle aspects of these services.

Pre-service—The entire pastoral staff and participants meet thirty minutes before the first service to go over the corporate worship folder and pray. All staff attend the meeting whether or not they have an up-front part in the service. Details completed, mention is regularly made about ourselves authentically engaging in worship as we lead it. For example, we must sing the hymns with our minds and hearts engaged, rather than thinking of our next duty. This goes for everything: the choir anthems, the prayers, the reading of Scripture, even listening to the announcements. We have a saying at College Church: "Our people will become in macrocosm what we are in microcosm." Our individual and corporate ethos must be one of engagement and authenticity if we are to expect our people to adopt the same stance.

Often we all sense ourselves buoyed and sustained for the day as we conclude our pre-service meeting in prayer. After prayer, we disperse to rotating spots in the congregation to greet our people during the prelude. We have found this as beneficial as greeting after services because it enhances our congregation's sense of warmth and connectedness before a time of corporate worship that is largely vertical. After the benediction many people are in a rush to get to classes or pick up children, but they are much more relaxed when gathering for corporate worship. Also we are able to greet people who, for various reasons, exit around us.

Welcome and Silence—Announcements are made at the time of welcome, and as every pastor knows, they are notorious time consumers. They go best when we insist that they be written out and timed—not to be read, of course, but so that they may be given with a relaxed economy. We plan them in terms of seconds, not minutes. Generally, they all can be done in less than two minutes.

After the welcome we ask the congregation to bow in silent preparation for corporate worship. The time is brief, perhaps ten seconds, but it helps us "center down" (as the Quakers say). My experience is that many in the Free Church tradition are afraid of silence. One very dear retired pastor in my congregation (now deceased) would say, "Pastor, can't we have the organ play during those silent times?" He even asked that I have the organ play while I prayed! No, we need times of silence—to listen and think. We carefully work silence into our meetings, before and after

174

prayer. And when serving communion we will sometimes serve the bread or the cup in several minutes of silence.

Apostles' Creed—You will note that the congregation weekly affirms the Apostles' Creed. Often it is in answer to the ringing question "Christian, what do you believe?"—"I believe. . . ." We employ the Creed for three reasons: (a) to affirm weekly the essentials; (b) to emphasize (because we are a church with no denominational affiliations) that we are in the stream of historic orthodoxy; and (c) to provide a familiar reference to visitors from Catholic and mainline churches whom we hope to evangelize. The congregation's response is not perfunctory, but resounding.

Congregational Prayer—I agree with Horton Davies's comment on free prayer: "Free prayers, under the guidance of a devout and beloved minister who knows well both his Bible and his people, have a moving immediacy and relevance that set prayers rarely attain."[1] At the same time, if prayers are not prepared, they can become a stream of clichés and repetitions that numb the mind and ice the heart.

So I prepare. I do not write them out in full, but I outline my prayers and make careful lists of petitions. The Puritan foil, the *Book of Common Prayer*, is a magnificent source of ideas and "prayer starters," as is the Presbyterian *Book of Common Worship* and other denominational sources. Hughes Oliphant Old's *Leading in Prayer: A Workbook for Ministers* is an excellent resource.[2] He draws from the *Didache*, the *Apostolic Constitutions*, the *Geneva Psalter*, and various Reformed and Puritan sources such as Luther, Calvin, Matthew Henry, Isaac Watts, and Richard Baxter to provide an indispensable resource. The long lists of his own Scripture-based prayers provide examples of how to do it.

Next to preaching, I spend most of my preparation time on prayer. My hope is not to pray a beautiful prayer, like the Boston preacher whose prayer the papers reported as "the most eloquent prayer ever offered to a Boston audience." My goal rather is to be so filled with the Word and the needs of my people that we are all borne up to God.

My typical prayers include a time for silent confession and conclude with us *praying* in unison the Lord's Prayer. Congregational prayer has a dynamic potential for edification as it not only corporately leads in worship of God but also teaches people how to pray.

---

1. Horton Davies, *Christian Worship* (New York: Abingdon, 1957), 68.

2. Hughes Oliphant Old, *Leading in Prayer: A Workbook for Ministers* (Grand Rapids: Eerdmans, 1995).

God at Work—This heading provides the place for the many variations that are a part of our corporate worship pattern. *God at Work in Families* is where infant baptisms and dedications take place. *God at Work in Missions* provides a three-minute missionary focus. *God at Work in Our Lives* is a place for a four-minute testimony. The variations go on.

Reading Scripture—Those who read Scripture are likewise asked to prepare well for this ministry. "After all," we say, "whether the preaching is good or bad, we can be sure this is the Word of God!" To this end my pastoral staff and I, along with our ministerial interns, periodically set aside a couple of hours to practice the public reading of Scripture under the instruction and critique of a professional speech instructor from nearby Wheaton College. My colleagues enjoy it—especially when "the boss" is corrected! Here mention must be made of Thomas McComiskey's *Reading Scripture in Public.*[3] As a respected Old Testament scholar, he employs both theological acumen and pastoral sensitivity in his thoroughgoing treatment of the subject. Helpfully, each chapter concludes with practical exercises.

We give prominence to the reading of Scripture by asking the congregation to stand for the reading of God's Word. At the completion of the reading the reader says, "This is God's Word," and the people respond with "Amen!" and then sing the "Gloria Patri." Such care and emphasis has served to enhance our people's focus on the centrality of God's Word. (See Appendix C for an account of the profound effect of the bare reading of God's Word.)

Music—College Church is blessed with immense musical resources that have developed over the years through the intentionality of our music leadership. At present, there are six choirs: the Chancel Choir, Cherubs (grades 1–2), Boys and Girls Choirs (grades 3–6), Junior High and Senior High, plus "God's Children Sing" (a music and worship curriculum for ages 4–5). We also have four instrumental groups: brasses, handbells, and combinations of our string and woodwind musicians. Our pastor of worship and music constantly refreshes the musicians to their biblical responsibility so that those who lead do so to God's glory. (See Appendix D.)

---

3. Thomas Edward McComiskey, *Reading Scripture in Public* (Grand Rapids: Baker, 1991).

Morning Corporate Worship Services

Example A: Morning Worship, April 11, 1999

The preaching text for that morning was 2 Timothy 2:8–13, in which Paul affirms that the resurrection is at the heart of the gospel he preaches: "Remember Jesus Christ, raised from the dead, descended from David. This is my gospel ..." (v. 8). Providentially, this passage from an ongoing series on the Pastoral Epistles fell on the Sunday following Easter, which provided us with a natural and exciting opportunity to continue the celebration of Easter while at the same time expounding the full text of the passage.

The tune chosen for the doxology was LASST UNS ERFREUEN, which with its "Alleluias" expresses resurrection joy. We use this tune from Easter to Pentecost. The haunting anthem "Christ Is Now Arisen" focused powerfully on the scriptural theme, as did the bell choir's "Alleluia! The Strife Is O'er." The progression of the three hymns "The Day of Resurrection," "Good Christian Men Rejoice" (which might have seemed out of place had this passage been preached in another season), and "Jesus Lives and So Shall I," all worked to build ringing unity. The final hymn became a resounding congregational response to the Word preached.

Morning Worship, April 11, 1999

*[As you are seated, please move to the center of the pew,
so others can join you in worship.]*

Prelude   *Morning*   Edvard Grieg

O Sons and Daughters Let Us Sing   arr. F. Gramann
And we with holy church unite
As evermore is just and right
In glory to the King of Light.

Jubilation Ringers, Bryan Park, conductor

Choral Call to Worship

Shout for joy to the Lord, all the earth.
Serve the Lord with gladness;
come before him with joyful songs. (Ps. 100:1–2)

Welcome †   Pastor Marc Maillefer

Silence

Invocation
9:00—Pastor David White
10:40—Pastor Niel Nielson

Doxology *
LASST UNS ERFREUEN

Praise God from whom all blessings flow;
Praise Him, all creatures here below;
Alleluia! Alleluia!
Praise Him above, ye heav'nly host;
Praise Father, Son, and Holy Ghost;
Alleluia! Alleluia! Alleluia! Alleluia! Alleluia!

Apostles' Creed *

I believe in God, the Father Almighty, Maker of heaven and earth;
and in Jesus Christ, His only son, our Lord, who was conceived
by the Holy Spirit, born of the virgin, Mary, suffered under Pontius
Pilate, was crucified, dead, and buried; He descended into hell;
the third day He rose again from the dead. He ascended into heaven,
and sitteth on the right hand of God the Father Almighty;
from thence He shall come to judge the living and the dead.
I believe in the Holy Spirit; the holy, catholic church;
the communion of saints; the forgiveness of sins;
the resurrection of the body; and the life everlasting. Amen.

Hymn #168 *†   *The Day of Resurrection*

Congregational Prayer/Lord's Prayer
(See inside back cover of hymnal)   Pastor Kent Hughes

Hymn #170 †   *Good Christian Men, Rejoice and Sing*

Anthem   *Christ Is Now Arisen*   Lee Scott
Chancel Choir   Greg Wheatley conducting

Now the song is begun, for the battle is done, and the victory won:
Now the foe is scattered: Death's dark prison shattered:
Sing of joy, joy, joy; sing of joy, joy, joy;
And today raise the lay, Christ is now arisen!
They that followed in pain shall now follow to reign,
    and the crown shall obtain;
They were sore assaulted, they shall be exalted:
Sing of life, life, life; sing of life, life, life;
Earth and skies bid it rise, Christ is now arisen!
For the foe nevermore can approach to that shore,
    when the conflict is o'er;
There is joy supernal; there is peace eternal;
Sing of joy, joy, joy; sing of joy, joy, joy;
Earth and skies bid it rise, Christ is now arisen!

Then be brave, then be true, ye despised and ye few,
>for the crown is for you:
Christ, who went before you, spreads His buckler o'er you.
Sing of strength, strength, strength, sing of strength, strength, strength;
Earth and skies bid it rise, Christ is now arisen!
Lo, the vict'ry is won, and the foe is scattered, death's dark prison
>shattered!
Hallelujah! Earth and skies bid it rise, Christ is now arisen!
Hallelujah! Come today, raise the lay, Christ is now arisen!

Tithes and Offerings **

Offertory †   *Alleluia! The Strife Is O'er*   arr. F. Gramann
Jubilation Ringers

Death's mightiest powers have done their worst
And Jesus hath his foes dispersed
Let shouts of praise and joy outburst. Alleluia!
On the third morn he rose again Glorious in majesty to reign
O let us swell the joyful strain. Alleluia!

Scripture Reading *   2 Timothy 2:8–13   9:00—Mrs. Diane Jordan
(P. 1178)   10:40—Mr. Bill Ladd

Gloria Patri *   GREATOREX
Hymn #575

Glory be to the Father, and to the Son, and to the Holy Ghost;
As it was in the beginning, is now, and ever shall be,
>world without end.
>>Amen. Amen.

Sermon   *The Essential Memory*   Pastor Kent Hughes

Hymn #159 *   *Jesus Lives and So Shall I*

Benediction *   Pastor Kent Hughes

[Please be seated for a moment of reflection]

Postlude   *Good Christians All, Rejoice and Sing*   H. Willan
Ed Childs, organ

*[Reception for visitors in the Fireside Room
immediately following each service.]*

* Congregation standing

† Ushers will assist worshipers to seating

** 10:40 a.m.; Children dismissed for Wonders of Worship: K, Room 001; Grades 1–2, Room 205

Example B: Morning Worship, June 20, 1999

The preaching text for that summer morning was 2 Timothy 3:14–17, which contains a foundational text on the inspiration of Scripture, "All Scripture is God-breathed and is useful for teaching, rebuking, correcting and training in righteousness" (v. 16). We didn't have to look hard for a theme!

You will observe that the opening hymn does not address the theme. This is because we could find no hymn that perfectly touched the theme and yet worked well in the opening slot. A slavish devotion to theme can, ironically, create dissonance if the tune and tempo are inappropriate. Thus, we chose the stately Trinitarian hymn "Holy God, We Praise Thy Name" to focus our minds God-ward. The theme was made the major emphasis of the Congregational Prayer. Then, with the special hymn "Powerful in Making Us Wise" from Psalm 119 (provided on an insert in the worship folder), the Word-focus was heightened.

The Chancel Choir further expanded on the theme with "Send Your Word," based on the text of a Japanese hymn which *intones* the prayer

Send your Word, O Lord, like the rain. . . .
Send your Word, O Lord, like the wind. . . .
Send your Word, O Lord, like the dew. . . .

Following the sermon, the congregation sang "O Word of God Incarnate" to emphasize that to be Word-centered is to be radically Christ-centered.

Morning Worship, June 20, 1999

The prelude is a gift to God's people,
prepared as a bridge between our busy lives and this hour of worship.

Prelude   *Oboe Concerto #1*, adagio and allegro   G. F. Handel
                     Nate Elwell, oboe; Ellen Elwell, piano

Choral Call to Worship

Shout for joy to the Lord, all the earth. Serve the Lord with gladness; come before him with joyful songs. (Ps. 100:1–2)

Welcome †   9:00—Jim Johnston
                                     10:40—Pastor Adam Rasmussen

Silence

Invocation   9:00—Mr. Jay Thomas
                                                 10:40—Pastor Niel Nielson

Doxology *   Hymn #572

Apostles' Creed *   *[See inside back cover of the hymnal]*

Hymn #9 †   *Holy God, We Praise Thy Name*

God at Work in India   9:00—STAMP/India

Hymn (White Insert) †

Congregational Prayer/Lord's Prayer

Lord's Prayer   *[See inside back cover of the hymnal]*

Anthem   *Send Your Word*   T. Keesecker
                 Chancel Choir

> Send your Word, O Lord, like the rain, falling down upon the earth.
> We seek your endless grace, with souls that hunger and thirst,
>   sorrow and agonize.
> We would all be lost in dark without your guiding light.
> Send your Word, O Lord, like the wind, blowing down upon the earth.
> We seek your wondrous power, pureness that rejects all sins,
>   though they persist and cling.
> Bring us to complete victory; set us all free indeed.
> Send your Word, O Lord, like the dew, coming gently upon the hills.
> We seek your endless love.
> For life that suffers in strife with adversities and hurts,
>   oh send your healing power of love;
> We long for your new world.

Text by Yasushige Imakoma, tr. by Nobuaki Hanaoka[4]

Tithes and Offerings

Offertory †   *Oboe Concerto #1*, largo   G. F. Handel

**Scripture Reading ***2 Timothy 3:14–17 (p. 1179)*   Mrs. Diane Jordan

Gloria Patri *   Hymn #575

Sermon   *Continue in the Word*   Pastor Kent Hughes

Hymn #219 *   *O Word of God Incarnate*

Benediction *   Pastor Kent Hughes

[Please be seated for a moment of Reflection]

Postlude   H. E. Singley III, organ

*[Reception for visitors in the Fireside Room
immediately following each service.]*

*If you would like to pray or share a need with church leaders, they will be
available at the front of the Sanctuary following the service.*

* Congregation standing

† Ushers will assist worshipers to seating

Example C. Morning Worship, November 7, 1999

We schedule communion about every five weeks, but we do not inter-
rupt our sequential expositions with a special communion message. Often
the scheduled text fits perfectly, and rarely is there any difficulty in making the segue to the table. On this particular Sunday, Daniel 4:1–37, which
exalts God's sovereignty in the humbling of King Nebuchadnezzar, worked
beautifully.

Because we have multiple morning services, some of the regular features of corporate worship have to be set aside or economized. The welcome is restricted to a maximum of 60 seconds, and the congregational
prayer is abbreviated and subsumed into the prayer over the bread.
Shorter hymns are used if possible.

The opening hymn, "All Creatures of Our God and King," which
emphasizes God's sovereignty, beautifully anticipated the humbled
monarch's declaration in its final stanza, which begins "Let all things their
Creator bless / And worship him in humbleness." The Chancel Choir and
orchestra provided an eschatological parallel to Nebuchadnezzar's declaration by singing Bach's "Alleluia! O Praise the Lord Most Holy," which is
based on Revelation 5:12.

Following the sermon, the congregation rose to sing George Herbert's
two-verse hymn "Let All the World in Every Corner Sing: My God and
King!" thus providing a brief, rousing response to the text. The sermon
concluded with a call to humble ourselves before almighty God as did the
Babylonian king, for this has always been the pattern of saving grace—

and therefore the perpetual posture of those who would come to the Lord's Table.

Communion was introduced with the words of institution from 1 Corinthians 11:23, 24 before the bread and 11:25 before the cup.

We normally make no attempt to sustain the sermon theme with the hymn excerpts sung before the bread and the cup. The excerpts vary widely, and one of them is typically sung a cappella. Periods of silence precede and follow both partakings.

The concluding hymn, "The God of Abraham Praise," provided a return to the sermonic theme. Its stately synagogue melody and Trinitarian emphasis provided a fitting conclusion. As Nebuchadnezzar praised Daniel's God, so we sang to Abraham's and Israel's God.

Morning Worship, November 7, 1999

Let the first sound of music be a call to silent worship.

Prelude   *My Heart Ever Faithful*   J. S. Bach
College Church Orchestra

Welcome †   9:00—Pastor Marc Maillefer
10:45—Pastor Jim Johnston

Silence

Choral Call to Worship †   *Taste and See*   G. Wheatley

Taste and see how good the Lord is;
blessed is the man that trusteth in Him. (Ps. 34:8)

Invocation   9:00—Pastor David White
10:45—Pastor Jim Johnston

Doxology *   Hymn #572

Apostles' Creed *   *[See inside back cover of the hymnal]*

Hymn #59 *   *All Creatures of Our God and King*

Tithes and Offerings **

Offertory †   *Alleluia! O Praise the Lord Most Holy*   J. S. Bach
Chancel Choir with Orchestra

Alleluia! O praise the Lord most holy!
Alleluia! Lord most high.

He is worthy to receive power, wealth, and glory,
wisdom, might, and honor, blessing now and ever more.
For He is the true and righteous Lord of all in heaven and earth.
King of kings and Lord of lords, we do worship at Your throne.[5]

Scripture Reading *   *Daniel 4:1–37*   9:00—Pastor Randy Gruendyke
        (p.877)   10:45—Pastor Niel Nielson

Gloria Patri *   Hymn #575

Sermon   *The Lord Is King*   Pastor Kent Hughes

Hymn #24 *   *Let All the World in Every Corner Sing*

Silence

The Lord's Table

Meditation for the Bread   *Now*   Carl Schalk

Now the silence, now the peace, now the empty hands uplifted;
Now the kneeling, now the plea, now the Father's arms in welcome;
Now the hearing, now the Power, now the vessel brimmed for pouring,
Now the body, now the blood, now the joyful celebration;
Now the wedding, now the songs, now the heart forgiven leaping;
Now the Spirit's visitation, now the Son's epiphany,
     now the Father's blessing,
Now.

Text by Jaroslav Vajda[6]

Hymn before the Bread   *Beneath the Cross of Jesus*   Hymn #151, v. 2

Upon that cross of Jesus mine eye at times can see
The very dying form of One who suffered there for me;
and from my smitten heart with tears two wonders I confess—
The wonders of redeeming love and my unworthiness.

Meditation for the Cup   *Meditation on SEYMOUR*   See Hymn #238

Hymn before the Cup   *Alleluia! Sing to Jesus*   Hymn #174, vs. 3

Alleluia! Bread of Heaven, Thou on earth our food and stay;
Alleluia! Here the sinful flee to Thee from day to day;
Intercessor, friend of sinners, earth's Redeemer, plead for me,
Where the songs of all the sinless sweep across the crystal sea.

---

5. Copyright © 1971 Concordia Publishing House. Reprinted with permission.

6. © 1969 Hope Publishing Company, Carol Stream, IL 60188. All rights reserved.
Used by permission.

Care and Share Hymn *The God of Abraham Praise* Hymn #36

Benediction * Pastor Kent Hughes

Choral Benediction *Romans 14:19* E. Thompson

Let us therefore follow the things which make for peace
and the building up of one another. Amen.

Postlude *Toccata on leoni* arr. G. Young
H. E. Singley III, organ

If you are visiting, we would like to greet you personally.
Please join us in the Fireside Room for a cup of coffee
immediately after the service.

If you would like to pray or share a need with church leaders,
they will be available at the front of the Sanctuary following the service.

* Congregation standing

† Ushers will assist worshipers to seating

** 10:45 a.m.   Service: Children dismissed for Wonders of Worship:
K, Room 001; Grades 1–2, Room 205

Evening Corporate Worship Services

We have two primary goals in our Evening Service: to engage the people in congregational singing, and to preach an expository sermon. The service is generally a simple bipartite structure—the song-service followed by the sermon. Song services might be thematic, based on the sermon text; thematic, based on another theme of Scripture; highlights from a particular hymn writer; or, as in the case of the first example below, songs that express praise and devotion to Jesus Christ.

The music in the evening service is more eclectic, so that from time to time nearly every musical style is employed. But we do not pursue a "blended" ideal. Rather, we want our singing and musical expression to be "us," not a proportioned balance or a blend. Evening worship naturally provides more opportunity for mutual encouragement, testimonies, and congregational participation in prayer. This regular evening fare is punctuated by seasonal services, missions conferences, special evangelistic emphases, and nights of prayer.

Example D. Evening Worship, May 9, 1999

In an evening series called "The Storyline of the Bible," the sermon on this Sunday placed the Old Testament prophets in the context of the entirety of Scripture. Instrumental music included the piano prelude "Scaramouche" (by 20th-century French composer Darius Milhaud) and American folk hymns played on the Appalachian dulcimer.

The extended time of singing at the beginning of the service wove hymns with familiar choruses and moved the ambience of the service from the brilliance of the two-piano prelude to the intimacy of the dulcimer. Along the way, the congregation sang words and melodies that spoke a well-rounded testimony of affirmation, affection, and action. The prolonged time of singing was made suitable for the congregation by its variety of mood, the familiarity of the songs, and by designating some hymn verses to be sung by men or women alone.

In this service we made no attempt to develop the preaching theme; our purpose was to engage in a vision of a God who is both transcendent and immanent. Following the sermon, then, we affirmed that this is the God who spoke in various times and in many ways, but in these last days has spoken through his Son and, by his written Word, continues to speak today.

Storyline of the Bible: Prophets

(Sermon 8 in a 13-part series)
Evening Service, May 9, 1999

Prelude   Debbie Hollinger, Melody Pugh, piano

Welcome & Prayer   Pastor Jim Johnston

Congregational Singing   Pastor Chuck King
> * Hymn #62—*All Hail the Power of Jesus' Name*
> * Page 3—*Glorify Thy Name*
> * Page 4—*How Majestic Is Your Name*
> * Page 5—*Great Is the Lord*
> * Hymn #67—*Fairest Lord Jesus*
> * Hymn #87—*I Love Thee, I Love Thee*

Announcements & Offering   Pastor Kent Hughes

Offertory	Carole Ehrman, dulcimer
Sermon	Pastor David White
Hymn of Response #223	*God Hath Spoken by His Prophets*
Benediction	David White
Postlude	H. E. Singley III

* Note: The text and music for these songs was included in an Evening Worship handout.

Example E. Evening Worship, October 3, 1999

As with the morning corporate worship services, we strive to maintain the same biblicism, unity, and creative nuance in making our Lord's Day evenings worship in the Word from beginning to end. As mentioned above, these times are less structured, more casual and spontaneous. The music is more eclectic.

In this evening setting, the sermon text was Acts 4:23–31, "Who Is in Control?" Following on the heels of an instrumental prelude, the congregation was led in a spontaneous, unaccompanied, joyous "He's Got the Whole World in His Hands." This familiar spiritual set the character of an informal pastiche of music—including hymns, spirituals, and choruses.

"God of Creation, All Powerful" is sung to a familiar Irish melody, while "Children of the Heavenly Father" is Swedish. The folk character of the congregational songs was picked up in "Simple Gifts" (Shaker), performed by "One Voice," an a cappella men's group of Wheaton College. Led by a College Church intern from Princeton, New Jersey, "One Voice" was the catalyst for an a cappella movement on campus much like that at Princeton University. "Ain't Got Time to Die" (African American) sung by "One Voice" continued the pleasant folk character of the evening while also reinforcing a joyful commitment to the God who is in control. Praise and worship choruses rounded out the evening: "He Is Able," itself folk-like in character, and the powerful Jude Doxology engaged our affections at the conclusion of the service.

Evening Service, October 3, 1999

Prelude   H. E. Singley III

Congregational Singing   *He's Got the Whole World in His Hands*
                            Songbook, pg. 2   *God of Creation, All-Powerful*

Simple Gifts   Jared Alcantara & Friends
                            Songbook, pg. 3   *He Is Able*

Hymn #41   *Children of the Heavenly Father*

Announcements & Offering

Offertory   *Ain't Got Time to Die*   Jared Alcantara & Friends

Who Is In Control?   Acts 1:23–31   Pastor Niel Nielson

Songbook, p. 4   *Jude 24 & 25*

Benediction   Pastor Niel Nielson

Postlude   H. E. Singley III

*Assisting in congregational singing this evening
is Kevin Casey with guitar and banjo.*

Appendix B

Wonders of Worship

Wonders of Worship provides an opportunity for children from kindergarten to second grade to learn about and practice worship. We spend the whole year focusing on "who," "where," "when," "why," and "how" we worship.

The first month we focus on "What is worship?" and answer that it is:

1. God-centered: a gift we give to God, our only response to the holy King.
2. Bible-centered: the Bible is wholly true; the whole Bible talks about worship; its two parts are the Old Testament (the Savior is coming) and the New Testament (the Savior is come).
3. The high point of our week: we can worship anytime, anywhere, but corporate worship is the culmination of all we do.
4. Active work: we use our heads, our hands, our hearts.

We then focus on the rationale of our God-centered worship, or "Whom do we worship, and why?" Our informing Scripture is Isaiah 6, Isaiah's vision of the Holy One on his throne, robes filling a temple, smoke, shaking doorposts, and six winged seraphs calling back and forth. The children memorize Isaiah 6:3, "Holy, holy, holy is the Lord Almighty; the whole earth is full of his glory." They also love memorizing three verses of the hymn "Holy, Holy, Holy." They ask to sing this hymn almost every Sunday and sing it with exuberance, seriousness, and reverence as they recall Isaiah's vision and his response. When they learn the verse about "all the saints adore thee, casting down their golden crowns around the glassy sea," we study Revelation 4. Again the children often respond in an almost stunned silence and awe as they consider the worthiness of the Lord and our great calling to respond in worship forever.

Heading into the Advent season, we learn from John 12:41 that Isaiah's vision was of Jesus himself. From "Pursuing Christ" we learn the catechism question: "Who is King over all things? The Lord Jesus Christ is King over all things."[1] It is a moving thing to see how seriously and worshipfully the children sing, "O come let us adore him" as they consider the eternal King of Isaiah 6 and Revelation 4 lying in a manger on our behalf.

---

1. "Pursuing Christ: A Biblical Profile of Christian Maturity," an unpublished statement prepared by College Church, Wheaton, in 1996.

Appendix C

Reading the Word

British evangelist and Bible teacher John Blanchard describes how he has prepared for the public reading of God's Word and the powerful results:

There are times when I have felt that the Bible was being read with less preparation than the notices—and with considerably less understanding. I hesitate to use the following illustrations because of my part in it, but I do so as a reminder to my own heart of the seriousness of the issue. A year or two after my conversion I was appointed as a Lay Reader in the Church of England, to Holy Trinity Church, Guernsey. There were two other, more senior, Lay Readers on the staff, with the result that on most Sundays the responsibilities could be evenly shared out. As it happened, the Vicar almost always asked me to read the Lessons, following a Lectionary which listed the passages appointed to be read on each Sunday of the year. My wife and I lived in a small flat at the time, but I can vividly remember my Sunday morning routine. Immediately after breakfast I would go into the bedroom, lock the door, and begin to prepare for reading the Lesson that morning. After a word of prayer I would look up the Lesson in the Lectionary, and read it carefully in the Authorized Version, which we were using in the church. Then I would read it through in every other version I had in my possession, in order to get thoroughly familiar with the whole drift and sense of the passage. Next I would turn to the commentaries. I did not have many in those days, but those I had I used. I would pay particular attention to word meanings and doctrinal implications. When I had finished studying the passage in detail, I would go to the mantelpiece, which was roughly the same height as the lectern in the church, and prop up the largest copy of the Authorized Version I possessed. Having done that, I would walk very slowly up to it from the other side of the room, and begin to speak, aloud: 'Here beginneth the first verse of the tenth chapter of the gospel according to St. John' (or whatever the passage was). Then I would begin to read aloud the portion appointed. If I made so much as a single slip of the tongue, a single mispronunciation, I would stop, walk back across the room, and start again, until I had read the whole passage word perfect, perhaps two or three times. My wife would tell you that there were times when I emerged from the bedroom with that day's clean white shirt stained with perspiration drawn from the effort of preparing one Lesson to be read in the church. Does that sound like carrying things too far? Then let me add this: I was told that there were times when after the reading of the Lesson people wanted to leave the service there and then and go quietly home to think over the implications of what God has said to them in his Word.[1]

1. John Blanchard, *Truth for Life* (West Sussex: H. E. Walter Ltd., 1982), 87–88.

Appendix D

———

When Music Equals Worship

Charles King, the Pastor of Worship and Music at College Church, writes a weekly column to the Chancel Choir. The following is his instruction.

We enjoy a rare and glorious privilege . . . to sing God's praises and his Word in the assembly of his people. But is this worship? Well, yes and no.

Music-making, even music-making that is supremely centered on the biblical revelation of our glorious God, is not by itself "worship." Or at least is not by itself "authentic worship." It may be idolatry, it may be self-centered, it may be culturally significant, it may even be extraordinarily emotional. *But when is music-making worship?*

It is no secret that those who prepare and "lead" also get the greatest benefit from their labors. There are three elements of worship in this task:

Labors: Our worship is our work at what we do for God's glory. In a very real biblical sense, Thursday rehearsals are a "worship time"! Worship is giving God his due with the devotion of our bodies, time, and energy.

Preparation: Our worship is what we do with our hearts and hands. "Who may ascend the hill of the Lord? He who has clean hands and a pure heart . . . [S]uch is the generation of those who seek him" (Ps 24). So for us it is not only the musical work, but our heart's and our life's connection to what we sing.

Leading: Making music in corporate worship is never for ourselves, but always to draw others into the joyous understanding of what we have learned and sing. Leading is worship when it is "the fruit of lips that confess his name" (Heb. 13).

Ours is a special joy and obligation. May we become "living sacrifices, holy and pleasing to God."

Sing on!

Chapter 4

REFORMED WORSHIP IN THE GLOBAL CITY

TIMOTHY J. KELLER

The Problem: Worship Wars

One of the basic features of church life in the United States today is the proliferation of corporate worship and music forms. This, in turn, has caused many severe conflicts within both individual congregations and whole denominations. Most books and articles about recent trends tend to fall into one of two broad categories.[1] "Contemporary Worship" (hereafter CW) advocates often make rather sweeping statements like "Pipe organs and choirs will never reach people today." "Historic Worship" (hereafter HW) advocates often speak similarly about how incorrigibly corrupt popular music and

---

1. As one of many examples, see Michael S. Horton, "The Triumph of the Praise Songs," *Christianity Today* 43/8 (1999): 28. He speaks of "Reformers," who value tradition and look for greater unity among churches through common liturgical forms, and of "Revolutionaries," who promote contemporary music and encourage broad diversity in worship style.

culture is, and how their use makes contemporary worship completely unacceptable.[2]

1. Contemporary Worship: Plugging In?

One CW advocate writes vividly that we must "plug in" our worship to three power sources: "the sound system, the Holy Spirit, and contemporary culture."[3] But several problems attend the promotion of strictly contemporary worship.

First, some popular music does have severe limitations for corporate worship. Critics of popular culture argue that much of it is the product of mass-produced commercial interests. As such, it is often marked by sentimentality, a lack of artistry, sameness, and individualism in a way that traditional folk art was not.

Second, when we ignore historic tradition, we break our solidarity with Christians of the past. Part of the richness of our identity as Christians is that we are saved into a historic people. An unwillingness to consult tradition is not in keeping with either Christian humility or Christian community. Nor is it a thoughtful response to the postmodern rootlessness that now leads so many to seek connection to ancient ways and peoples.

Finally, any corporate worship that is strictly contemporary will become dated very quickly. Also, it will necessarily be gauged to a very narrow market niche. When Peter Wagner says we should "plug in" to contemporary culture, which contemporary culture does he mean? White, black, Latino, urban, suburban, "Boomer," or "Gen X" con-

---

2. Representative figures who emphasize historic continuity, tradition, high culture, and theological exposition in worship are Marva Dawn, *Reaching Out without Dumbing Down* (Grand Rapids: Eerdmans, 1995), and David Wells, "A Tale of Two Spiritualities," in *Losing Our Virtue* (Grand Rapids: Eerdmans, 1998). See also the Web page for "Church Music at a Crossroads": http://www.xlgroup.net/cmac. Examples of those urging a move to contemporary worship with emphasis on "visual communication, music, sensations, and feelings" are Lyle Schaller, "Worshiping with New Generations," in *21 Bridges to the 21st Century* (Nashville: Abingdon, 1994), and C. Peter Wagner, *The New Apostolic Churches* (Grand Rapids: Regal, 1998).

3. See C. Peter Wagner, in "Another New Wineskin—the New Apostolic Reformation," in *Next* (Leadership Network: Jan–Mar 1999), 3. This is a good description of tradition-eschewing contemporary worship.

temporary culture? Just ten years ago, Willow Creek's contemporary services were considered to be "cutting edge." Already, most younger adults find them dated and "hokey,"[4] and Willow Creek has had to begin a very different kind of "Buster" service in order to incorporate teenagers and people in their twenties.

Hidden (but not well!) in the arguments of CW enthusiasts is the assumption that culture is basically neutral and that thus there is no reason why we cannot wholly adopt any particular cultural form for our gathered worship. But worship that is not rooted in any particular historic tradition will often lack the critical distance necessary to critique and avoid the excesses and distorted sinful elements of the particular surrounding culture. For example, how can we harness contemporary Western culture's accessibility and frankness but not its individualism and psychologizing of moral problems?

2. Historic Worship: Pulling Out?

HW advocates, on the other hand, are strictly "high culture" promoters, who defend themselves from charges of elitism by arguing that modern pop music is inferior to traditional folk art.[5] But problems also attend the promotion of strictly traditional, historic worship.

First, HW advocates cannot really dodge the charge of cultural elitism. A realistic look at the Christian music arising from the grassroots folk cultures of Latin America, Africa, and Asia (rather than from commercially produced pop music centers) reveals many of the characteristics of contemporary praise and worship music—simple and

---

4. The critique of Willow Creek as a "dated" and "Boomer" model can be found in Sally Morganthaler, "Out of the Box: Authentic Worship in a Postmodern Culture," *Worship Leader* (May–June 1998): 24ff. This and an interview with musician Fernando Ortega in *Prism* (Nov–Dec 1997) are indications of some major cracks in the foundation of evangelical assumptions about what kind of services will reach young secular people. However, if a church abandons "Boomer" contemporary music for more alternative rock, won't it be in the same position in another ten to fifteen years that Willow Creek is in now? More historic worship forms have a better claim to durability.

5. Marva Dawn does an excellent job of distilling Ken Myers's concerns about pop music in her chapter, "Throwing the Baby Out with the Bath Water" in *Reaching Out*, 183ff.

accessible tunes, driving beat, repetitive words, and emphasis on experience.[6] Much of high culture music takes a great deal of instruction to appreciate, so that, especially in the United States, a strong emphasis on such music and art will probably only appeal to college-educated elites.

Second, any proponent of "historic" corporate worship will have to answer the question, "Whose history?" Much of what is called "traditional" worship is very rooted in northern European culture. While strict CW advocates may bind worship too heavily to one present culture, strict HW advocates may bind it too heavily to a past culture. Do we really want to assume that the sixteenth-century northern European approach to emotional expression and music (incarnate in the Reformation tradition) was completely biblically informed and must be preserved?

Hidden (but not well!) in the arguments of HW advocates is the assumption that certain historic forms are more pure, biblical, and untainted by human cultural accretions. Those who argue against cultural relativism must also remember that sin and fallenness taints *every* tradition and society. Just as it is a lack of humility to disdain tradition, it is also a lack of humility (and a blindness to the "noetic" effects of sin) to elevate any particular tradition or culture's way of doing worship. A refusal to adapt a tradition to new realities may come under Jesus' condemnation of making our favorite human culture into an idol, equal to the Scripture in normativity (Mark 7:8–9).[7] While CW advocates do not seem to recognize the sin in all cultures, the HW advocates do not seem to recognize the amount of (common) grace in all cultures.

---

6. See Horton, "The Triumph of the Praise Songs," 28.

7. Too often, advocates for "high culture" or "pop culture" worship music try to make their advocacy a matter of theological principle, when their conviction is really more a matter of their own tastes and cultural preferences. For example, when pressed, HW advocates admit that jazz is not really a product of commercial pop culture but qualifies as a high culture medium that grew out of genuine folk roots, requires great skill and craft, and can express a fuller range of human experience than rock and pop music. See, for instance, Calvin M. Johansson, *Music and Ministry: A Biblical Counterpoint* (Peabody: Hendrickson, 1984), 59–62, on "Folk Music and Jazz." On their own principles, then, there is no reason for traditionalists not to allow jazz music in worship, yet I see no HW worship proponents encouraging jazz liturgies! Why not? I think that they are going on their own aesthetic preferences.

3. Bible, Tradition, and Culture

At this point, the reader will anticipate that I am about to unveil some grand "Third Way" between two extremes. Indeed, many posit a third approach called "blended worship."[8] But it is not as simple as that. My major complaint is that both sides are equally simplistic.

CW advocates consult the Bible and contemporary culture, while HW advocates consult the Bible and historic tradition. But in this essay I propose that we forge our corporate worship best when we consult *all three*—the Bible, the cultural context of our community,[9] and the historic tradition of our church.[10] The result of this more complex process will not be simply a single, third "middle way"; there are at least nine worship traditions in Protestantism alone.[11] That is why the book you are

---

8. Unfortunately, for many people "blended" worship consists of a simple, wooden, fifty-fifty division between contemporary songs and traditional hymns. Simply to sew pieces of two different kinds of liturgical traditions together is often quite jarring and unhelpful. It is more of a political compromise than the result of reflection about your community's culture and your church's tradition. A better example of a "Third Way" is Robert E. Webber, *Blended Worship: Achieving Substance and Relevance in Worship* (Peabody: Hendrickson, 1996). In many ways my essay agrees with Webber's basic thrust, yet even he tends to lump ancient and contemporary elements together artificially rather than interweaving them in a theological unity. I would not use the term "blended worship" as a category because it usually connotes the political compromise mentioned above. On the problems of fifty-fifty music division, see the comments at the end of the paper, under "Music for Corporate Worship, " page 236.

9. A good case for a balanced view of consulting culture within an evangelical view of the authority of Scripture is made by Andrew F. Walls in his chapters "The Gospel as Prisoner and Liberator of Culture" and "The Translation Principle in Christian History" in his *The Missionary Movement in Christian History: Studies in the Transmission of the Faith* (Edinburgh: T & T Clark, 1996).

10. A good case for a balanced view of consulting tradition within an evangelical view of the authority of Scripture is made by Richard Lints, *The Fabric of Theology: A Prolegomenon for Evangelical Theology* (Grand Rapids: Eerdmans, 1993), 83–101. He writes that Christian humility makes us recognize the reality of our biases and prejudices when coming to Scripture. This means it is unbiblical (in our doctrine of sin) to think we can find the biblical "way" without consulting our own tradition and other traditions to check our own scriptural findings. See also John Leith, *Introduction to the Reformed Tradition* (Atlanta: John Knox, 1981), ch.1: "Traditioning the Faith."

11. James F. White, *A Brief History of Christian Worship* (Nashville: Abingdon, 1993), 107, identifies the Protestant worship traditions as follows: sixteenth century: Anabaptist, (Continental) Reformed, Anglican, Lutheran; seventeenth century: Quaker, Puritan/Reformed; eighteenth century: Methodist; nineteenth century: Frontier; twentieth century: Pentecostal

reading provides examples of culturally relevant corporate worship that nonetheless deeply appreciates and reflects its historic tradition.

This more complex approach is extremely important to follow. The Bible simply does not give us enough details to shape an entire service when we gather for worship. When the Bible calls us to sing God's praises, we are not given the tunes or the rhythm. We are not told how repetitive the lyrics are to be or how emotionally intense the singing should be. When we are commanded to pray corporate prayers, we are not told whether those prayers should be written, unison prayers or extemporary.[12] So to give any concrete form to our gathered worship, we must "fill in the blanks" that the Bible leaves open. When we do so, we will have to draw on tradition; on the needs, capacities, and cultural sensibilities of our people; and on our own personal preferences. Though we cannot avoid drawing on our own preferences, this should never be the driving force (cf. Rom 15:1–3). Thus, if we fail to do the hard work of consulting both tradition and culture, we will—wittingly or unwittingly—just tailor music to please ourselves.

In summary, I believe the solution to the problem of the "worship wars" is neither to reject nor to enshrine historic tradition but to forge new forms of corporate worship that take seriously both our histories and contemporary realities, all within a framework of biblical theology. I will show how to do this within my own Reformed tradition, first looking at the basic principles of the Reformed theology of worship and then applying them in the contemporary situation.

---

12. John M. Frame, *Worship in Spirit and Truth* (Phillipsburg: Presbyterian and Reformed, 1996) shows how great a variety of forms the basic biblical elements can take. Some have argued against the use of choirs and solos on the basis of the "Regulative Principle," namely, that they are not prescribed by Scripture. But Frame asks, If some are allowed to pray aloud while the rest of the congregation meditates, why can't some be allowed to sing or play aloud while the rest of the congregation meditates? (p. 129). Why would song be regulated in a different way than prayer and preaching? Some have argued against using hymns and non-scriptural songs on the basis of the Regulative Principle. But Frame asks, If we are allowed to pray or to preach using our own words (based on Scripture), why can we not sing using our own words (based on Scripture)? (p. 127). Why would song be regulated in a different way than prayer and preaching? Some have argued against the use of dance in worship, but aside from many apparent references to dance in worship in the Psalter, Frame asks, If we are exhorted to raise hands (Neh 2:8; Ps 28:2; 1 Tim 2:8), clap hands (Ps 47:1), and fall down

The Reformed Worship Tradition

The historic tradition of Reformed worship, especially the Continental liturgical branch, can, I believe, inform and shape gathered worship in a very contemporary setting.

1. The Variety of Reformed Corporate Worship

One writer says, "For the first time in over 400 years, a consensus as to what constitutes Presbyterian worship is nowhere to be found"[13]— but that is an oversimplification. In the sixteenth century, two Swiss Reformers sought to renew gathered worship along biblical lines. Ulrich Zwingli created a service that was centered almost completely on the preacher's teaching and praying. It had little or no liturgy, music, or congregational participation. John Calvin, however, designed a service with more fixed liturgical forms, more music, and more congregational participation. As is well known, Calvin also desired that every service would combine the Lord's Supper with the Word preached.

These approaches were sufficiently distinct to lead the liturgical historian James F. White to describe them as two different worship "traditions" within the Reformed community.[14] Zwingli's approach was the seedbed for the worship of the Puritans, expressed in the Westminster Confession and Standards, as well as that of later "Free Church" worship.[15]

(1 Cor 14:25), is it not expected and natural that we accompany words with actions? (p. 131). We can't preach, surely, without using our bodies to express our thoughts and words, so how can we arbitrarily "draw the line" to exclude dance? Frame points out that the real way to make decisions about these issues (such as dance) is wisdom and love—namely, what will edify? In other words, if you think that dancers in leotards will be too distracting and sexually provocative for your congregation, just say so— don't try to prove that the Bible forbids it. It is a bad habit of mind to seek to label "forbidden" what is really just unwise.

13. Terry L. Johnson, *Leading in Worship* (Oak Ridge: Covenant Foundation, 1996), 1.

14. James F. White, *A Brief History*, 107.

15. This is the view of Peter Lewis, "'Free Church' Worship in Britain," in *Worship: Adoration and Action*, ed. D. A. Carson (Grand Rapids: Baker, 1993), who points out that the extemporary prayer, the lack of emphasis on artistic variety and quality, and the sermon-as-worship-climax were all passed down from the Puritans to the Free Churches. Lewis is more positive about the Puritan tradition than is Guillermo W. Mendez, who sees hidden in the tradition many European cultural assumptions, for

Continental Reformed worship, following Calvin, was admittedly more rooted in early Christian tradition.[16]

It is critical to remember that "from the beginning, there were two different liturgical conceptions within the Reformed wing of the Reformation."[17] This may partly explain why Reformed evangelical churches have been as divided by the "worship wars" as the rest of the U.S. church.[18] There has never been complete consensus. Reformed HW advocates sometimes speak as if a use of the "Regulative Principle"— a strictly biblical standard for gathered worship forms—will solve the "wars" and bring us back to a single, simple kind of service. But Zwingli and Calvin,[19] both working with the same biblical commitments, came to such different conclusions that they birthed two distinct corporate worship traditions.[20] On the other hand, Reformed CW advocates often do not take sufficient notice of how the Reformed tradition could and should influence gathered worship today.

Having identified two worship traditions within the Reformed tradition, I now want to concentrate on what we can learn from Calvin rather than Zwingli. Why? First, I believe we can learn from the

---

example: "Awe, admiration and quiet pondering are the only possible human responses to God's majesty. That means that all non-silent human responses are less spiritual . . . and cognitive handling of Scripture is more pleasing to God than praise. . . . [T]he impression is left that knowledge has devoured experience." See "Worship in the Independent/Free Church/Congregational Tradition: A View from the Two-Thirds World," in *Worship: Adoration and Action,* 172.

16. Hughes Oliphant Old, *The Patristic Roots of Reformed Worship* (Zurich: Theologischer Verlag, 1976).

17. Klass Runia, "Reformed Liturgy in the Dutch Tradition," in *Worship: Adoration and Action,* 100.

18. Two articulate examples of the two opposing Reformed "sides" on worship are (HW advocate) Terry L. Johnson, *Leading in Worship,* and (CW advocate) John M. Frame, *Contemporary Worship Music: A Biblical Defense* (Phillipsburg: Presbyterian and Reformed, 1997).

19. See Edmund P. Clowney, "Presbyterian Worship," in *Worship: Adoration and Action,* 115. Clowney makes a good case that Calvin held to the Regulative Principle of worship, though Calvin's conception of nonessential "circumstances" was broader than that of many other proponents of this principle.

20. See n. 12 above on how the Regulative Principle cannot produce a single, simple form of worship.

process that Calvin used to shape his worship for the gathered community. As I said above, our current "worship wars" are due in great part to our unwillingness to consult the Bible, culture, and tradition together. I think Calvin did this much more effectively than did any of the other Reformers. His process for forging corporate worship is therefore highly instructive for us. Second, I believe Calvin's product—the actual worship tradition he gave us—has traits that are very relevant to contemporary "postmodern" people.[21]

Calvin's corporate worship tradition resonates with many of the concerns of postmodern people. They have a hunger for ancient roots and a common history; Calvin emphasizes this through liturgy in a way that neither traditional Free Church worship nor contemporary praise worship does. They have a hunger for transcendence and experience; Calvin provides an awe and wonder better than the cognition-heavy Free Church services in the Zwinglian-Puritan tradition and better than the informal and breezy "seeker services." Postmodern people are much more ignorant of basic Christian truth than their forebears and need a place to come to learn it, yet they are also more distrustful of "hype" and sentimentality than older generations. Calvin's worship tradition avoids the emotional manipulation that so frightens secular people about charismatic services, even though they desire the transcendence that contemporary-praise worship appears to offer.

Though we must not adapt too much to postmodernism, much of what it seeks is based on a valid, postmodern critique of modernity's idols (e.g., individualism, sentimental views of human nature, rationalism) and therefore can justifiably be taken into account as we plan our worship as a gathered community. Calvin will give us many resources for doing so.

---

21. Of the making of books about postmodernity there is no end! But three accessible and helpful ones (for me) have been Gene Veith, *Post-Modern Times* (Wheaton: Crossway, 1994), Stanley Grenz, *A Primer on Postmodernism* (Grand Rapids: Eerdmans, 1996), and Richard Lints, "The Theological Present," in his *The Fabric of Theology* (Grand Rapids: Eerdmans, 1993). In tone of voice, Veith is more negative, Grenz is more positive, and Lints is more scholarly. Together they give a good overview without taking too much time.

2. The Sources of Calvin's Corporate Worship

We said above that CW and HW advocates have overly simplistic processes for arriving at their corporate worship forms. How did Calvin arrive at his?

No one questions that Calvin considered the Bible to be the supreme authority and source for God-honoring worship. But Calvin also understood that the Bible had not given us a New Testament "Directory of Worship" like Leviticus had provided for pre-Christian worship.[22] The Bible may give us basic elements of corporate worship, but it leaves us free with regard to modes, forms, and the order of those elements (traditionally called the concrete "circumstances" of worship). Therefore, the reformer did not claim the ability to create a pure biblical corporate worship "from scratch." Rather, he first consulted ancient tradition and produced a simplified liturgy of Word and Eucharist based on patristic worship. Calvin's reliance on church tradition has been well documented by Hughes Old, so there is no need to make that case any further.[23]

Not only did Calvin engage with ancient Christian tradition, but he also consciously consulted the capacities of the congregants. The Latin of the medieval Mass was only accessible to "the learned" classes schooled in "high culture," but Calvin would not choose high culture over intelligibility to the common person.[24] The preaching and the singing were to be done so that they were accessible even to the unlearned.[25] Calvin went so far as to write that the liturgy he presented to the church was "entirely directed toward edification."[26] This refusal of Calvin to choose between transcendence and accessibility is

---

22. John Calvin, *Institutes,* IV.x.30. Cited in Clowney, "Presbyterian Worship," 117.

23. Hughes Oliphant Old, *The Patristic Roots of Reformed Worship.*

24. This must be borne in mind by those who rightly fear the loss of transcendence and the sentimentality of evangelical worship. They emphasize the dangers of popular culture, but their emphasis and preference for high culture may lose touch with Calvin's concern for accessibility and the intelligibility of worship for the person with less formal education.

25. Calvin, *Commentary on 1 Corinthians,* 449.

26. Calvin, *Opera Selecta,* 2:15, quoted in Leith, *Introduction,* 176.

striking.[27] When Calvin faced the question of how to arrange the concrete "circumstances" of worship (such as whether we should pray standing or kneeling, in unison or individually, etc.) he wrote that we must be wholly directed by the concern for edification, for the love of those present. "If we let love be our guide we are safe."[28]

The present relevance of Calvin's process for shaping gathered worship is obvious. Critics of the "seeker services" insist that gathered worship services are strictly "for God" and not for the people present, that in gathered worship "God alone matters."[29] But Calvin refused to pit "the glory of God" against the "edification" of the participants. The basic elements of gathered worship are laid out by God in his Word, but our arrangement and utilization of them is strongly controlled by what helps and touches those who come.[30]

3. The Balance of Calvin's Corporate Worship

What is worship? Is worship *primarily* what happens on Sundays when we do specific activities of singing, praying, offering, confessing, and so on? Or is worship *primarily* the way we live all of life for the honor of the Lord in such a way that Sunday gatherings are no more "worship" than any other time in the week? Within Protestantism, this is an old debate. "Low church" advocates have traditionally leaned toward the

---

27. Happily, I find Calvin at this point to have many affinities with the insights of David Peterson, "Worship in the New Testament," in *Worship: Adoration and Action,* as well as those of Don Carson in the first chapter of this book. They point out how usual is the New Testament description of the weekly services of the church as being for "edification."

28. Calvin, *Institutes,* IV.x.30. Quoted in Clowney, "Presbyterian Worship," 116.

29. The first quote in this sentence is from John H. Armstrong, "The Mad Rush to Seeker-Sensitive Worship," in *Modern Reformation* 4/1 (Jan/Feb 1995), 25. The second is by C. W. Gaddy, *The Gift of Worship* (Nashville: Broadman, 1992), quoted in Dawn, *Reaching Out,* 80.

30. A strict Willow Creek model assumes that a church cannot do both evangelism and worship in the same service. That is why the model provides for "seeker services" on the weekend and mid-week services for worship. Ironically, the most severe critics of "seeker-sensitive" worship share the same premises (as can be seen in Armstrong, "The Mad Rush"). The premise is that you cannot really combine the vertical and horizontal—you cannot have transcendent adoration and effective edification and evangelism in the same service. Calvin's statements undermine this premise, I believe.

second view and insisted that Sunday services are not distinctive from "all of life" worship, while "high church" advocates have held to a view that it is supremely in the gathered corporate service that "real" worship actually happens.

In today's church, this debate has taken on new forms. The CW and charismatic churches have a new form of the old view—that worship really happens in the service of corporate praise rather than out in the world during the week. The alternative to this view has recently been put forth very articulately by low-church evangelical Anglicans in Australia and Britain.[31] This view argues that Christ completely fulfills all the "cultic" elements of worship—the temple, the priesthood, the sacrifices, the Sabbath, the Passover—so that now the language of worship is applied to how all Christians live all of life (1 Pet 2:5; Rom 12:1; Heb 13:16, 17). This view contends, then, that our gathered meetings are not in any distinctive way "worship." The main reason that Christians gather now is for edification.

It is not my place here to make any detailed arguments about these two views. Don Carson does that in his chapter in this book and comes to a "middle" position that I essentially agree with.[32]

On the one hand, to say that we meet on Sunday only for edification is a mistake. Worship, as Carson writes, " is ascribing all honor and worth to . . . God precisely because he is worthy, delightfully so."[33] We are therefore only truly worshiping when we are serving God with our entire beings, including our hearts, which must be "affected" by God's glory. The fullest definition of worship, then, is something like "obedient action motivated by the beauty of who God is in himself." If this is worship, it is more than being moved "affectively," but it is not less. For example, when we gather to listen, pray, and praise as a community, we are seeking to "remember" the gospel (cf. 1 Cor 11:25). "Remember" cannot simply be a cognitive action. It is talking about

---

31. See, for example, David Peterson, *Engaging with God* (Leicester: Apollos, 1992) and "Worship in the New Testament" in *Worship: Adoration and Action.*

32. See also a very balanced and exegetically thoughtful view of the subject in Herman Ridderbos, *Paul: An Outline of His Theology* (Grand Rapids: Eerdmans, 1975), 481ff.

33. See Chapter 1 above, "Worship under the Word," 26.

getting a "sense of the heart" of the truth so that our lives can be more conformed to what we believe. Corporate praying, corporate singing, corporate offering, and hearing God's Word all do have a distinctive worship function.[34]

On the other hand, it is also a great mistake to load into the Sunday service all that the Bible has to say about worship. While I fear that the "edification only" view will lead to an academic, classroom approach to worship without an expectation of transcendence, so this opposite view is in danger of leading us toward emotional hype or toward a performance mentality in corporate worship services. If worship only "happens" in the "big event," then we will be overly concerned to give people a huge emotional or aesthetic experience.

There is another danger to differentiating corporate worship too much from "all of life" worship. You can become far too inflexible about what occurs within the worship service. For example, among many traditionalists in my denomination, it is allowable for a woman to teach a Sunday school class or small group, but not to speak from the

---

34. John Frame, from a Reformed perspective, nicely strikes this middle "balanced" view of worship in chapter 3 of *Worship in Spirit and Truth*. He gives full weight to the exegesis of Peterson and the fact that the coming of Christ has fulfilled the ceremonies and rituals, so that "essentially, what is left is worship in the broad sense: a life of obedience to God's word, a sacrifice of ourselves to his purposes. All of life is our priestly service, our homage to the greatness of our covenant Lord" (p. 30). However, Frame does not agree that Christians therefore no longer meet for any kind of distinctive corporate worship, though he admits that there is some danger in calling Sunday services "worship" (p. 32). He points out that many of the things we do in gathered meetings, such as offerings and praise (Heb 13:15–16), prayers (Rev 5:8; 8:3–4), and the reading and hearing of the Word (Heb 4:12) all have bestowed on them worship or "cultic" terminology by the NT writers. Also, we are still exhorted to "draw near" to God (Heb 10:19–22; cf. 12:28–29)—is that not worship in some sense distinctive from the normal work of obeying God? Frame even gives an illustration to explain the difference between corporate worship and "all of life" worship. If you serve the king in his palace, you are doing so all the time. Yet certainly when the king himself comes into the room where you are working and has a conversation with you, "your service takes on a different character ... becomes somewhat ceremonial. You bow, and you remember as best you can the language of homage. ... Something like this happens in our relationship to God. All of life is worship ... but when we meet him, something special happens" (p. 33). So Frame concludes that all of life is worship, but there is something distinctive about corporate praise and worship.

pulpit during corporate worship. This is because, in their view, the Sunday "worship" is something very different and set off from the lives that we live during the rest of the week. Since the formal worship service is seen as *real* worship, it must be regulated much more strictly than all the rest of life. However, the "middle" balanced view we are putting forth here means that there is no scriptural distinction between "formal" and "official" worship services and other gathered meetings of the church.[35]

As far as I can tell, Calvin himself rode out a "middle" way in this issue.[36] For example, Calvin believed that Christ so fulfilled the Sabbath that the Old Testament regulations regarding Sabbath observance are not really binding on worshipers today at all. (The Puritans and the Westminster Confession, of course, disagreed sharply with him.) On the other hand, Zwingli seemed to view the Sunday gathering as mainly a time of teaching and edification, indistinguishable from a class. Calvin, however, knew that one purpose of the service was transcendence, a corporate experience of God. Therefore, he introduced more liturgical elements and gave more emphasis to music.

In short, Calvin believed that there was *corporate* worship and that it was distinct from, and supportive of, the worship of Christians in all of life. If this balance is not maintained, you will get either an overly cognitive or overly emotional shape to your worship. (Note: This is why

---

35. Frame effectively criticizes the view that there is such a thing as a "formal" worship service that is more regulated by the Word of God than any other part of life. This is one of the unfortunate results of failure to recognize how Christ has transmuted Christian worship so as to include all of life (see *Worship in Spirit and Truth*, 37–49). It is ironic that the two major protagonists in the "worship wars"—the contemporary charismatic praise-and-worship movement and those advocating return to traditional worship—both seem to hold a similar (unbalanced) view of worship that sees the worship service as being sharply different from the rest of Christian living and gathering.

36. On the one hand, Calvin certainly understood the principle that for the Christian "all of life" is worship. See his comment in the *Institutes* on the "sum of the Christian Life" as seen in Rom 12:1: "Here then, is the beginning of this plan: the duty of believers is 'to present their bodies to God as a living sacrifice, holy and acceptable to him,' and in this consists the lawful worship of him (Rom12:1)" (III.vii.1). On the other hand, Calvin is of course very interested in what he calls "public" prayers and worship (for example, IV.x.29).

I often use the somewhat inelegant term "corporate worship" in many headings in order to maintain this balance.)

4. The Core of Calvin's Corporate Worship

Nicholas Wolterstorff's excellent article identifies a core commitment that is central to all the distinguishing traits of Calvin's corporate worship.[37] If we could return to the sixteenth century and attend both a Catholic service and a service led by Calvin, we would immediately be struck by obvious differences. First, we would notice how much simpler Calvin's service was. The medieval liturgy was extremely elaborate. Second, we would notice how much the Bible was read and preached in Calvin's liturgy. In the Mass the "homily" had virtually disappeared. Third, we would notice the increased participation of Calvin's congregation in singing, praying together, reading, and listening. In the medieval Mass, lay people passively watched the actions of priests and musicians. There was very little common prayer. The congregants prayed silently, individually, as priests behind a screen prayed inaudibly in Latin.[38] They were not even offered the eucharistic cup.[39]

What caused this difference? A superficial answer might be that the Reformed "style" was more democratic and intellectual, but that is to give a sociological address to a theological principle. Wolterstorff identifies the conception of grace as the central difference between medieval gathered worship and that of the Swiss Reformers. Aquinas, for example, insisted that the sacraments are literally the cause of grace, regardless of the state of piety of the priest or recipient.[40]

---

37. Nicholas Wolterstorff, "The Reformed Liturgy," in *Major Themes in the Reformed Tradition,* ed. Donald McKim (Grand Rapids: Eerdmans, 1991), 280–81.

38. See Robert M. Kingdon, "The Genevan Revolution in Public Worship," in *Princeton Seminary Bulletin* 20 (1999): 167. Kingdon states that the essential difference between Calvin's service and medieval worship was that "above all, they had to deploy a different set of sense. [Protestants] were expected to absorb what is most essential in religion through hearing [the Word] rather than through seeing [the Mass]" (p.180). Listening to a sermon takes far more engagement than watching the performance of the Eucharist.

39. See White, *A Brief History,* chs. 3 and 4.

40. *Summa Theologica,* III, Q. 62, art.1. Cited by Wolterstorff, "Reformed Liturgy," 282.

The whole goal of the service was to use the instruments of grace to reach God.

This view of grace had the practical effect of losing the action of God himself in the service. Nowhere in the service was God heard to speak or seen to act or initiate. Even the physical movement (of the priest with his back to the people, approaching God with the sacrifice of Christ) was all from us toward God. There was never movement from God toward the people. The priests used the instruments on behalf of the people to satisfy God.

The "core commitment" of Calvin's corporate worship was his rediscovery of the biblical gospel of unmerited and free grace. God's grace comes to us as *a word to believe*, rather than as a deed to be performed. This new emphasis on the "graciousness of grace" made Calvin's corporate worship distinct from the medieval Mass. Calvin believed that medieval corporate worship was "performing the sacrament" in order to get God to bless the people. That was why the emotional, ritual, mystical, and sacramental aspects were completely dominant. But on the other hand, Calvin avoided the completely nonsacramental, rational, nonmystical meetings of the Zwinglians (and to a great degree the Anabaptists). It could be that he realized that there was a "worship-as-performance" error on the Protestant side. Could not congregants fall into "performing the Word" in order to get God to bless them?[41]

Calvin's balance of "corporate worship elements" (singing, sacrament, common prayer) with the preaching of the Word all flowed out of his emphasis on the sovereign free grace of God in the gospel. What follows is a sketch of some of the salient traits of this gathered worship.

5. Traits of Reformed Corporate Worship

(a) Its Voice—*Simplicity.* Calvin believed that simplicity of form and language should be valued over spectacle on the one hand and sentimentality on the other.

---

41. For evidence that the Zwinglian service lent itself to worship-as-performance, see below, n. 54, and discussion in Wolterstorff, "Reformed Liturgy."

Medieval worship worked directly on people's emotions through pomp, ceremony, and spectacular architecture and performances. But Calvin wrote that corporate worship must "omit . . . all theatrical pomp, which dazzles the eyes . . . but deadens their minds." So concerning ceremonies, "it is necessary to keep fewness in number, ease in observance, dignity in representation."[42] The Reformers saw how the medieval spectacle tended to make worshippers passive observers and to stir the emotions without changing the understanding and life. Most of all, the "spectacle" represented a lack of confidence in God's gracious action. Does God need a great performance before he will give us his favor? Therefore, Calvin asked not for mediocrity but for a lack of ostentation—in ceremony, music, and architecture.

Calvin also spoke of "dignity in representation," however. This was a warning against the modern opposite to ceremony—what today we might call "folksiness" or sentimentality. Often it is a reverse form of pride: "We are not like the snobs who need all that artistic finery." In an effort to be nonpretentious, many churches produce a service with a deliberate lack of concern for quality of music, reading, singing, and speaking. "Worship leaders" speak completely "off the cuff," sharing spontaneous thoughts. As a result of the mediocrity and informality, there is no sense of awe, no sense of being in the presence of the Holy. Calvin knew the difference between simplicity and sentimentality.

Sentimentality is subtle. C. S. Lewis once told a young writer: "Instead of telling us a thing is 'terrible,' describe it so that we'll be terrified. Don't say it was a 'delight,' make us say 'delightful' when we've read the description. You see, all those words ('horrifying,' 'wonderful,' 'hideous,' 'exquisite') are only saying to your readers, 'Please, will you do my job for me.'"[43] Lewis complains that authors of gushy and sentimental words are tyrannical because they tell the readers how they must feel rather than letting the subject work on them in the same way it did the author. Sentimental worship leading works in exactly the

---

42. The two quotes are from *Institutes*, IV.xv.19 and IV.x.14. See John Leith, who discusses these quotes under the heading of "Simplicity" in *Introduction*, 176.

43. *Letters of C. S. Lewis*, ed. W. H. Lewis (New York: Harcourt, Brace, and World, 1966), 271.

same way that Lewis describes. With typical comments—"Isn't he just wonderful?" "Isn't it such a blessing?"—the leader tells people how they ought to feel about God instead of telling them about God.

Both spectacle and sentimentality work directly on people's emotions rather than trusting God's Spirit to bring truth "home."[44] The "moderately liturgical" form of Calvin's corporate worship was a practical upshot of his concern to be simple, avoiding spectacle on the one hand and sentimentality on the other.[45] Reformed gathered worship does not have as many prescribed forms, fixed parts, and historical references (e.g., creeds) as "higher" churches (Anglican and Lutheran), but it has more than the Free Church or the charismatic churches. The mild liturgy means that it is not as dependent on casual and spontaneous remarks by the pastor and other leaders.

(b) Its Goal—*Transcendence*. Calvin believed that the goal of gathered worship was to bring people face to face with God. His aim was not that people would simply learn information about God, but that they would truly hear God speak and know his presence in the service.

Calvin's gathered worship was famously *soli Deo gloria*.[46] Worship was God-centered, and its purpose was to honor God. But nothing honors him more than the "fear of God." This "fear" is not servile scaredness, but rather awe and wonder.[47] Calvin's theology shows a remarkable

---

44. See Ken Myers, *All God's Children and Blue Suede Shoes: Christians and Popular Culture* (Westchester, Ill.: Crossway, 1989), 84–85, for a good summary of what is wrong with sentimentality: (1) Sentimental emotions are fleeting and not change-associated. (2) They are welcomed just for emotion's sake, as a good in themselves, instead of as a due response to truth. (3) They thus always are taken with a grain of salt. Sentimentality creates deep cynicism. No one takes it very seriously.

45. In the broadest sense, *liturgy* simply means "the shape of the worship service." In that (better) sense of the word, all worship traditions have a liturgy. I am using the word in another valid sense, as "ceremonies, symbols, and fixed responses." In this sense, Anglican worship is more "liturgical" than Reformed, which is more so than Free Church worship. Wolterstorff has a fine discussion of the meaning of *liturgy* in "Reformed Liturgy," 274–75.

46. The primary principle of Reformed worship is that "worship must above all serve the glory of God" (Hughes Oliphant Old, *Worship That Is Reformed According to Scripture* [Atlanta: John Knox, 1984], 2).

47. Psalm 130:3–4 is a famous text that proves the "positive" content in the biblical term "fear of the Lord." Here the psalmist says, essentially, "I fear you because of

balance between objective and subjective knowledge. He taught that head and heart are coherently bound up in the act of worship:

> A good affection toward God is not a thing dead and brutish but a lively movement, proceeding from the Holy Spirit when the heart is rightly touched and the understanding is enlightened.[48]

Years later, Jonathan Edwards surely was speaking in Calvin's tradition when he said that worship has not occurred when the "external duties" are performed of "reading, praying, singing, hearing sermons, and the like" even when "zealously engaged in," but only when our "hearts [are] affected, and [our] love captivated by the free grace of God," and when "the great, spiritual, mysterious, and invisible things of the gospel ... have the weight and power of real things in their hearts."[49]

Thus, for Calvin the goal of gathered worship is to make God "spiritually real" to our hearts. That is where truths (that we may have known intellectually) now by the Spirit's influence become fiery, powerful, and profoundly affecting (e.g., Rom 8:15–16). They now thrill, comfort, empower (or even) disturb you in a way they did not before (Eph 1:18–22; 3:14–21). It was not enough, for Calvin, to be told about grace. You had to be *amazed* by grace.

How, then, do we fit the first trait (simplicity) together with this second trait? How can we bring people into transcendent awe and wonder in God's presence when Calvin forbade the most obvious ways to "create" that sense of awe—the use of the spectacular or the maudlin? This is accomplished in the following ways.

First, the sense of transcendence is dependent on the quality of speaking, reading, praying, and singing. Sloppiness drains the "vertical" dimension out of gathered worship immediately.[50] There was

---

your forgiveness." This means that "the fear of God" contains joyful amazement as well as humble and sobering awe.

48. Quoted in Leith, *Introduction*, 176.

49. Jonathan Edwards, *Religious Affections*, ed. John Smith (New Haven: Yale, 1959), 163, 263, 291–92.

50. In America the metaphorical terms "vertical" and "horizontal" with regard to worship have widespread usage. "Vertical" has to do with our relationship to God, with the sense of awe and the fear of the Lord. "Horizontal" has to do with our relationship to one another, with the sense of community and unity in the Lord.

nothing "sloppy" about Calvin's approach! His use of music is a case in point.

Mark Noll points out that in the Reformation Lutherans and Catholics used "complex music and professional performance," while Anabaptists eschewed all "worldly" forms of music in favor of unaccompanied congregational song. The Anabaptists' reason for doing this was what Noll calls their "populist" sentiments.[51] They felt that less professionalism made music less "worldly" and more spiritually "pure." The other great Swiss Reformer, Zwingli, made his service almost completely oriented toward cognition and the mind, and eliminated most music because of its emotional power.[52]

Calvin, however, took a middle way. Because professional musicians could turn the congregants into an audience instead of a community, he chose not to use choirs or soloists. But he by no means shared the view that artistic excellence was elitist.[53] Instead, he took care to hire excellent poets to put the Psalms in metric form and excellent composers to put them to music. Far from shunning excellence, the early Reformed practice was to turn the congregation into a well-trained choir under trained "singing masters."[54] Mediocre music and language can only provide a "horizontal" reference. Our hearts may be

---

51. Mark Noll, *Turning Points* (Grand Rapids: Baker; Leicester: IVP, 1997), 17.

52. Leith, *Introduction,* 177.

53. Calvin's service book (1545) included a hymn—an indication that he did not think it a sin to sing hymns. However, as a "quality control," he limited worship music to the singing of metrical psalms. He also avoided organs, most instruments, and even elaborate polyphony. As we saw above, these restrictions were not grounded in the same disdain of artistic excellence that led the Anabaptists to unaccompanied song. It was due to his concern for simplicity and intelligibility. (As we have seen, musical quality is important for transcendence.) Therefore, while Anabaptist theology of art would preclude accompaniment and choirs per se from worship, Calvin's theology does not. His "middle way" between the Anabaptists and the Lutherans points the way for Reformed worship today to include the judicious use of accompaniment, ensembles, and solos—provided Calvin's over-arching purposes of simplicity, transcendence, and edification are honored. The music must not turn the church into an audience enjoying the music but into a congregation singing the Lord's praises in his presence.

54. See Anne Heider's program notes to *Goostly Psalms: Anglo-American Psalmody 1550–1800,* by His Majestie's Clerkes; Paul Hillier, conductor—a compact disc on the Harmonia Mundi label. See also *A Land of Pure Delight: William Billings Anthems and Fuging Tunes* by the same artists on the same label.

warmed by the sincerity of the singer or speaker, but excellence has a "vertical" reference, lifting the heart toward the transcendent.

The second way we get transcendence with simplicity is the demeanor or heart attitude of those leading in the gathered worship. If their tone is merely joyful and warm, the service will have an exclusively "horizontal" reference. It may be very sweet and cozy, but it will not inspire transcendent awe. However, if their tone is only dignified and sober, this will simply create somberness or awkwardness.[55] There will be no wonder, which is a constituent part of transcendent awe. Transcendence is served best when both delight and awe are evident in the leaders' demeanor and heart. Then the congregation will sense that it is being ushered into God's presence.

Why would this be the case? Again, this flows from the gospel of grace. The gospel means (as Luther said) that we are *simul justus et peccator,* that is, in Christ we are simultaneously righteous yet sinful. If we have a more antinomian view of salvation, believing that we are all accepted because God is vaguely loving, then we may be existentially aware of God's love but not of his holiness. There will be no awe. That can lead to the exclusively warm, "folksy" demeanor. If, on the other hand, we have a more legalistic view of salvation, believing that we are accepted because we live and believe everything "exactly right," then we may be existentially aware of God's holiness but not of his bounteous mercy. There will be no wonder. That can lead to an overly stiff and dignified manner.[56]

---

55. While an exclusively warm and happy attitude by the worship leaders can give a good sense of unity and community in the Lord (the "horizontal"—see n. 182), an exclusively dignified and serious attitude does not bring a sense of transcendence and the fear of the Lord. Rather, it creates an atmosphere of remoteness, grimness, and severity. I make this additional comment because many writers and church leaders who rightly disdain the loss of transcendence (especially in "contemporary" worship) may move to the other extreme. They encourage dignity and seriousness but without a deep joy mixed in with it. Such a spirit will not help people into the presence of God.

56. Of course, all terms such as "dignified" are somewhat culturally elastic. What would be considered proper decorum in one culture can be considered stiff and remote in another culture. This is often the case even between generations in the same culture: what my parents' generation considered respectful, my children's generation considers harsh and severe. But though these terms are elastic, they are not infinitely so. There are attitudes and behaviors that in all cultures would be considered undignified, disrespectful, shallow. So we cannot glibly say that it is all relative. Allowances and adjustments must be constantly weighed and made.

In neither case are the leaders really *amazed* at grace. Only when there is a profound awareness of the holiness of God and of the costliness of the sacrifice he provided will there be a joyful awe that is at once warm and forceful. Only a joyful yet awe-filled heart—an exuberant decorum—can keep pomp and sentimentality from mimicking the two true poles of biblical worship: awe and intimacy.[57]

(c) Its Order—*Gospel reenactment*. By the "order" of Reformed gathered worship, we are not speaking so much about the exact sequence of Calvin's service, but of the foundational rhythm and flow of his liturgy.

To the "right" of Calvin's service was the medieval liturgy, which had almost completely lost the sense of God's speaking to us.[58] All the action was taken up with the priest on the congregation's behalf. To the "left" of Calvin was Zwingli, whose service was nearly completely taken up with the preacher, on God's behalf, speaking to the congregation. Ironically, both kinds of services made the people passive. Why? Because there was no "rhythm" of reception and response. In the medieval service there was much responding, but no place where people heard a word of grace. In the Zwinglian service there was a great deal of listening, but no place for response. The sermon ended the service. So in both services there was no rhythm of reception and response in faith, of receiving grace and thankful action.

Wolterstorff contrasts Calvin's attitude toward the Lord's Supper with Zwingli's. Zwingli's opening prayer for the Eucharist asks that we might rightly perform our praise to God, while Calvin's opening prayer asks that we might rightly receive that which God has to give us. "How ironic that in his understanding . . . Zwingli is allied with the medievals against Calvin!"[59] He argues that Zwingli had more of the medieval concept of grace-as-performance than the Calvinist concept of grace-

---

57. This paragraph is based on a typically brilliant, pithy comment by Derek Kidner on Psalm 66:2: "The gloriousness [of praise] will be that of 'spirit and truth . . . ,' the grandeur and vitality of worship that . . . is never trivial, [but] never pretentious" *Psalms 1–72* (Leicester: IVP, 1973), 234.

58. Cf. the section above, "The Core of Reformed Worship," and Wolterstorff's article, "Reformed Liturgy."

59. "Reformed Liturgy," 292–93.

as-received-gift. That view of grace accounts for Zwingli's imbalance of Word without the response of sacrament as well as the Catholics' imbalance of the sacrament over the Word.[60] All such imbalances come from a lack of orientation to free grace and an orientation toward performance. If we fail to grasp grace, we will seek to perform either through Word-obedience or Eucharist-usage. Instead, Calvin saw the entire service, not as a performance for God by the celebrants, but as a rhythm of receiving God's word of grace and then responding in grateful praise. That is how the gospel operates. We do not perform duties, anxiously and wearily hoping that some day we will deserve to enter his kingdom and family. Rather, we hear the word of our acceptance now; and transformed by that understanding, we respond with a life of thankful joy (Rom 5:1–5).

For Calvin, then, each service reenacted the reception of the gospel. How did that work? There were two basic features to Calvin's order of service. The first, and most obvious, was that unlike the medieval and the Zwinglian services, Calvin provided a balance between hearing the gospel in the first half of the service, the "Service of the Word," and responding in grateful joy in the second half of the service, the "Service of the Table," the Eucharist. If we separate the Eucharist from strong preaching, the Lord's Table becomes something to perform, and the gospel-response of thanks is muted in the liturgy's structure. If we separate the preaching from the Eucharist, the Word becomes something to perform, and the gospel-response of thanks is also muted. We know that the leaders of Geneva did not let Calvin celebrate the Lord's Supper every week as he wished. We today could respond to Calvin's concern by having the Eucharist very frequently. [61]

But Calvin's theme of "hear-and-respond" was not confined to the sacrament. The second basic feature of his service was the repeated

---

60. There was also, in the medieval and Zwinglian services, an imbalance of "head" and "heart," or thinking and emotion. The medieval emphasized artistic magnificence, rite, mysticism, and emotion; while Zwingli emphasized thinking, learning, and rationality.

61. At Redeemer Presbyterian Church, we have for many years celebrated the Lord's Supper in the morning service on the first Sunday of each month, and in the evening service on the third Sunday of each month. Since many parishioners attend both, we essentially offer the Eucharist every other week.

cycle within the service of hearing-repentance-renewal in grace. The following chart throws Calvin's liturgy into relief. [62]

Zwinglian	Calvinian	Medieval
Invocation	Scripture Sentence	Choral Introit
Scripture	Confession/Pardon	*Kyrie*
Sermon	Singing of Psalms	Collects
Prayer	Illumination Prayer	OT reading
Creed/Decalogue	Scripture Readings	Antiphonal chant
Benediction	Sermon	Epistle reading
	Psalm sung	
	Offerings	Alleluia
	Intercession Prayer	Gospel reading
	Creed (sung)	Sermon
	Words of Institution	Gloria
	Exhortation	Dismissal
	Communion (with singing or Scripture reading)	Psalm 43
		Nicene Creed
	Prayer	Offertory Prayer
	Benediction	*Agnus Dei*
		Consecration
		Communion
		Collect
		Dismissal

Unlike the typical evangelical service of singing followed by preaching, Calvin's liturgy shows the "rhythm" of corporate worship based on the gospel.[63]

---

62. The Medieval and Zwinglian liturgy is based on the information in White, *A Brief History*, 89, while Calvin's liturgy is based on information in Leith, *Introduction*, 185ff.

63. See John Murray, "The Church—Its Identity, Functions, and Resources," in *Works* (Edinburgh: Banner of Truth, 1976), 3:239: "There are two aspects to worship, God's address to us and our response to his address. The former consists particularly in the reading and preaching of the Word, and the latter in adoration, reception, thanksgiving, and prayer." Murray does not mention Calvin's belief that the Eucharist is both God's address to us and our response to him.

First, there is an "Isaianic" cycle. God's Word is read (a Scripture sentence), and the congregation responds with a confession of sin. God's words of pardon are then a gracious response of God to repentance. After this, the singing of a psalm is in turn a response of thanks and praise to God for his mercy. We have here a very close approximation of the experience of Isaiah 6.

Next, there is a "Mosaic" cycle. Prayer for illumination asks for God to appear through his Word read and preached as he did to Moses in the burning bush. The aim is not simply instruction and information, but the knowledge of his glory. To respond to God's Word, there is the offering and prayers of intercession.

Finally, there is an "Emmaus" cycle, in which Jesus becomes known to us in the breaking of the bread. The exhortation over the table was included so that the Lord's Supper was not seen as only a response. The supper itself is a gospel-word, an embodied sign of Christ's work for us. So within this third cycle, we have both God's address to us (the sung creed, the Words of Institution, the exhortation) and our response of grateful joy to him (in the Communion, the prayers, and the singing). These cycles of deeper repentance leading to deeper grace and joy is the "gospel rhythm" that shapes Calvin's liturgy.

Summary: In conclusion, we have said that the *voice* of Calvin's gathered worship is *simplicity of form* because of our confidence in God's grace (cf. 1 Cor 2:2–5). The *goal* is *entering the presence of God,* in our amazement at God's grace (cf. Exod 33:18). The *order* consists of cycles of *gospel reenactment* for the reception of God's grace afresh. "Let us then approach . . . with confidence, so that we may receive mercy and find grace to help us in our time of need" (Heb 4:16).

6. Tests of Reformed Corporate Worship

If we are truly receiving grace in the presence of the living God, three results should occur. If they do not, we must radically reexamine what we are doing.[64]

---

64. I must admit that Calvin and the Reformers did not give the following "tests" as much emphasis and development as they deserved. I believe, though, that these tests are implicit in the Reformed tradition that Calvin left us. That is why other Reformed theologians have taught these to us. I think it is therefore fair to include these tests as part of the historic Reformed tradition of worship that Calvin left us. But because I am not able to cite him very much in this section, I will be fairly brief.

(a) Doxological evangelism. Calvin's refusal to choose between the glory of God and edification (see "Sources of Calvin's Corporate Worship" above) lays the groundwork for what Edmund Clowney calls "doxological evangelism."[65]

Clowney points out that Israel was called to make God known to the unbelieving nations (Ps 105:1) by singing his praises (Ps 105:2). The temple was to be the center of a "world-winning worship." The people of God not only worship before the Lord but also before the nations (cf. Isa 2:1–4; 56:6–8; Ps 47:1; 100:1–5; 102:18; 117). God is to be praised before all the nations, and *as* he is praised by his people, the nations are summoned and called to join in song.

This pattern does not essentially change in the New Testament, where Peter tells a Gentile church to "declare the praises" of him who called us out of darkness. The term cannot merely refer to preaching but must also refer to gathered worship. Two case studies of this are in Acts 2 and 1 Corinthians 14. In Acts 2, the nonbelievers initially hear the disciples praising God (v. 5), which leads them to ask what the worship is all about (v. 12) and how they can find God (v. 37). In 1 Corinthians 14:24–25, a nonbeliever in the midst of gathered worship falls down in conviction that God is real. These two case studies show that nonbelievers are expected in gathered worship, that nonbelievers should find the worship comprehensible (that is the point of Acts 2:11 and 1 Cor 14:23–24), and that nonbelievers may be convicted and converted through corporate worship.

Despite these biblical exhortations, preachers and other leaders typically lead in congregational worship as if no non-Christians are present. This only ensures that Christians will not feel safe in bringing nonbelieving associates. But if we do not follow Calvin at other points, our corporate worship will also not be challenging or comprehensible to nonbelievers even if they are brought. A lack of simplicity (especially sentimentality) or a lack of transcendence (especially mediocrity) will bore, confuse, or offend nonbelievers. On the other hand, if

---

65. This term is taken from a seminal work on the whole subject of "evangelistic worship" by Edmund Clowney, "Kingdom Evangelism," in *The Pastor-Evangelist* (Phillipsburg: Presbyterian and Reformed, 1985), 15–32. This whole section is a summary of his teaching.

a service aims very strictly at being *only* evangelistic, the Christians will not have their hearts engaged in worship, and the main power of "doxological evangelism" is lost. Non-Christians will not see a people formed and sustained by glorious praise.

In summary, if the Sunday service aims primarily at evangelism, it will bore the saints. If it aims primarily at education, it will confuse unbelievers. But if it aims at *praising the God who saves by grace,* it will both instruct insiders and challenge outsiders. Good corporate worship will naturally be evangelistic.

(b) *Community building.* The passage in 1 Peter 2 not only tells us that we are to worship before the nations, but it tells us to declare his praises as "a chosen people . . . a holy nation" (v. 9).[66] Christian worship is both a cause and an effect of our being a very distinct community.

It has been typical of sociologists to divide religious groups into two forms—"church" and "sect."[67] A "sect," we are told, has a very strong, distinct group identity because it is negative toward the world, stressing purity and the holiness of God. A "church," however, has begun to lose its distinctive identity. It is much more positive toward the world, stressing the acceptance and love of God.

Miroslav Volf, in a study of 1 Peter, shows that the biblical church transcends these categories.[68] On the one hand, it did not "demonize" the surrounding world, but rather gave respect to worldly authority (2:13–21) and showed patience when persecuted (3:8–17). On the other hand, it never lost sight of being "aliens and strangers" (2:11).

How could the church keep a strong, distinct identity without either "affirming" or "denying" the world? It was because "she did not forge her identity through rejection [demonization] of her social environment, but through the acceptance of God's gift and its values."[69] As

---

66. Again, I rely on the exegesis of Edmund Clowney. See *The Message of First Peter: The Bible Speaks Today* (Leicester: IVP, 1992).

67. Ernst Troeltsch in his highly influential *The Social Teachings of the Christian Churches* followed Max Weber and was largely copied even by H. Richard Niebuhr in his classic *Christ and Culture.*

68. See Miroslav Volf, "Soft Difference: Theological Reflections on the Relation between Church and Culture in 1 Peter," *Ex Auditu* 10 (1994): 15–30.

69. Ibid., 30.

we have seen, it is preeminently in corporate worship where the truth of the gospel becomes "spiritually real" to us and renews us according to its power.

True worship, then, is the key to forging strong identity without the separatism and legalism that marks so many "sects." But then "community building" also becomes a second test of real worship. If the great preaching and music simply draw a crowd of people who have nothing to do with each other the rest of the week, we have created spectacle, not a worshipping community.

(c) *Character for service.* Edwards, in his *Religious Affections,* said that the acid test of a heart with its affections truly raised toward God (his definition of worship) is love toward one's neighbor, working for the common good in society. A real experience of the triune God, said Edwards, that divine "society or family of three," will necessarily lead to love of neighbor.[70] Corporate worship is only true and effective when it leads us to the "all of life" worship of doing justice and living generously (Heb 13:16). Wolterstorff makes the point that God's action in the service perfectly mirrors his action in the world, so that if our hearts are truly forged anew by gospel reenactment, we will, like him, move out into the world in welcome of the poor, the stranger, the marginalized.[71] This is one of the reasons that Calvin wanted alms for the poor incorporated into regular corporate worship. Our actions in gathered, corporate worship will strongly influence our actions in scattered, "out in the world" worship.[72] Paul's complaint to Peter about his cultural biases was not that he was simply breaking God's law, but that his prejudice was not "in line with the truth of the gospel" (Gal 2:14).

Amy Plantinga-Pauw writes: "While contemporary Reformed culturalists are quick to insist that faith in God must result in a thirst for

---

70. *Religious Affections,* 263.

71. See Wolterstorff's other article, "Worship and Justice," in *Major Themes in the Reformed Tradition,* ed. McKim.

72. James White, in *A Brief History* (p. 165), explains how the more egalitarian worship form of the Quakers (in which anyone present in the service could speak) had a "spillover" effect into the abolitionism and social justice work of the Quakers in the world.

love and justice on earth, they have been slower to acknowledge that a full-orbed earthly ethic can only originate from thirst for God."[73] It is not just faith in general, but worship in particular that will be the fountain of strength and desire to work for peace and justice in the world.

Practice: Contemporary and Reformed Worship

1. Reformed and Contemporary

How does the historic Reformed tradition interact with contemporary Western culture when it comes to corporate worship? Speaking very broadly, there are four possible ways. The first two are characterized by minimal or no real interaction. First, there is "Reformed worship," in which an unchanged sixteenth-to-seventeenth-century Reformed tradition is maintained without any real interaction with contemporary realities. This is characterized by traditional hymns and instruments, much talking up front, and substantial preaching. Second, there is "Contemporary worship," in which the typical "praise music service" does not interact with the Reformed tradition. This is characterized by a "worship band-team," a long stand of singing with interludes of devotional commentary, followed by the sermon.

The next two models are characterized by good interaction of tradition and culture. On the one hand, there is what I will call "Reformed Contemporary Worship." This is a more contemporary mode with significant HW elements integrated in. This form relies musically largely on CW songs and on instruments (a "band") that best render such music. However, this form also uses many historic hymns and other theologically substantial lyrics put to contemporary tunes and arrangements. There is also much more "simplicity" of voice, avoiding the typical sentimentality of contemporary "worship leading." Finally, the service follows a basic shape of "gospel reenactment." Though there are fewer fixed liturgical forms, there are acts of

---

73. See Amy Plantinga-Pauw, "The Future of Reformed Theology: Some Lessons from Jonathan Edwards," in *Toward the Future of Reformed Theology,* ed. David Willis and Michael Walker (Grand Rapids: Eerdmans, 1999), 469.

entrance and praise, confession of sin and assurance of pardon, more readings of Scripture and use of Creeds, and greater emphasis on the sacrament.[74]

Lastly, there is what I will call "Contemporary Reformed Worship." This is a more historic mode with CW elements integrated. It relies musically mainly on "high culture" forms and historic hymns, and it uses the instruments (orchestral "ensembles" and organ) that best render such music. However, this form makes careful use of contemporary and folk selections that lighten and sweeten the tone. Drawing on Calvin's tradition, it is characterized by more frequent Communion, moderate liturgy, and an orientation toward silence, joyous awe, and wonder.

As I have said before, there is no one "middle way" or "third way." Neither of these approaches is a simple fifty-fifty compromise; but rather they both work to integrate Bible, culture, and tradition in such a way that the result is a coherent whole. Our own congregation, Redeemer Presbyterian Church, has a morning service (called "Contemporary Reformed") that is Reformed worship with contemporary influences, while our evening service (called "Reformed Contemporary") is customary worship with Reformed influences. One of Redeemer's first two daughter churches, the Village Church in downtown Manhattan, uses a more "Reformed Contemporary" format (though it is more liturgical than our evening service), while another daughter church, Trinity Presbyterian of Westchester County, uses a "Contemporary Reformed" format.

What follows is a more specific case study of how corporate worship is led, planned, and designed at Redeemer Presbyterian Church in New York City.[75]

---

74. See Webber, *Blended Worship*, Appendix II. His version of "blended worship" comes closer to what I am describing as "Reformed Contemporary Worship."

75. Redeemer Presbyterian Church meets in the Upper East Side and Upper West Side of the borough of Manhattan in New York City. (1) Denominational profile: Redeemer is a member of the Presbyterian Church in America (PCA). (2) Sociocultural context: The population of Manhattan is 1.5 million, and in our ministry area (midtown and downtown) it is nearly 70 percent single. Those singles state their "religious preference" as 40 percent Catholic, 21 percent Jewish, 6 percent Protestant, and 33

2. Leading in Corporate Worship

"Leaders" in corporate worship include all those who will be "up front"—praying, reading the Scripture, singing, preaching, praising, and even giving "notices" or "announcements." In a thoroughly non-liturgical service or in a highly liturgical service there is less need for the leaders to prepare. (They either make some off-the-cuff remarks, or they simply read elaborate prayers and formulas.) In our approach to corporate worship, the leaders not only have much material to prepare, but they also have a great deal of spiritual preparation to do. Their attitude of heart and demeanor is as important as what they say. The remarks and spirit of the leader are therefore extremely important. The following are guidelines and instructions that we use with our leaders.

(a) Demeanor. First, if we have a sense of awe before God's glory, we shouldn't be too charming, cute, or folksy, drawing attention to ourselves. Instead of folksiness, there should be dignity and a sense of wonder. Second, if we have a sense of freedom in God's love, we won't be nervous, intimidated, or self-conscious. Instead of tautness, there should be a sweetness and peace. Third, if we have a sense of humility before God's grace, we won't be pompous, authoritarian, severe, or "ministerial." Instead of pomposity, there should be authenticity and humility.

(b) Emotion. First, we should neither hide nor over-control our feelings behind a reserved, formal, and deadpan exterior. One sign of genuineness is that there is a full range of emotions. We should not always be happy or sad or intense or tender. Unless our feelings are

---

"other/no preference." (Compare this with the rest of the United States, which is more than 50 percent Protestant and 12–15 percent "no preference.") Fifty percent consider themselves "very liberal" compared to less than 20 percent nationally who give that answer. (3) Our congregation's Sunday attendance in late 2001 was 3,800 adults in corporate worship. Of these, 75 percent are Manhattan residents, 80 percent are single, 98 percent are professionals, with an average age of 30. We are 50 percent Anglo, 35 percent Asian, and 15 percent of other ethnic groups. We estimate that 20–35 percent of our attenders are nonchurched and/or non-Christians.

deeply engaged, how can we lead others to worship? But second, we should not let our feelings have full scope, leaving the congregation behind.[76] If we indulge our individual feelings, how can we lead others to worship? Third, we should not talk overly about how we feel or about our experiences and convictions ("I believe that . . ."). And we should not tell others how they are supposed to feel at the moment ("Don't you just really want to . . . ?" or "Isn't the Lord just so good?"). Both are manipulative and "bathetic," working directly on the feelings instead of pointing to the Lord. Instead of hiding, discussing, or forcing feelings, we should reveal a full range of emotions as we lead. It should be clear to others that we have strong emotions that we are keeping in check, rather than hiding an empty heart under sentimental language or hearty gestures.

(c) Language. First, language should not be too archaic. It is dangerous to seek transcendence and dignity by using antiquated language, which can be stuffy, preachy, grandiloquent, pedantic, and over-stated rather than simple, immediate, clear, vivid, and direct.[77] It is especially easy to lapse into such language because the King James Version of many texts of Scripture will come to mind as we pray and speak. Instead of saying, "we have been unchaste in our hearts," say "our thoughts have been impure." Don't pray

> Almighty God, we come before you now. Because of our transgressions, we are not worthy of you, but forgive us for Christ's sake. Give us fervent hearts to worship you in a faithful and worthy manner. Let your Word be mighty in us to the pulling down of strongholds, and to the casting down of imaginations and everything that exalts itself against the knowledge of God.

But rather,

---

76. If you let your emotions have full scope, you will draw attention to yourself. Generally, when you let your personal emotions go too far, you (at best) have forgotten the corporate aspect of worship and are absorbed in your own response to God. At worst, you are showing off, doing "spiritual bragging."

77. Instead of using archaic ("fair" instead of "beauty") or florid language ("beauteous" instead of "beauty"), use "Strunk-White" English. This refers to the rules of

Almighty God, gracious Father, we are not fit for your presence, but we look to Jesus Christ, who takes away our sin. Through him we would now come to you, listening to your voice, trusting in your love, delighting in your Word, and leaning on your arm. We joyfully beg to see your face! Now cleanse our minds of all error and our hearts of all idols, that we may shine in the world with your radiant light.

Second, on the other hand, language should not be too colloquial. Just as archaic language loses the accessibility and intimacy of worship, so colloquial language loses the transcendence. Colloquial language is casual, familiar, highly idiomatic, and sentimental instead of stately, elegant, and "unembroidered." Colloquial language has little resource for expressing emotion except to use "bathetic" words. "Lord, you are so incredible." "The Lord is so exciting."

An overly informal style of address would be this:

Lord God, it is just so good to be here today with you, Father. Here with the family of brothers and sisters who love you. And we just ask that you would be really near to us, and help us to really lift up your Name. Lord, you are just incredible.

Third, language should be free from technical jargon, and especially evangelical subculture terminology. There are innumerable phrases that we fall back on because they sound "spiritual," but they are sentimental and undecipherable to non-initiates. For example: "Let us come *unto* the Lord." "Let's just *lift up* the name of Jesus." "We pray for a *hedge of protection* around him, Lord." Overuse of the word *blessing* is another example of jargon. Key theological terms like *justification* can be introduced and explained. Subcultural talk, however, is at best highly exclusionary and at worst very phony, a ruse to hide a lack of actual heart engagement.

---

composition in the little volume *The Elements of Style* (2nd edition; New York: Macmillan, 1972) by William Strunk and E. B. White. Their rules of composition include "use the active voice," "put statements in positive form," "use definite, concrete language," "omit needless words," "express co-ordinate ideas in similar form," "keep related words together," "place the emphatic words of a sentence at the end." (If only I had followed these rules as I wrote this essay!)

3. Planning Corporate Worship

Weekly Preparation. Our bulletins contain our entire liturgy—all prayers, music, and responses are fully written out. We use no overheads, no hymnals. This is partially a physical necessity (we do not own any buildings), but we find it is also simpler for people unfamiliar with Christian worship. In order to enhance the quality of our singing and corporate worship, we have developed a limited number of confessional prayers, calls to worship, confessional responses, and hymns or songs to sing. Without repetition our people can't learn the music or come to deeply understand the concepts. Therefore, we put our prayers and liturgies and opening hymns into about twenty-five "templates" that are repeated twice a year. These templates keep us from having to "start from scratch" each week in developing liturgies.

Each Monday the music director brings the week's templates for the next two or three weeks to the corporate worship planning meeting, which consists of pastors, music directors, and other staff. The staff has already put the preacher's sermon title, Scripture text, reflection quotes, and final hymn selection into the working draft of the next week's liturgy. After the staff evaluates yesterday's services in some detail, they turn to the upcoming liturgy draft and begin to make revisions. Many of the revisions are made in order to keep each part of the service "in line" with every other part and with the sermon. Many other revisions have to do with variables such as the number of people to be baptized, a special offering, and so on.

Basic Liturgies. We have two basic liturgies at Redeemer, one that has the sermon earlier in a more strictly "Calvinian" manner, and one that has the sermon later in the service. In turn, each of these liturgies has two basic "music modes" in which it can be produced. One music mode is mainly characterized by classical music/hymns, but with carefully selected and occasional folk/contemporary music added. The other music mode is mainly characterized by jazz music/praise songs, but with carefully selected and arranged traditional hymns added. (See the next section on "Worship Music.") What follows is Liturgy #1—the less Calvinian manner—in a classical music mode.

LITURGY #1

Praise Cycle

Preparation *(Scripture)*

Hymn of Praise

Responsive Call to Worship *(Scripture)*

Invocation

Lord's Prayer

Doxology *(Old Hundredth)*

Silent Adoration

Renewal Cycle

Scripture (Call to Renewal)

Prayer of Confession

Silent Confession

Confessional Response

Words of Encouragement *(Scripture)*

[Baptisms, Membership Vows, Testimonies]

Prayer (Pastoral or Prayers of the People)

Hymn

Commitment Cycle

Words of Welcome

Scripture (before the Sermon)

Sermon

Call to Offering

Offering and Offertory

Hymn

Exhortation

Benediction and Dismissal

Commentary on Liturgy #1: Each of the three cycles consists of hearing God's Word of grace through Scripture and responding through the offering up of our lives. But each cycle facilitates a hearing-and-offering of a different kind. The first cycle is to recognize the presence and greatness of God. The second cycle is to pull our hearts' affections off things we worship besides God. The third cycle is to set our hearts' affections on God and live out of that new awareness.

The Praise Cycle is designed to shake participants free from distractions and remind them that God alone is worthy of worship, and of the possibility of meeting God in his presence. It begins with the *Preparation.* A leader gives a 60-to-90-second exhortation on the nature and practice of gathered worship. It is based on a verse of Scripture or on a Scriptural idea already in the service—in the hymn about to be sung or in some other item in the liturgy. The "worship prep" must go from friendly ("Hello, welcome to Redeemer. Let me help us get ready for worship") to rousing and intense in just a few seconds. For example: "Worship is not *less* than learning, but it is far more than that. It is not *less* than inspiration, but it is far more than that. You are here to meet God. That means anything could happen. You might remember what happened today twenty years from now as the day your eyes were opened to something you'd always been blind to. Are you ready for that? Are you looking for that?"

The opening *Hymn of Praise* is of course majestic and "big" and focused on praise and adoration. We may use orchestral ensembles along with organ. The hymn is a response to the preparation. The *Responsive Call to Worship* is the second (and the main) place in the praise cycle that the people hear the Word from God regarding his greatness and worth. The call is Scripture broken into four or six responsive segments. The leader must lift up the voice and heart and be obviously in full-hearted praise. The call is shouted, and the Scripture is chosen to be shout-able.

Invocation.[78] The leader responds to the scriptural call on behalf of the people, usually using the call's themes and phrases. The invoca-

---

78. See Hughes Oliphant Old, *Leading in Prayer: A Workbook for Worship* (Grand Rapids: Eerdmans, 1995) for an excellent selection of prayers of invocation based on Scripture texts.

tion builds energy quickly. It is not quiet and pedantic, but it gathers momentum and is usually done in only two breaths. It must be filled with longing and delight at the riches before us. It moves into a unison *Lord's Prayer.* Immediately thereafter comes the climax of the first cycle and the response to the whole—the *Doxology.* This is done each week to the tune of the "Old Hundredth," two verses, with the second verse modulated up a key from the first. Whenever possible we have trumpets and other instruments supplementing the organ. It is often the "biggest" sound and voice that the congregation musters all day.

The final part of the cycle usually consists of *Silent Adoration.* Silences are (at least twice) very real parts of corporate worship. They are not "transitions." We take our times of silence very seriously. The people are urged to take a full minute to praise God in silence. We find that the pure silence is sometimes more startling and attention-grabbing than anything else has been. It actually forces people to ask, "Am I actually worshiping?" in a way the other parts of the service do not. The leader briefly introduces the minute by urging people to either praise God directly, or to revisit part of the service so far (hymn, call to worship, doxology, or the preparation) and ask God to open their hearts to make these themes living realities.

In some settings (the time of day and the physical space make a difference), we find that a sweet and quiet song of praise can be sung before the silent adoration. At the end of this cycle, the people have crossed the first mountain range in the journey. The leader may simply say "Amen" and seat people (who have been standing since the beginning of the hymn), or close with a brief summarizing prayer that ties together the themes of the whole first cycle. It all usually takes about 10 to 15 minutes.

The Renewal Cycle is designed to provide opportunity for analysis of what our hearts are now worshiping *instead* of God. Then we repent and hear God's word of grace in the gospel. While the first cycle moves from inertia to dynamic shout, this second cycle moves from a quiet sorrow to the sweetness and relief of grace and pardon. It begins with *Scripture of Renewal.* A lay person reads a Scripture passage that is selected to be the basis for the cycle of renewal. The leader then explains the text and how it can be a guide for us during repentance.

The tone of this brief, one-minute exhortation is sober yet warm and hopeful. The renewal Scripture can sometimes look ahead to the rest of the service with its sermon theme, but that is not necessary.

The *Prayer of Confession* is always a written prayer, prayed in unison by the congregation. This is immediately followed by *Silent Confession*. The leader invites the participants either to return to the written prayer of confession to make it one's own in silent reflection, or to go and confess "free form" about personal wrongs and sins. After silent confession, the congregation responds musically to God through a *Confessional Response* or *Hymn*. Musicians at the church have composed several short (two or three line) phrases that are usually sung twice. The music tends to be bright, soft, and lyrical, with a "folk" feel. Instrumentation would be lighter, such as strings or solo instrument and piano rather than organ and trumpets. Immediately after the confessional response, the leader reads the *Words of Encouragement*. We always print a Scripture passage that talks of forgiveness and pardon.

If we have no vows that Sunday (see the next item), we may simply choose the second hymn to look back to the confession and thus be itself a confessional response. The "middle hymn" then can have more of a "folk" feeling to it. It can be more accessible, contemporary, and melodic than the first and last hymns. If the hymn comes after vows and testimonies, it may in its theme look back to the work of the church (if testimonies are about life in the Body) or back to the joy of salvation (if there have been adult baptisms) or ahead to the sermon.

Vows and Testimonies. Other appropriate responses to God's word of pardon are vows and covenant-making. One week a month we have new members take their vows, at that time doing both infant and adult baptisms. In addition (or in substitution), we have testimonies of changed lives. Very often, some ministry in connection to the church wishes to make itself better known to the congregants. Rather than have "commercials" or even "announcements," we regularly have people from various ministries speak of how God's grace is operating in their lives. At certain times of the year we hear from people whose lives have been influenced by fellowship groups, or ministries to the poor, or diaconal work, or international missions, or other volunteer ministries, or we hear from those who have been converted. Testimonies are written out and reviewed by staff before they are given.

The final part of the renewal cycle is *Prayer.*[79] This is always a prayer of intercession for the needs of the church and the needs of the world, but it may take different forms, depending on the elements of this cycle. If there are no testimonies or vows, and there is no observance of the Lord's Supper, the prayer might immediately follow the sung *Confessional Response.* In that case, the prayer is a direct response to God's word of pardon. Then we go to God with our needs and the needs of the world because we have confidence in his grace. If, on the other hand, the prayer comes after baptisms, vows, or testimonies, it will focus more on those new commitments. The prayer is sometimes simply prayed by a pastor, but we prefer to have it provided by one or two lay persons. The second cycle ordinarily takes 15 to 20 minutes and concludes with a hymn.

The Commitment Cycle centers on hearing God's Word through the sermon. After the sermon there are opportunities for investing our substance, our hearts, and our lives in him. It begins with *Words of Welcome.* These are "announcements" but are kept as part of the worship service. They serve as one of the very few places in the service where there is some relief from the emotional intensity of the rest of the liturgy. It is almost literally a place to "catch your breath," a place to cough. The announcements are only there to truly be "Words of Welcome." They put a human face on the congregation to newcomers. They must be done with the humble humor that admits our congregation's flaws ("We are trying to work on the sound system—we know the problems some of you are having in the back!") and values ("Please realize that if you are not in a small group, we may not discover your needs or concerns as fast. So join a group!"). Also, our church's "worldview" is very much on exhibit at this time—its view of the city, for example.

The *Scripture and Sermon.* The Scripture is read by the preacher, and with a Scripture sentence, declaration, or prayer for illumination

---

79. Besides Old, *Leading in Prayer,* which has a good selection of prayers of intercession, see Arthur Bennett, *The Valley of Vision* (Edinburgh: Banner of Truth, 1975) for a wide variety of excellent prayers put into modern language from older sources.

between the end of the Scripture reading and the sermon.[80] The preacher might simply say, "This is the Word of God," or give a very brief prayer.

Offering and Offertory. After the sermon is the *Call to Offering.* It is necessary to forcefully take the congregation "in hand" here if the offering and offertory are going to be truly a part of corporate worship. We exhort people to make use of the offering as a time to ask, "What has God been saying to me in this service, and what should I do about it?" We have a musical offering to go with the people's offering. This should be carefully chosen to fit the sermon theme.

The *Closing Hymn* is chosen for themes that have to do with the sermon. The moment the hymn is over, the preacher gives a brief (30-second) but ardent *Exhortation,* urging seekers to stay for classes dealing with the basics of Christianity, urging Christians to stay for discipleship classes, and inviting people to come forward for prayer with officers who are in the front of the auditorium. For example: "You noticed that I assumed the authority of the Bible and that may raise many questions in your mind. Well, I urge you to stay for a class on that very subject, which begins in twenty minutes: Why Trust the Bible? There are very good reasons to do so. Please stay. Your questions won't be dismissed; you won't be browbeaten!" The *Benediction* and *Dismissal* sends people out with a shout: "Thanks be to God!"

---

80. See Old, *Leading in Prayer,* for an excellent selection of brief prayers of illumination, based on Scripture texts.

LITURGY #2

Praise Cycle

Preparation *(Scripture)*

Hymn of Praise

Responsive Call to Worship *(Scripture)*

Invocation

Lord's Prayer

Doxology *(Old Hundredth)*

Silent Adoration

Renewal Cycle

Call to Renewal

Prayer of Confession

Silent Confession

Words of Encouragement *(Scripture)*

Scripture (before Sermon)

Sermon

Commitment Cycle

Offering and Offertory

[Offertory Music]

Community Life

Prayers of the People

Hymn

Invitation to the Table

Creed

Eucharistic Prayer

Giving of the Bread and Cup *(Scripture)*

[Hymns and Songs]

Prayer of Dedication

Hymn

Benediction and Dismissal

Commentary on Liturgy #2: This liturgy more literally follows Calvin's order of having the sermon earlier in the service, in the Renewal Cycle, giving the people more chance to digest and respond to the message. Once a month the Lord's Supper is the heart of the Commitment Cycle. One other Sunday of the month, baptisms and member vows become the heart of the commitment cycle. In the other weeks the Prayers of the People are longer and more elaborate than in Liturgy #1. Also there are two songs or hymns that follow the hymn, not just one.

Here are the differences from Liturgy #1: In this liturgy the *Prayers of the People* are more elaborate and participatory. Several lay people may pray prayers they have written, or they may lead the congregation in a responsive, written, unison prayer. These prayers are for the needs of the church and the world, but they also are tied in to the sermon theme. They give people a chance to ask God to help them apply the message to their lives. Also in this liturgy the "Words of Welcome" are called *Community Life*. This consists of several carefully worded notices, but they are tied in to the prayers about to come. The leader says: "This is how we live out this truth in our community life."

The *Lord's Supper* must be led in a special way in an evangelistic, urban church. Since we live in a post-Christian society, we expect the presence of many people in the service who should not be partaking. But our goal is nonetheless to include them so that the Supper becomes either a converting or a renewing ordinance for them. We say something like this: "If you are not in a position to take the bread and cup, then take Christ! It is the best possible time to do business with him, no matter what your spiritual condition or position. He is present." We have found that it is very normal for people to become converted in the monthly Communion service, even though they are not communing. If they have been listening to the Word for some time, the Lord's Supper service forces them to ask: "Where do I stand with God?" in a way that other services do not. We print in the liturgy the prayers that are used in the service. (See appendix.)

To take us from our discussion of planning corporate worship to a more thorough discussion of music styles, let me offer (without commentary) another example of Liturgy #1, this one in a contemporary rather than a classical music mode. Again, both examples of Liturgy #1 are distinguished from Liturgy #2 in that their sermons come later in the service and therefore have a less Calvinian manner.

LITURGY #1 (Contemporary)

Praise Cycle

Preparation

Songs of Praise (3)

Approaching God (Invocation)

Renewal Cycle

Call to Repentance

Song of Renewal (1)

Prayer of Confession

Silent Confession

Words of Encouragement

Songs of Renewal (2)

Commitment Cycle

[Testimony]

[Vows/Baptisms]

Prayers of the People

Song of Response

Words of Welcome

Scripture

Sermon

Call to Offering

Offering and Offertory

Song of Praise (1)

Benediction and Dismissal

It is interesting to note that, at least in Manhattan, our "contemporary music" service has not been more effective than our classical music service in including nonbelievers. If anything, the reverse has been the case.

4. Music for Corporate Worship[81]

In earlier parts of this essay I have laid the groundwork for a more moderate approach to contemporary music than either CW or HW advocates commonly take. Nevertheless, at Redeemer we believe that a wooden "fifty-fifty" division between praise songs and traditional hymns is usually not helpful. In this final section, I lay out our church's specific guidelines for choosing music for the worship services.

(a) Reasons for "Excellence" in Music. First, we have made it a basic principle that music in corporate worship must be of high technical and artistic quality as well as theologically sound and fitting for some of the traits and tests of corporate worship. Many churches believe only the latter concern is nonnegotiable. Why have we decided that they are both absolutely necessary?

Transcendence. As we said above, excellent music is more important for Reformed than for other kinds of corporate worship because the goal is transcendence without spectacle and ritual. Without great music it is hard to capture transcendence and yet have simplicity. Nothing contributes to a hushed sense of awe better than music that is startlingly good.

Evangelistic inclusion. The better the aesthetics, the more it includes both insiders and outsiders, both newcomers and old-timers. Mediocre music may be edifying to long-time Christians for two reasons. First, they may know the performers and think "Ah, how great to have that faithful member using her gifts in this way!" Second, they are much more likely to know and understand the Christian lyrics. But nonbelievers or seekers who enter and listen to a mediocre or poor musical performance will not be helped to sense God's presence or be struck by the beauty of the words. They will at best be unmoved, and at worst distracted or made to feel awkward by the performance.

---

81. Much of what is in this section is the work of our Worship Arts director, Dr. Tom Jennings.

Contextualization. Technology is making people everywhere more and more used to excellence in music. It is obvious that Manhattan's general resident population is remarkably musically literate. That is why we can occasionally offer a provocative, more atonal piece of high-culture music that should probably not be tried in most places. However, in general all parts of the United States and much of the rest of the world are more and more "wired," and therefore it will become less and less possible for churches to present mediocre art in their services.

(b) Reasons for Selection of Music. There are several reasons why we are not strictly "contemporary" or strictly "historic" or compromising with a "fifty-fifty" blend of contemporary and historic music.

First, *musical form and style are not neutral.* Contemporary worship advocates usually insist that music style is neutral and a matter of taste and that there is no reason why we cannot use any form of music.[82] However, contemporary advocates actually do "draw lines," recognizing that some music is inappropriate for gathered worship.[83] Some of the tunes and arrangements of popular music are too saccharine, syrupy, or bombastic. (On the other hand, we have found this to be true of a number of "traditional" hymns as well.) Nobody is really a musical relativist.

Second, *musical style boundaries, however, are very elastic.* Traditional worship advocates insist that music style is not neutral and that it carries connotations that may not be appropriate for gathered worship. They then eliminate pop music with arguments about its superficiality and sentimentality. But others have noted that jazz and folk music require a great deal of skill, can be marked by excellence, and can express a fuller range of human feeling. They have not grown out of commercialism and modernity, and thus they are deemed appropriate for gathered worship.[84] But the boundaries between pop music and (the more substantial) folk, jazz, or black gospel are really very fuzzy. There are many individual pieces that are hard to classify. How

---

82. Dawn, *Reaching Out,* 183.

83. Donald Miller, *Re-Inventing American Protestantism* (Berkeley: University of California Press, 1997), 84–85.

84. Calvin M. Johansson, *Music and Ministry: A Biblical Counterpoint* (Peabody: Hendrickson, 1991).

can the anti-contemporary-music party set definitive and unambiguous boundaries? They can't. Our position, then, is a midway one. Each piece of music has to be judged on its own merits. Music that people may consider "pop" is acceptable if it can be performed excellently, if the words of its text are rich and doctrinally illuminating, and if it conveys the gospel. We have no broad-based definition of "pop music" that eliminates a piece automatically before we apply these tests.

Third, *music styles have integrity*. As I said before, we do not think it is easy to mix classical and contemporary music equally in the same service. The first obstacle is the instrumentation. We are committed to quality and excellence, but can an organ, brass, and tympani accompany "Lord, I Lift Your Name on High" as well as can a guitar and snare drum? On the other hand, can guitar, saxophone, and drum accompany "A Mighty Fortress" as well as organ and brass? The answer in both cases is no. And it would be extremely jarring to go from organ-and-brass to saxophone-and-drum in the same service.

The second obstacle is that, since musical style is not neutral, we should recognize that folk/contemporary music has a frame of reference that is different from Bach. They set different tones. Each one conveys certain theological themes better than the other. One kind of music is better for certain occasions, for certain architecture and settings, and even for certain styles of preaching than is the other. Therefore, we have generally found it best to let one kind of music dominate any particular service. Nevertheless, as I said above, judicious mixing of classical and folk in a service is both possible and desirable. In a HW service, a folk or popular chorus can sweeten and lighten the tone at the end of a time of praise, after a confession of sin, or during the Lord's Supper. On the other hand, the CW service almost has to borrow some historic hymns, since modern choruses tend to harp on the same themes over and over. (It is nearly impossible to find certain themes, like the holiness of God or social justice, in them.) However, to honor the integrity of musical forms, it is best for traditional hymn lyrics either to be put to contemporary tunes or at least to contemporary arrangements.

(c) Reasons for Selection of Musicians. First, we use only professional and/or trained musicians for our corporate worship services, and

we pay them all. The reason for this has to do with our commitment to excellence. We are one of many congregations today that hire only professional clergy for their staff. Ministers (and other staff, such as counselors) are expected to be schooled and trained specifically for their work and then paid for it by the church. However, many of these same congregations single out and treat musicians differently. At Redeemer, we do not. We retain the services of the best musicians we can find just as we do the best counselors, preachers, and educators we can find.

Second, we often include non-Christian musicians in our services who have wonderful gifts and talent. We do not use them as soloists, but we incorporate them into our ensembles. We believe this fits a Reformed "world-and-life view." The dualistic view in many evangelical churches is that a godly, sincere Christian who is an average musician is more pleasing to God than a non-Christian professional musician. But Reformed theology teaches that God's natural gifts in creation are as much a work of grace as God's gifts in salvation. In the film *Amadeus*, Antonio Salieri can see that Mozart, though "unworthy" in many ways, has been chosen by God's grace to receive an artistic gift. Musical talent is the gift of God, and to ask a musician to offer up that gift in a service of worship is a good thing both for him or her and for us. (See Exodus 31, which considers artistic talent to be a gift of the Spirit, and James 1:17.)

I believe Calvin's own approach to music provides guidance for an approach somewhere in the middle, between, on the one hand, the evangelical church that pays its ministers but not its musicians, and, on the other hand, the mainline church that has non-Christians singing or playing as "just another gig." When we incorporate non-Christians into our services, we pray that the gathered worship itself will have an impact on them. We model for them the difference between just performing and seeking to "catch the conscience" with our music. When we invite non-Christians to use their talents in corporate worship, we are simply calling them, along with every creature, to bring their "peculiar honors" and gifts to praise their Creator.

Appendix A

Sample Worship Services

First Worship Service

Morning Worship   **3 September 2000**

REFLECTION

Love offers honey to a bee which has no wings.
—John Trapp, *Seventh-Century Puritan*

What the poor need, even more than food and clothing and shelter (though they need these, too, desperately), is to be wanted. It is the outcast state their poverty imposes upon them that is the more agonizing.
—Mother Teresa, *Something Beautiful for God*

I am not hard-hearted; far from it—full of pity on the contrary and with a ready tear to boot. Only, my emotional impulses always turn toward me, my feelings of pity concern me. It is not true, after all,
that I never loved. I conceived at least one great love in my life, of which I was always the object.
—Jean-Baptiste Clamence, the Parisian lawyer who "confesses" his way through Albert Camus' *The Fall*. Try as he might to be the complete man, Clamence finds himself perennially dominated by self-love.

The cross is a revelation of God's justice as well as of his love. That is why the community of the cross should concern itself with social justice as well as loving philanthropy. It is never enough to have pity on the victims of injustice, if we do nothing to change the unjust situation itself. Good Samaritans will always be needed to succour those who are assaulted and robbed; yet it would be even better to rid the Jerusalem-Jericho road of brigands.
—John R. W. Stott, *The Cross of Christ*

PRELUDE   *Sonata in C Major*   A. Corelli
                        I. Adagio, II. Allegro

PREPARATION   Tim Pettit

PRAISE   *Worship Christ, the Risen King*   HYMN

Rise, O church, and lift your voices,
Christ has conquered death and hell.
Sing as all the earth rejoices;
resurrection anthems swell.
Come and worship, come and worship,
worship Christ, the risen King!

See the tomb where death had laid him,
empty now, its mouth declares:
"Death and I could not contain him,
for the throne of life he shares."
Come and worship, come and worship,
worship Christ, the risen King!

Hear the earth protest and tremble,
see the stone removed with pow'r;
all hell's minions may assemble,
but cannot withstand his hour.
He has conquered, he has conquered,
Christ the Lord, the risen King!

Doubt may lift its head to murmur,
scoffers mock and sinners jeer;
but the truth proclaims a wonder
thoughtful hearts receive with cheer.
He is risen, he is risen,
now receive the risen King!

We acclaim your life, O Jesus,
now we sing your victory;
sin or hell may seek to seize us,
but your conquest keeps us free.
Stand in triumph, stand in triumph,
worship Christ, the risen King![1]

CALL TO WORSHIP   from Psalm 98

Minister: The LORD has made his salvation known and revealed
             his righteousness to the nations.

All: He has remembered his love and his faithfulness to the
             house of Israel; all the ends of the earth have seen the
             salvation of our God.

Minister: Shout for joy before the LORD, the King!

All: Let the sea resound, and everything in it, the world, and all who live in it.

Minister: Let the rivers clap their hands, let the mountains sing together for joy; let them sing before the LORD, for he comes to judge the earth.

All: He will judge the world in righteousness and the peoples with equity.

PRAYER OF ADORATION   (Concluded by the Lord's Prayer)

Our Father, who art in heaven, hallowed be thy name.
Thy kingdom come, thy will be done, on earth as it is in heaven.
Give us this day our daily bread, and forgive us our debts as we forgive
our debtors. And lead us not into temptation, but deliver us from evil.
For thine is the kingdom, and the power, and the glory, forever and ever.
Amen.

DOXOLOGY

All ye who are of tender heart,
Forgiving others take your part.
Sing his praises, Alleluia!
Ye who long pain and sorrow bear,
Praise God and on him cast your care!
O praise him! O praise him!
Alleluia! Alleluia! Alleluia!

Let all things their creator bless,
And worship him with humbleness!
O praise him, Alleluia!
Praise, praise the Father, praise the Son,
And praise the Spirit, Three in One,
O praise him! O praise him!
Alleluia! Alleluia! Alleluia!

SILENT PRAISE AND THANKSGIVING

RENEWAL

PRAYER OF CONFESSION

Minister: Almighty God, you are generous in abundance. You have given to us gifts that we do not deserve. You have called us from death to life, granted us forgiveness through the death and resurrection of your Son, Jesus Christ, given us the Holy Spirit, and made us your children.

All: You have provided for us, both spiritually and materially. Yet we have failed to be thankful and to rejoice in your goodness. We have ignored you and neglected to give you the praise that is due your name.

         Forgive us for our ingratitude. Give us eyes that see your hand at work in all areas of our life. Enable us to realize that every good thing comes from you. And deepen our gratitude

so that we might serve you with undivided and joyful hearts.
In the name of Jesus Christ our Lord. Amen.

PRIVATE CONFESSION

WORDS OF ENCOURAGEMENT   —Acts 4:12

Salvation is found in no one else, for there is no other name under heaven
given to men by which we must be saved. (NIV)

*[Children ages 5–10 may be dismissed to join the Children's
Worship. Nursery and pre-school programs are already in progress
and may also be joined as the hymn begins.]*

HYMN   *Jesus, Thou Joy of Loving Hearts*

Jesus, thou joy of loving hearts,
thou fount of life, thou light of men,
from the blest bliss that earth imparts,
we turn unfilled to thee again.

They truth unchanged hath ever stood;
thou savest those that on thee call;
to them that seek thee thou art good,
to them that find thee all in all.

We taste thee, O thou living bread,
and long to feast upon thee still;
we drink of thee, the fountainhead,
and thirst our souls from thee to fill.

Our restless spirits yearn for thee,
where'er our changeful lot is cast;
glad when thy gracious smile we see,
blest when our faith can hold thee fast.

O Jesus, ever with us stay,
make all our moments calm and bright;
chase the dark night of sin away,
shed o'er the world thy holy light.

COMMITMENT

PRAYER

ANNOUNCEMENTS

SCRIPTURE READING   —Luke 10: 25–37

SERMON   *Enduring Truths from Four Neighbours*   Rev. Terry Gyger

OFFERTORY   *Sonata in C Major*   A. Corelli
             III. Adagio non troppo

HYMN   *Lord, with Glowing Heart I'd Praise Thee*

Lord, with glowing heart I'd praise thee for the bliss thy love bestows,
for the pard'ning grace that saves me, and the peace that from it flows.
Help, O God, my weak endeavor; this dull soul to rapture raise:
thou must light the flame or never can my love be warmed to praise.

Praise, my soul, the God that sought thee, wretched wand'rer far astray;
found thee lost and kindly brought thee from the paths of death away.
Praise, with love's devoutest feeling, him who saw thy guilt-born fear,
and, the light of hope revealing, bade the blood-stained cross appear.

Praise thy Savior God that drew thee to that cross, new life to give,
held a blood-sealed pardon to thee, bade thee look to him and live.
Praise the grace whose threats alarmed thee, roused thee from thy fatal ease;
praise the grace whose promise warmed thee, praise the grace that
      whispered peace.

Lord, this bosom's ardent feeling vainly would my lips express:
low before thy footstool kneeling, deign thy suppliant's pray'r to bless.
Let thy love, my soul's chief treasure, love's pure flame within me raise;
and, since words can never measure, let my life show forth thy praise.

BENEDICTION

DISMISSAL

Minister: Let us go forth to serve the world as those who love our
                 Lord and Savior Jesus Christ.

All: Thanks be to God!

POSTLUDE   *Sonata in C Major*   A. Corelli
                IV. Allegro ma non troppo, V. Giga

  (Redeemer officers are available for prayer at the front after the service.)

WORSHIP MUSICIANS

                Mark Peterson—organ
                Scott McIntosh—trumpet

Second Worship Service

Evening Worship   3 September 2000

REFLECTION

Love offers honey to a bee which has no wings.
—John Trapp, *Seventh-Century Puritan*

What the poor need, even more than food and clothing and shelter (though they need these, too, desperately), is to be wanted. It is the outcast state their poverty imposes upon them that is the more agonizing.
—Mother Teresa, *Something Beautiful for God*

I am not hard-hearted; far from it—full of pity on the contrary and with a ready tear to boot. Only, my emotional impulses always turn toward me, my feelings of pity concern me. It is not true, after all, that I never loved. I conceived at least one great love in my life, of which I was always the object.
—Jean-Baptiste Clamence, the Parisian lawyer who "confesses" his way through Albert Camus' *The Fall*. Try as he might to be the complete man, Clamence finds himself perennially dominated by self-love.

The cross is a revelation of God's justice as well as of his love. That is why the community of the cross should concern itself with social justice as well as loving philanthropy. It is never enough to have pity on the victims of injustice, if we do nothing to change the unjust situation itself. Good Samaritans will always be needed to succour those who are assaulted and robbed; yet it would be even better to rid the Jerusalem-Jericho road of brigands.
—John R. W. Stott, *The Cross of Christ*

PRELUDE   *Change of Heart*   Marcus Miller

PREPARATION   David Bisgrove

SONGS OF PRAISE   *Lord, with Glowing Heart I'd Praise Thee*

Lord, with glowing heart I'd praise thee for the bliss thy love bestows,
For the pard'ning grace that saves me, and the peace that from it flows;
Help, O God, my weak endeavor; this dull soul to rapture raise;
Thou must light the flame, or never can my love be warmed to praise.

Praise, my soul, the God that sought thee, wretched wand'rer far astray;
Found thee lost, and kindly brought thee from the paths of death away;
Praise, with love's devoutest feeling, Him who saw thy guilt-born fear,
And, the light of hope revealing, bade the blood-stained cross appear.

Praise thy Saviour God that drew thee to that cross, new life to give,
Held a blood-sealed pardon to thee, bade thee look to him and live;
Praise the grace whose threats alarmed thee, roused thee from thy fatal ease,
Praise the grace whose promise warmed thee, praise the grace that whispered
    peace.

Lord, this bosom's ardent feeling vainly would my lips express;
Low before thy footstool kneeling, deign thy suppliant's prayer to bless:
Let thy love, my soul's chief treasure, love's pure flame within me raise,
And, since words can never measure, let my life show forth thy praise.

(Francis Scott Key)

He Is Exalted

He is exalted, the King is exalted on high; I will praise Him.
He is exalted, forever exalted, and I will praise His name!
He is the Lord, forever His truth shall reign;
heaven and Earth rejoice in His Holy name.
He is exalted, the King is exalted on high.

(Twila Paris/© 1985 Straightway Music) CCLI 48102

All for Jesus

All for Jesus, all for Jesus! All my being's ransomed pow'rs:
All my thoughts and words and doings, All my days and all my hours.

Let my hands perform His bidding, Let my feet run in His ways;
Let my eyes see Jesus only, Let my lips speak forth His praise.

Since my eyes were fixed on Jesus, I've lost sight of all beside,
So enchained my spirit's vision, Looking at the Crucified.

O what wonder! how amazing! Jesus, glorious King of kings,
Deigns to call me His beloved, Lets me rest beneath His wings.

(Mary D. James)

APPROACHING GOD

PRAYER OF CONFESSION

PRIVATE CONFESSION

CONFESSIONAL RESPONSE   *One Thing I Ask*

One thing I ask, one thing I seek,
That I may dwell in Your house, O Lord.
All of my days, all of my life,
That I may see You, Lord.

Hear me, O Lord, hear me when I cry,
Lord, do not hide Your face from me.
You have been my strength, You have been my shield,
And You will lift me up.

(Psalm 27:4, 7–9/© 1989 Mercy Publishing) CCLI 48102

PRAISE   *Walk with Me*

Walk with me, Lord. Walk with me.
Walk with me, Lord. Walk with me.
While I'm on this pilgrim journey,
I want Jesus to walk with me.

You walked with Moses, won't you walk with me?
You walked with Moses, won't you walk with me?
While I'm on this pilgrim journey,
I want Jesus to walk with me.

In my trials, Lord, walk with me.
In my trials, Lord, walk with me.
When my heart is almost breaking,
I want Jesus to walk with me.

When I'm in trouble, walk with me.
When I'm in trouble, walk with me.
When my head is bowed sorrow,
I want Jesus to walk with me.

(James Ward)

PRAYER

SONG OF PRAISE   *Shout to the Lord*

My Jesus, my Savior, Lord, there is none like You;
All of my days I want to praise the wonders of Your mighty love,
My comfort, my shelter, tower of refuge and strength;
Let ev'ry breath, all that I am, never cease to worship you.
Shout to the Lord, all the earth, let us sing power and majesty,
    praise to the King;
Mountains bow down and the sea will roar at the sound of Your name.
I sing for joy at the work of your hand; forever I'll love you,
    forever I'll stand.
Nothing compares to the promise I have in you.

(© 1993 Darlene Zschech/Hillsong Music
[admin. in U.S. and Canada by Integrity's Hosanna! Music]/ASCAP) CCLI 48102

ANNOUNCEMENTS

SCRIPTURE READING   Luke 10:25–37

SERMON   *Enduring Truths from Four Neighbours*   Rev. Terry Gyger

OFFERTORY   *Christ for the World*

Christ for the world we sing;
The world to Christ we bring with loving zeal;
The poor and them that mourn, the faint and overborne,
Sin-sick and sorrow-worn, whom Christ doth heal.

(Samuel Wolcott)

SONG OF COMMITMENT   *Ever Closer*

Draw me closer, ever closer, Lord, to you.
Draw me closer, ever closer, me to you.
Love too pure for a heart like mine,
Grace too costly for me;
Tender mercies now unto eternity, eternity.

Draw me nearer, ever nearer, Lord, to you.
Draw me nearer, You who are dearer than my due.
Father of wonders, author of truth,
Worship and honor are Yours.
Glory and majesty, blessing and praise
To Jesus our Lord, to Jesus our LORD,

BENEDICTION

POSTLUDE   *Bordertown*   Grover Washington, Jr.
Gary Haase

WORSHIP MUSICIANS

Gary Haase—bass
Joel Frahm—saxophone
Chuck Jennings—guitar
Tom Jennings—piano
Buddy Williams—drums

Appendix B

Prayers for Those Not Taking the Lord's Supper

Redeemer Presbyterian Church welcomes all baptized Christians who are willing to forsake their sin and trust in Jesus Christ for salvation, and who are members of congregations that proclaim the gospel, to receive the Holy Communion with us. If you are not able to receive Communion, please use this time to meditate on one of the following prayers.

Prayer for Those Searching for Truth. Lord Jesus, you claim to be the Way, the Truth, and the Life. Grant that I might be undaunted by the cost of following you as I consider the reasons for doing so. If what you claim is true, please guide me, teach me, and open me to the reality of who you are. Give me an understanding of you that is coherent and convincing, and that leads to the life you promise. Amen.

Prayer of Belief. Lord Jesus Christ, I admit that I am weaker and more sinful than I ever dared admit, but through you I am more loved and accepted than I ever dared hope. I thank you for paying my debt on the cross, taking what I deserved in order to offer me complete forgiveness. Knowing that you have been raised from the dead, I turn from my sins and receive you as my Savior and Lord. Amen.

(WRITTEN BY THE REV. SCOT SHERMAN
OF REDEEMER PRESBYTERIAN CHRUCH)

SCRIPTURE INDEX

INDEX OF HYMNS AND SONGS

INDEX OF NAMES

SUBJECT INDEX